Culture

and the
Development of Management:
An International Example

John D. Theodore
Ph.D., Ph.D., D.B.A. CMC

Lyseis Public Policy Publishing
an imprint of Concrescent LLC

Culture and the Development of Management: An International Example

Published 2012 by Lyseis Public Policy Publishing,
an imprint of Concrescent LLC.

For information contact Concrescent LLC, Richmond CA, USA:
info@concrescent.net

ISBN: 978-0-9843729-4-2

Library of Congress Control Number: 2011944907

Contents

Acknowledgments

I want to thank a number of persons who have assisted me in completing this book. First, my sincere thanks to Dr. Gary Keller, Dr. Orlando Rivero, Dr. Daljit Singh, Professor Franklin Orellana, and Sherill Harriger for their technical and editing support. Furthermore, I want to express my appreciation to Ashley Hogan and Ashley Even for their secretarial support in typing the manuscript and providing assistance with the bibliographical section of the book. Finally, my profound thanks to many other persons who have provided me with assistance during the preparation of the book.

John Theodore
Clearwater, Florida, USA.

Dedication

This book is dedicated to Fatimita.

Chapter 1: Introduction

The great differences that exist among the nations of the world insofar as their economic development is concerned can be attributed to a variety of causal factors. To persons familiar with management, there is a tendency to equate the degree of development of management with a nation's culture. Management is influenced by beliefs, customs, institutions, objectives and techniques—the cultural factors in each nation. Consequently, there are significant cultural reasons why certain countries resort to only minimal management practices while others employ the most advanced ones. Therefore, tracing the impact of cultural factors upon the development of management in selected nations of the world will help us understand and improve their economic development.

Most management analysis in the past has approached management as being impacted by the internal environmental factors within a given enterprise, such as finance, production, etc. The impact of cultural factors on management development, especially on an international basis, had not been adequately treated until the third quarter of the twentieth century. Management studies were preoccupied with the contingency approach, which emphasized technological rather than cultural influence on organizational features and paid little attention to cultural variables until the 1970s.[1]

This work will demonstrate that cultural factors exert a major influence on the development of management by examining and assessing these factors in eleven nations. It will also show that a change in one or more cultural factors causes changes in the development of management.

The Nations under Examination

The nations we will discuss are representative of divergent cultures and different levels of management development, and have been chosen because of their model character: India, Ecuador, Brazil, Russia, Japan, Greece, Italy, France, Germany, the United Kingdom, and the United States. They are studied in sufficient depth to validate conclusions, but not as intensively as they might be because such discussion would comprise a multi-volume work.

This book is partially based on research that I started in the early 1970s and published in 1975 as *Management Development Stages*, which approached the development of management from the human resources perspective of the organization.² In *Management Development Stages*, the nations I examined were India, The Soviet Union, Japan, Italy, France, Germany, The United Kingdom, and the United States. India was one of the largest underdeveloped nations in the world, and, for the purpose of the study, it personified managerial underdevelopment. The Soviet Union represented the totalitarian approach to management and its development. Japan was the only non-Western nation that had reached a relatively advanced level of management development. It represented a different pattern in the development of management that was influenced by the nation's distinct cultural factors, and operated within the framework of a Western-type capitalist economic system.

The European Economic Community depicted a rapidly advancing phase in the development of management as the result of the dynamic evolution of its cultural factors. In 1975 the European Economic Community consisted of Belgium, Denmark, France, West Germany, The United Kingdom, Ireland, Italy, Luxembourg, and The Netherlands. For the purpose of the previous study, four of these nine members were included: The United Kingdom, West Germany, France, and Italy. Italy represented the Latin nations of South Europe; France represented the French-speaking members; West Germany represented the Germanic members; and the United Kingdom, the English-speaking members of the European Economic Community. (The term United Kingdom and Great Britain were used interchangeably used in the previous publication and are still used in the same manner in the present work). The United States personified the nation with the longest professional managerial tradition, and was the highest managerially developed country.

In this book, I have expanded upon my previous work and added three new countries to my analysis; Greece, Ecuador, and Brazil.

In 1971, I did a study on the development of management in Greece. My findings were published in Athens under the title *I Exelixis Tis Dioikiseos Ton Epiheriseon Eis Tin Ellada* (The Development of Management in Organizations in Greece). It examined the state of Greek management up to 1971, which was the period that the country had applied for membership in the European Economic Community. In this work, I have continued my examination of the development of management in Greece from 1971 to 2011. As in *Management Development Stages*, the development of management is also approached from the human resources perspective of the organization.

I am a specialist in Latin American Studies and have been teaching, consulting, publishing, and researching in Latin American nations for three decades, mostly in Ecuador. The current government of Ecuador is proposing macroeconomic development, whereas the private sector favors microeconomic growth based on the power and strength of private Ecuadorian organizations, instead of depending on the macroeconomic alternative that has had limited success. Ecuador has abundant natural resources, agriculture, fishing, mining, and petroleum available for microeconomic development, but the management of private organizations is substantially underdeveloped due to the negative impact of the cultural factors in that nation. The development of management in Ecuador has also been included in this publication and covers the same chronological periods as the other nations in the study. The development of management is also examined from the human element. Finally, the development of management in Brazil has also been incorporated into this work. Brazil is the largest nation in Latin America, having a strong political, economic, and social influence upon the entire region. Its presence as an emerging world economic power is gradually being felt around the world.

Definitions

Before we look at the criteria by which we will assess the nations in this study, let's define and examine the significance of the terms used in this book.

Culture refers to the specific learned norms of a society based on attitudes, values, beliefs, and frameworks for processing information and tasks.[3] The impact of culture on organizations is broad. It can affect all aspects of management of a firm including, but not limited to, strategy, hiring, pay, promotion, organization, and evaluation of performance.[4]

Cultural Factors include the impact of religion upon economic development, the education system, and the social structure. It also pertains to the impact of economic development, education system, and social structure upon the industrialization of the country, a condition that affects the development of labor unions and the corporate form of business. The impact of one cultural factor upon the others is reciprocal. For example, the education system provides curricula that help the development of industrialization, and industrialization — due to its changing operations and infrastructure — demands different curricula from the education system in order to sustain such changes. Also, social structure and change affect economic development and vice versa. All these factors affect the development of management in a direct or indirect manner. For example, the impact of the corporation upon the development of management is more direct than the impact of religion. However, both impact upon the development of management.

Management is defined as planning, organizing, staffing, directing, and controlling the activities of employees in order to accomplish organizational goals. Management pertains to the tasks and activities involved in directing an organization or one of its units: planning, organizing, leading, and controlling.[5] In this work, our discussion of management will be limited to the human elements in the organization, managers and employees.

Managers are people whose primary responsibility in the organization is to carry out the management process. In particular, a manager is the person who plans and makes decisions, organizes, leads, and controls human, financial, physical, and formative processes.[6] There are two types of managers, owner-managers and professional managers. Owner-managers are responsible for both the ownership and the management of their enterprises. They are usually found in small and less developed enterprises that exist in abundance in the managerially underdeveloped nations. Professional managers function in corporations characterized by the separation of management from ownership, as is the case in managerially developed countries. The emergence and strength of professional managers were affected by the corporate form of business.

The class origin of managers is affected by social structure and the education system. For example, in Russia under the Soviet Union, managers came from the upper social hierarchy and were members of the Communist Party. The managers of the Soviet Union contrasted sharply with the managerial group of modern industry elsewhere in the world because of the stress on political reliability.[7] In turn, the class origin of managers influences management authority, employee control, and management's view toward organizational change and development. Managers who come from a flexible social structure implement democratic authority and employee control, espouse modern managerial philosophies, and are inclined to initiate managerial changes.

Employees are the people who are working in the organization under the direction of managers. To distinguish employees from independent contractors, legal examiners focus on just one factor—the legal agreement between employers and employees that clarifies the employment status and the degree of control the business exercises over the employee.[8]

The Development of Management denotes a planned transformational change from an emphasis on the satisfaction of the employees' lower echelon needs to the satisfaction of their higher ones, as promulgated in Maslow's Hierarchy of Needs. Maslow indicated that each human being has seven needs to satisfy: physiological, safety, social, self-esteem, and self-actualization.[9]

Furthermore, management development also denotes the evolutionary development of management from Theory X beliefs to Theory Y beliefs as stated by Dr. Douglas McGregor in his influential book *The Human Side of Enterprise*. Under Theory X beliefs, the average person is viewed as disliking work and avoiding it, if possible. Under Theory Y beliefs, the exertion of physical and mental effort in work by employees is viewed as natural as play or rest.[10] Under Theory X beliefs, the managers must make all decisions by themselves. Employees cannot be left to themselves to carry out their work. Managers must punish the employees in order to make them perform effectively. Under Theory Y beliefs, the employees must be involved in the decision process and left to their own devices in carrying out assigned tasks. Managers must be supportive and encouraging, but not autocratic, in order to create effective employees.

I believe that managers who promote the satisfaction of the highest echelon needs of their employees and operate under Theory Y beliefs are the most advanced, and that the success or failure to attain such advanced management level is influenced directly and indirectly by the cultural factors of each nation. The management characteristics described in this work do not permeate all the enterprises in a certain nation, but depict its management modus operandi. For example, there are Indian enterprises characterized by democratic employee control, but the majority of the nation's enterprises practice autocratic control.

Management Education appertains to the availability of curricula in management and related fields. For example, in the United Kingdom today management education and training are facing the appropriateness of curricula and training programs for preparation and learning in the outside world.[11] Management education is influenced by the education system and, in turn, education influences management authority, employee control, and management's view about organizational change and development. Managers with adequate commensurate education implement democratic authority and control, and strongly favor organizational change and development.

Managerial Respect denotes the degree of prestige the profession of management has in the countries under examination and the extent the profession is accepted by the respective societies. The level of management as a prestigious profession is influenced by the extent of industrialization and the impact of the corporate form of business. In turn, it influences management authority and employee control. For example, in India, due to the limited extent of industrialization, the minimal role of the corporation, and the nature of the education system, the profession of the manager is not adequately respected, whereas in Germany respect for managers started in the late 1800s. Respect was accorded to managers who enjoyed the same high status as public-sector bureaucrats, while salaried managers dominated supervisory boards.[12]

Managerial Authority applies to the type of authority used by managers. Authority involves the rights, prerogatives, obligations, and duties associated with particular positions in an organization. A manager's authority includes the right to make particular types of decisions for the organization.[13] This is directly and indirectly influenced by strength of labor unions and the corporation.

Employee Control indicates the implementation of management authority, which can be autocratic, with the use of rules, regulations and formal authority; or democratic, which considers that employees share the values, expectations and goals of the organization and act in accordance with them.[14] Employee control is also directly and indirectly influenced by the strength of labor unions and the corporation.

Managerial Flexibility indicates the inclinations of management toward planned change and the development of the organization in order to acquire, adopt, and implement better managerial practices. Managers need to identify effective ways of management change for organizational survival. Organizational development has to do with techniques used to implement planned organizational change.[15] Imbedded into planned organizational change and development is the concept of learning organizations, which treats organizations as living entities that are learning effectively, efficiently, and on an evolutionary and incremental basis. Learning leads to performance enhancement; learning is transferred to the job and translated into improved performance.[16] This is also directly and indirectly influenced by the strength of labor unions and the corporation.

Criteria

The nations in this study will be assessed according to specific criteria, as defined and explained in the pages that follow.

Religion and Economic Development examines the extent that the dominant religion in the nations under examination supports economic development. The impact of religion upon economic development is a great concern today, especially in underdeveloped and developing nations of the world. There is also heightened interest in how religion affects development, how development institutions should approach faith-based ideas and institutions, and the impact of development on religious groups themselves.[17] A positive impact emanating from religion creates an economic system which favors, sustains, and develops industrialization as a major factor of the economic activities of a nation.

Furthermore, if the attitude of religion changes from negative to positive, then economic development takes place. For example, Max Weber indicated that economic development and economic prosperity improved in the nations that accepted the Protestant Reformation, breaking away from the Roman Catholic Church's negative attitude toward economic prosperity and development.[18] This event also took place in Japan when the Meiji oligarchy forced religion to change its position and allow economic development and industrialization to take place.

Religion and Education examines the role of religion in the nature, extent, and type of education in the country. The nature of education is influenced by the religious attitudes, beliefs, and practices, or the tenets of any other belief that replaces or supersedes religion, such as communism in the former Soviet Union. The Confucian religion, for example, emphasizes an education system that creates harmony and order in society.[19] Changes in the attitude of religion toward education cause changes in the education system. For example, as the result of the Reformation Movement in Germany, religious leaders saw the need for universal mandatory education for all children, not just the rich or those preparing to serve the church.[20]

Education has an impact upon the industrialization of the country that results in a more prosperous socioeconomic environment. Furthermore, the extent of education influences the level of knowledge, earnings, and strength of the people, and consequently, that of employees. For example, poorly compensated employees with inadequate education do not have sufficient strength to equitably interact with management; therefore, they are autocratically controlled by management. The type of education influences the specialization of the labor force. Educational curricula emphasizing economics and business administration are supportive of an industrial economy and society.

Religion and Social Structure examines the way religion affects social groupings formed to meet socioeconomic objectives and values in the countries under examination. Social stratification is formed as the result of the impact of religion. For example, in Soviet Russia the occupants of the highest social echelon were members of the Communist Party. These individuals also occupied responsible managerial positions and, therefore, influenced the development of management. Religion interacts with any other social phenomenon or process; it influences society and social phenomena, and it is influenced by them in turn.[21] For example, the social structure in India is tightly controlled by religion, and therefore the Brahmins occupy the highest echelon of the structure. The inhabitants of different nations arrange their social relationships and activities according to their attitudes, beliefs, and practices. Religion played a unique role among the privileged classes in agrarian societies. By contrast, religions which conceive of developmental forces in impersonal terms have enjoyed great growth, sometimes through persuasion, sometimes through coercion.[22]

Social Mobility denotes the movement of individuals and groups from one social class to another and from one level in a stratification system to another. Intergenerational mobility is the social movement experienced by family members from one generation to the next.[23] Changes in the view of religion toward social structure and mobility precipitate changes in those areas. A good example is the change of the Catholic Church's position toward the democratization of the Italian society after World War II.

Economic development, education, and social structure exert a powerful force upon industrialization by providing a strong economy and capable human resources that emanate from all socioeconomic stratifications and who have commensurate education in order to sustain and develop the industrial infrastructure of the country

Extent of Industrialization relates to the extent of industrial development in the nations under examination and the result of the impact of economic development, education, and social structure. Industrialization is the process of coordinating materials, persons, and machines to create finished products for the satisfaction of human needs. Industrialization necessitates a certain degree of economic development in order to take place. It does not simply come from purely agrarian or other similarly basic economies. Prior to the Industrial Revolution, domestic industry had been of great significance for economic development, especially during the early modern period, and was the predominant form of industry producing for mass markets from the fourteenth to the eighteenth century.[24] For industrialization to take place, it is necessary for the country to have an education system that can support the arrival of the new production system. Industrialization demands the improvement of public education, such as increased demand for the establishment of mechanical and commercial schools.[25] Finally, industrialization necessitates a social structure which can accept and support it upon its arrival. The British social structure facilitated the early Industrial Revolution, and this Revolution subsequently reflected and represented social changes in the country.[26] Industrialization precipitates the formation of labor unions for the protection of employees; it supports, sustains, and develops the corporate form of business, which possesses all the factors of production that are needed for the industrial network of a nation. Changes in the economy, education system, and social structure in Japan, Italy, and Germany precipitated rapid industrial development in those countries.

Labor Unions examines the power of labor unions resulting from the impact exerted by industrialization in the countries under examination. Although worker and employee organizations existed before the arrival of industrialization, it was industrialization that created labor unions as they are known and function today. As industrialization sped up during the first decades of the nineteenth century, the composition of the labor force began to change.[27] Even though labor movements are among the constants of industrialization, none seems more certain than the impulse toward collective action by workers.[28] The impact of labor unions first affects its members and then extends to the entire socioeconomic network of the population. Unions have had a lead role in establishing many of the most fundamental and valued features of society, and they have played an integral part in the expansion of the middle class that has been the key to assuring its social stability.[29] Early developmental changes in the industrialization process in the United Kingdom and the United States precipitated the early development of labor unions in both nations.

The major goals of labor unions are to create employment security and to provide better wages and benefits. Labor unions affect the development of management by providing security and satisfaction for the employees' physiological and safety needs, and by strengthening the employees' position in interacting with management, which in turn affects management authority and employee control. For example, in the United States, due to the support received from labor unions, the strength of employees made management authority and employee control mainly democratic. Labor unions are power centers for employees that countervail the power of organizations in order to establish the desired balance between employees and managers. Labor unions exert a direct impact upon the management, the managers, and the employees in the countries under examination.

The Corporation looks at the extent industrialization has contributed to the creation, sustenance and development of the corporate form of business. Corporations are one of the three legal forms of enterprise, the other two being proprietorships and partnerships. Corporations appeared long before the First Industrial Revolution, but industrialization precipitated their development because it demanded large-scale enterprises and large-scale capital. The genius of the corporation as a business form, and the reason for its remarkable rise over the last three centuries is its capacity to combine capital, and thus the economic power of unlimited numbers of people.[30] Only the corporate form of business provides these elements due to its broadly distributed ownership, limited liability, and the ability to attract investors by offering ownership (stocks) at reasonable prices. The most important organization in the world is the corporation, which is the basis of the prosperity of the West and the best hope for the future of the rest of the world.[31] Corporations affect the development of management because their large size includes all the factors of production in abundance and thus allows management and organizational specialization. Corporations also precipitate the emergence, sustenance, and development of professional managers by separating ownership from management. Early development changes in the industrialization process in the United Kingdom and the United States precipitated the early development of the corporate form of business in both nations. The development of corporations creates an infrastructure and power that countervails that of labor unions and thus creates the desired balance between employees and managers. The corporate form of business exerts a direct impact upon the management, the managers, and the employees in the countries under examination.

Finally, we examine **Management** in each country and how it is shaped by labor unions and corporations. Labor unions are viewed by employees as power centers that can help them overcome their dissatisfaction, and dissatisfaction is consistently associated with interest in unionizing. Gaps between expectations and achievements motivate employees to find ways to eliminate them with the assistance of unions, especially if the gap is perceived to be a threatening environment created by management.[32] On the other hand, corporations have had a tremendous impact upon the internal stakeholders of the organization. The presence of corporations greatly affected the governance of organizations and the way in which managers behave.[33] The early developmental process of labor unions and corporations in the United Kingdom and the United States precipitated the early development of management in both countries; whereas the late development of labor unions and corporations in Italy contributed to the late development of management in the nation. Furthermore, the inability to create an adequate number of corporations in Greece has substantially slowed down the development of management in the country.

References

Ahlstrom, David, and Garry D. Bruton. *International Management: Strategy and Culture in the Emerging World*. Mason, OH: South-Western Cenage Learning, 2010.

Anthony, M. J., ed. *Introducing Christian Education: Foundations for the Twenty-First Century*. Grand Rapids, MI: Baker Academic, 2001.

Armbruster, T. *Management and Organization in Germany*. Bodmin, Cornwall, United Kingdom: MPG Books, 2005.

Bakan, Joel. *The Corporation: The Pathological Pursuit of Profit and Power*. New York, NY: Free Press, 2004.

Bateman, T. S., and S. A. Snell. *Management: Competing in the New Era*, 5th ed. Boston, MA: McGraw-Hill/Irwin, 2002.

Bensel, F. R. *The Political Economy of American Industrialization: 1877-1900*. Cambridge, MA: Cambridge University Press, 2000.

Brody, D. *In Labor's Cause: Main Themes on the History of the American Worker*. Oxford, England: Oxford University Press, 1993.

Cochran, Thomas C. *The Inner Revolution: Essays on the Social Sciences in History*. New York, NY: Harper & Row, 1964.

Daniels, J. D., L. H. Radebaugh, and D. P. Sullivan. *Globalization and Business*. Upper Saddle River, NJ: Prentice Hall, 2002.

Dine, P. *State of the Unions: How Labor Can Strengthen the Middle Class, Improve Our Economy, and Regain Political Influence*. New York, NY: McGraw-Hill, 2007.

Directory of Education Online. http://www.directoryofeducation.net/colleges/worldwide/

Elkeles, Tamar, and Jack J. Phillips. *The Chief Learning Officer: Driving Value Within a Changing Organization through Learning and Development (Improving Human Performance)*. Amsterdam, Netherlands: Elsevier, 2006.

Fielding, J. R. *Discovering World Religions at 24 Frames Per Second.* Plymouth, England: Scarecrow Press, 2008.

Fossum, J. *Labor Relations: Development, Structure, Process.* Boston, MA: McGraw-Hill/Irwin, 2006.

Granick, D. *Management of the Industrial Firm in the U.S.S.R.* New York, NY: Columbia University Press, 1954.

Griffin, R. W. *Management*, 6th ed. Boston, MA: Houghton Mifflin, 1999.

Heaton, N., and C. Ackah. "Changing HR Careers: Implications for Management Education." *The Journal of Management Development* 26, no. 10 (2007): 959. doi:10.1108/02621710710833405

Hellriegel, D., S. E. Jackson and J. W. Slocum, Jr. *Management: A Contemporary-Based Approach.* Mason, OH: South-Western Publishing, 2005.

Johnson, R. L. *Religion in Society: A Sociology of Religion.* Upper Saddle River, NJ: Prentice Hall, 2009.

Kendall, D. *Sociology in Our Times.* Belmont, California: Wadsworth, 2003.

Kiely, R. *Industrialization and Development: A Comparative Analysis.* London, England: Routledge Taylor & Francis, 1998.

Kriedte, P., H. Medick, and J. Schlumborhm. *Industrialization Before Industrialization.* Cambridge, MA: Cambridge University Press, 1981.

Kreitner, R., and A. Kinicki. *Organizational Behavior*, 9th ed. New York, NY: McGraw-Hill/Irwin, 2010.

Lenski, G. L. *Power and Privilege: A Theory of Social Stratification.* Chapel Hill, NC: University of North Carolina Press, 1984.

Marshall, K., and M. V. Saanen. *Development and Faith: Where Mind, Heart, and Soul Work Together.* Washington, D.C.: The International Bank of Reconstruction and Development/The World Bank, 2007.

Maslow, Abraham H. *Motivation and Personality.* New York, NY: Harper & Row, 1954.

McGregor, D. *The Human Side of Enterprise.* New York, NY: McGraw-Hill, 1960.

Micklethwait, J., and A. Wooldridge. *The Company: A Short History of a Revolutionary Idea.* New York, NY: Random House, 2003.

Miller, R. L., and G. A. Jentz. *Business Law Today*, 6th ed. Mason, OH: South-Western Publishing, 2003.

Theodore, John D. *The Development of Managerial Practices in Select-*

ed Nations in the World. Edina, MN: Alpha Editions, 1991.

Weber, Max, Peter Baehrt, and Gordon C. Wells. *The Protestant Ethic and the Spirit of Capitalism: and Other Writings*. New York, NY: Penguin Books, 2002.

Wilson, J. F., and A. Thomson. "Management in Historical Perspective: Stages and Paradigms." *Competition & Change* 10 (December 2006), 356. doi:10.1179/102452906X160996

Yates, Michael D. *Why Unions Matter*, 2nd ed. New York, NY: Monthly Review Press, 2009.

Yukl, G. *Leadership in Organizations*, 7th ed. Upper Saddle River, NJ: Prentice Hall, 2010.

Endnotes

1   T. Armbruster, *Management and Organization in Germany* (Bodmin, Cornwall, UK: MPG Books, 2005).

2   John D. Theodore, *The Development of Managerial Practices in Selected Nations in the World* (Edina, MN: Alpha Editions, 1991).

3   J. D. Daniels, L. H. Radebaugh, and D. P. Sullivan, *Globalization and Business* (Upper Saddle River, NJ: Prentice Hall, 2002).

4   David Ahlstrom and Garry D. Bruton, *International Management: Strategy and Culture in the Emerging World* (Mason, OH: South-Western Cenage Learning, 2010).

5   D. Hellriegel, S. E. Jackson and J. W. Slocum, Jr., *Management: A Contemporary-Based Approach* (Mason, OH: South-Western Publishing, 2005).

6   R.W Griffin, *Management*, 6th ed., (Boston, MA: Houghton Mifflin, 1999).

7   D. Granick, *Management of the Industrial Firm in the U.S.S.R.* (New York, NY: Columbia University Press, 1954).

8   R. L. Miller and G. A. Jentz. *Business Law Today*, 6th ed. (Mason, OH: South-Western Publishing, 2003).

9   Abraham H. Maslow, *Motivation and Personality* (New York, NY: Harper & Row, 1954).

10 D. McGregor, *The Human Side of Enterprise* (New York, NY: McGraw-Hill, 1960).

11 N. Heaton and C. Ackah, "Changing HR Careers: Implications for Management Education," *The Journal of Management Development* 26, no. 10 (2007): 959. doi:10.1108/02621710710833405

12 J. Micklethwait and A. Wooldridge, *The Company: A Short History*

of a Revolutionary Idea (New York, NY: Random House, 2003).

13 G. Yukl, *Leadership in Organizations*, 7th ed. (Upper Saddle River, NJ: Prentice Hall, 2010).

14 T. S. Bateman and S. A. Snell, *Management: Competing in the New Era*, 5th ed. (Boston, MA: McGraw-Hill/Irwin, 2002).

15 R. Kreitner and A. Kinicki, *Organizational Behavior*, 9th ed. (New York, NY: McGraw-Hill/Irwin, 2010).

16 Tamar Elkeles and Jack J. Phillips. *The Chief Learning Officer: Driving Value Within a Changing Organization through Learning and Development (Improving Human Performance)* (Amsterdam, Netherlands: Elsevier, 2006).

17 K. Marshall and M. V. Saanen, *Development and Faith: Where Mind, Heart, and Soul Work Together* (Washington, D.C.: The International Bank of Reconstruction and Development/The World Bank, 2007).

18 Max Weber, Peter Baehrt, and Gordon C. Wells, *The Protestant Ethic and the Spirit of Capitalism: and Other Writings* (New York, NY: Penguin Books, 2002).

19 J. R. Fielding, *Discovering World Religions at 24 Frames Per Second*, (Plymouth, England: Scarecrow Press, 2008).

20 M. J. Anthony, ed., *Introducing Christian Education: Foundations for the Twenty-First Century*, (Grand Rapids, MI: Baker Academic, 2001).

21 R.L. Johnson, *Religion in Society: A Sociology of Religion* (Upper Saddle River, NJ: Prentice Hall, 2009).

22 G. L. Lenski, *Power and Privilege: A Theory of Social Stratification* (Chapel Hill: University of North Carolina Press, 1984).

23 D. Kendall, *Sociology in Our Times* (Belmont, California: Wadsworth, 2003).

24 P. Kriedte, H. Medick, and J. Schlumborhm, *Industrialization Before Industrialization* (Cambridge, MA: Cambridge University Press, 1981).

25 F. R. Bensel, *The Political Economy of American Industrialization: 1877-1900* (Cambridge, MA: Cambridge University Press, 2000).

26 R. Kiely, *Industrialization and Development: A Comparative Analysis* (London, England: Routledge Taylor & Francis, 1998).

27 Michael D. Yates, *Why Unions Matter*, 2nd ed. (New York, NY: Monthly Review Press, 2009).

28 D. Brody, *In Labor's Cause: Main Themes on the History of the*

American Worker (Oxford, England: Oxford University Press, 1993).

29 P. Dine, *State of the Unions: How Labor Can Strengthen the Middle Class, Improve Our Economy, and Regain Political Influence* (New York, NY: McGraw-Hill, 2007).

30 Bakan, *The Corporation: The Pathological Pursuit of Profit and Power*.

31 J. Micklethwait and A. Wooldridge, *The Company: A Short History of a Revolutionary Idea* (New York, NY: Random House, 2003).

32 J.Fossum, *Labor Relations: Development, Structure, Process* (Boston, MA: McGraw-Hill/Irwin, 2006).

33 J. F. Wilson and A. Thomson, "Management in Historical Perspective: Stages and Paradigms," *Competition & Change* 10 (December 2006), 356. doi:10.1179/102452906X160996

Chapter 2: India

Religion and Economic Development

The principal religion in India is Hinduism, practiced by the majority of the population. The Hindu religion teaches renunciation of worldly concerns and professions and is against greed, materialism, and the soul-destroying character of an industrialized society. Consequently, the majority of Indians traditionally view economic development negatively. Also, the Hindu religion stresses the philosophy of selfless action, love and sacrifice, with a basic emphasis on concepts of service and spirituality.[1]

The Hindus accept their status in life, their occupation, their caste, and their degree of wealth as the result of their *Karma*. The Hindus' passive acceptance of what is has acted as a deterrent to economic development, for the Hindu religion is by far the most pervasive and dominant force in the lives of the people.

Furthermore, economic development is also equated with slums, low wages, and long working hours. Longer working hours are considered especially reprehensible, for people believe that work would detract from time that could be better spent on cultural and spiritual activities. They also believe that industrialization will engender a harried sense of urgency and competition, resulting in tensions which would lead to a neurotic condition of individuals as well as of society. It is commonly assumed by economists and environmentalists alike that greater economic openness will lead to increased pollution in the country, as free trade will increase environmental degradation.[2]

The government of India and some private sectors of the economy have been making efforts to increase economic development, which is now slowly taking place. The nation is now facing a new political situation that has gripped the public imagination, and a culture that is, in the face of new global challenges, trying to maintain its identity.[3]

The impact of religion upon economic development has been negative because it has been viewed as inimical to India's religious tenets. Although the government and some private sectors are making great efforts to create economic development, the process is moving slowly due to the religious tenets that prevail in the nation.

Religion and Education

As the result of the country's strong religious dominance, education in

India has traditionally leaned toward religious studies and the fine arts, making it hard for the education system to contend with the prevailing religion of the culture.[4] Furthermore, except for the Brahmin hierarchy, the rural and urban populaces have been disinterested in formal education mainly because of the rigid caste system.[5]

Following India's independence, the apathetic attitude of the populace towards education slowly began to change, and social attitudes started to concentrate not on the type of education that a person should have, but rather on the fact that everyone should receive an education. This strong belief has been held by parents, local politicians, provincial officials, private societies, and some teachers. According to the Constitution adopted in 1950, the Central Government was given the requisite powers with respect to higher and professional education.[6] The concept of universal education, however, has impeded the demand for specialized education, which is required for industrial development. The government wants to place emphasis on science and technology, with the growth of comprehensive education as a secondary consideration.

Elementary education is compulsory between the ages of six and fourteen, but it is not universally enforced in the country. The number of schools still remains severely limited and so is the number of students enrolled in relation to the number of students eligible for matriculating in elementary education. Secondary and upper secondary education consists of two years of study in each level. The degree of vocational education has been inadequate and ill-prepared. Worst of all, it does not meet the demands of today's labor market in the country.

The character of education in India has traditionally been dichotomous — on one side is the ideal of education for all, while on the other side is the drive to specialization. The University Education Commission has recommended that general education and vocational preparation co-exist and be developed in conjunction with each other at an early stage.[7] Considerable efforts have been made to develop technological education at the university and diploma levels, but there has been little done to train craftsmen. Until the 1950s, there had been practically no facilities to train workers in a skill, even in the larger industrial centers. There had been no part-time classes in colleges or polytechnic institutions, and no training institutes for young apprentices. In general, the lack of interest demonstrated by industry and government concerning any type of vocational training resulted in a lag between industry's need, industrial expansion, and the number of skilled workers who are available.

Several industries started apprenticeship schemes in the 1980s and 1990s and have been successful in training a number of craftsmen. Also, a number of industrial training institutes have been started in the last two decades. The objective of the vocational training program is to integrate the worker with industry. The Central Board of Workers' Education, comprised of representatives of national and state government; business and labor organizations; and educators make up the society which established training programs in the past. The society established a larger number of regional and sub-regional workers' education centers and has trained several million workers.

The interest in the extent of higher education has increased since 1985. The number of universities and university students has increased during the same period, and the same is true with the number of professional and technical colleges. There are currently 205 colleges and universities in the country.[8] However, serious problems still exist in the education system, such as a tremendous conflict between those who have access to education and those who do not.

In conclusion, the education system in India has been heavily influenced by the nation's religious tenets. The general curricula have been mainly dedicated to religious and classical studies and are not available to all. The government has made great efforts to provide sufficient education for all, but this effort has not yet materialized. The type of education currently offered is general in nature, and specialized curricula are limited and difficult to attain. The majority of the Indian people do not have access to higher education.

Religion and Social Structure

Most Indians belong to the low socioeconomic stratification, while only a very small portion of the entire society belongs to the upper socioeconomic class. Generally speaking, the Indian social structure is strongly affected by Hinduism and it is composed of two systems. One is the caste system that consists of a large group of families having the same name, usually associated with a specific occupation and claiming common descent from a mythological ancestor. The other, the joint family system, is a clan or large group of relatives descended from a common ancestor who work together in a communal structure of joint income and expenditures and hold property in common.

In the caste system, everyone is born into a certain caste which they may not leave, thus preventing any degree of social mobility. Hindu society contains thousands of castes and sub-castes, with each caste having its own particular occupations and its own customs and rituals which often determine the minutest details of daily life. The concept of mobility between castes within an individual's life time makes no sense to traditional Hindus. Hindus see mobility between castes as something that is achieved through spiritual progression and reincarnation.[9] The caste system evolved many centuries ago under the auspices of Hinduism to protect Hindu society from decay, but with the passage of time the system became hereditary and arbitrary, and its rigidity and inequities have inhibited social and economic growth.

When India became independent in 1947, laws were enacted to make the caste system illegal; consequently, the caste system has been very slowly declining. For example, inter-caste dining is common, inter-caste marriages are increasing, and discrimination against members of the lowest castes is now a legal offense. Mobility of labor and a new middle class comprised of engineers, businessmen, and technical persons from all castes has recently emerged. The future of the caste system is directly connected to the economic growth of India, but attempts to dissolve the caste system have been met with resistance, which indicates that its elimination is highly unlikely in the near future.

The joint family system which represents cooperative production and consumption is the economic structure of rural society, which comprises more than 70 percent of India's population. It regulates the proper division of labor, for each person contributes according to their own ability and shares in the fruits of the labor of all. It provides economic security for the young, the old, and the deserted. It avoids economic waste and helps to conserve economic resources. The major negative aspects of the joint family system are that it is the extended family that forms the basis of Indian social life which diminishes incentive to work, and it also serves to hinder initiative, enterprise, and thrift.[10] The system encourages cottage labor in the villages and inhibits the mobility of labor, thus creating non-competing groups and static cost levels. Caste barriers also prevent the merger and cooperation of the various factors of production and impede large-scale enterprises and production. The joint family system has also inhibited the mobility of classes by preserving the accepted tradition of the son following his father's work and way of life.

The disintegration of the joint family system has begun, but disintegration without an effective substitute will have detrimental effects in rural society. There will no longer be a welfare system for the needy, and mutual help will disappear. It will be necessary for rural society to evolve from the joint family system to the individualistic type. Evidence shows that the government should establish a welfare system because both the caste system and the joint family system are declining and evolving toward a more Western and industrial economy. With this decline, the Indian economy will expand to a greater degree.[11]

A dominant characteristic of Indian society is its resistance to change. This resistance was succinctly expressed by Jawaharlal Nehru, India's late prime minister, who initiated many changes: "The old enchantment seems to be breaking today and she is looking around and waking up to the present. But however she changes, as change she must, that old witchery will continue and hold the hearts of her people."[12]

During the last six decades of the twentieth century, signs appeared that religious and social beliefs were weakening to the extent that they could be in harmony with economic progress. As the Western influence increased and the traditional social ideas declined, an increasing acceptance of the use of more modern methods and techniques appeared, especially in the urban areas.[13] Today, there is a strong effort to modernize the Indian society, and it is time to liberate India by empowering people and promoting more local governance. This is the best way to spread prosperity to larger sections of the population because it will unleash the natural enterprise of the people.[14] However, India at large has not been ready yet to accept change; the social structure is still unfavorable, and social mobility remains very limited.

Formed under the influence of Hinduism, India's social structure still remains mainly unchanged. The absence of social mobility allows only the occupants of the very small top social echelon to occupy important positions, while the clear majority of the population still remains trapped in social positions due to the caste system, immobility, rigidity, and antiquated environments.

Extent of Industrialization

The underdeveloped economy, the rigid social structure, and the inadequate education system have retarded the development of industrialization in India. The education system is not providing the necessary educational services for industrial development, whereas the social structure remains rigid and inhibits the movement of capable persons from reaching deserving positions. Finally, the economy in general across the vast population has not reached a solid pre-industrial infrastructure.

The history of organized industry began in 1854, when Britain initiated the cotton mill industry in Bombay. During and after World Wars I and II, somewhat more liberal policies were adopted, such as the discrimination protection policy introduced in 1922 that gave impetus to industrial development. Several industries rapidly expanded, and a number of new industries arose, such as steel, sugar, cement, glass, industrial chemicals, and soap. However, their production has never been adequate in quantity for meeting even the low level of internal demand, nor is it diversified in character.

In 1938, Nehru wrote about the lack of industrialization:

> *Is it desirable or possible for us to stop the functioning of big-scale machinery in our country? … It is obvious that we cannot do so. If we have railways, bridges, transport facilities, etc., we must produce them ourselves or depend on others. If we want to have the means of defense we must not only have the basic industries but a highly developed industrial system.[15]*

Independence from the British brought with it a host of political and economic problems that had to be remedied without delay. In the 1960s the government of India attached great significance to growing industrialization. For this purpose, the Indian Planning Commission was created and was charged with drawing up five-year plans to solve the existing economic problems and to increase economic development. In the long run, the rate of industrialization and the growth of the national economy would depend on the increasing production of coal, electricity, iron, steel, heavy machinery, heavy chemicals, and other industries that would increase the capacity for capital formation.[16]

Today, the industrial sector accounts for 30 percent of all economic activities, services occupy about 50 percent, and agriculture about 20 percent, an excessively high percentage. Many industrial firms are under government ownership and control, a situation that makes their operations less effective and efficient. The state ended up without the requisite institutional capacity, despite the national leadership's awareness of its necessity, and despite the leadership putting it on the agenda.[17] Privatization has been initiated, but it has not gained adequate ground. Indian industries are also characterized by industrial clusters that draw their sustenance through functioning as informal production entities. Informality is the key *modus operandi* that is imbedded in the labor process and production/technology sphere, flouting fiscal environmental regulations and working in markets that buttress the net profit accruing to the owners of the firms.[18]

To summarize, India's underdeveloped economy, rigid social structure, and the inadequate education system have retarded the development of industrialization in the country.

Labor Unions

Sporadic and slow industrialization has not contributed to the development of labor unions in India. Consequently, labor unions have been very weak and were developed with a technology that emphasized semi-skilled and unskilled labor.

Prior to 1947, management was still making unilateral decisions on all matters; however, since India's independence there has been some awakening of the workers, followed by an increase in the growth of trade unions and a rise in the level of expectations of workers. The labor movement was initially like a vicious cycle because most unions were weak, their membership small, and their resources limited; therefore, employees were reluctant to recognize unions as effective bargaining agents. The result was that the smaller unions sought the protection of the industrial courts, where they could obtain recognition of their status and, more importantly, achieve some results on behalf of their members. It was evident that the trade union movement could not achieve its objectives because the industrial structure was not supported by a full-fledged socialist democracy with firm foundations. The government found it difficult to assure fundamental rights to the working class.[19] The Indian government made abortive attempts to promote the development of trade unionism along progressive guidelines to promote the economy. Because of the weakness of labor unions, Indian employees were not able to satisfy their physiological and safety needs and remained unprotected when they interacted with management.

Indian labor unions still remain weak at this time. A process of deregulation and disorganization of the labor force has allowed industrialists to evade labor law. The main means by which labor laws are circumvented is the subcontract labor system, under which workers are provided on demand through a labor contract without any legal or moral obligations between the employee and the employer.[20] Today, labor unions are looked upon either as an unnecessary factor in decision-making or as a necessary legal formality; they have too much political influence.[21]

Currently, there are a very large number of trade unions; the most important include: All India Central Council of Trade Unions, All India

Trade Union Congress, Indian Federation of Trade Unions, Indian National Trade Union Congress, and the Labour Progressive Federation.[22]

The slow and irregular industrialization of India has retarded the development of strong and functional labor unions. Labor unions consistently have been very weak and developed with a technology that emphasized semi-skilled and unskilled labor. Although industrialization continues to take place under the same slow and irregular basis, trade unions do not serve the interests of their members or that of Indian people because they remain weak and are easily manipulated by the interests of internal or external political elements.

The Corporation

Because of the limited degree of industrialization, the corporate form of business has always played a very minor role in the social and economic life of India. The managing agency system—which operated from Britain—was the progenitor of the corporation; later on the corporation appeared in the country to a very limited extent.[23] The ratio of public to private corporations is high, a situation that indicates the strong presence of government control upon the corporate form of business. Government corporations do not and can not function as private enterprises because private management is missing. At the beginning of the 1990s, India had little more than 100 relatively large state-owned enterprises and more than 2500 smaller public traded private-sector companies, emphasizing that the corporate form of business in relation to proprietorships and partnerships is very small.[24]

The prevailing socioeconomic conditions dictate that private corporations—which are based on a close family management network—provide employment to the male family members, a situation that does not allow for the separation of management from ownership; consequently, the influx of new ideas and methods is eliminated and managerial inbreeding is fostered. The Indian government has made phenomenal efforts to change the situation with minimal results. Corporations have a different role to play in India, one with more obligations and nuances attached, than those in nations where economic well being has already been achieved.[25]

Because of the limited extent of industrialization, the corporate form of business in private organizations also remains limited. The majority of corporations are owned and controlled by the government. Therefore, the corporate form of business does not have a positive impact upon the development of management in India.

Management in India

Because of the negative impact of labor unions and the corporate form of business, Indian management remains underdeveloped, a situation that reflects upon the human factor in the country's organizations.

Most Indian managers work in small organizations and are either family members or friends of the owners. Consequently, these organizations are not professional in the sense that the managers are members of the owners' families.[26] The tradition of being a member of the family, either genetically or by marriage, is a part of the Indian culture that dates back to the formation of the nation. While the economy was governed by significantly different regimes, family business groups continued to dominate the Indian organizational landscape.[27] Managers take pride in identifying themselves as family members of the owners of the organization they are working for. However, many are not commensurately prepared and there does not seem to be any career planning in place. Since their capacities and capabilities are not recognized and given due credit, these individuals become unmotivated and demoralized.[28] Delegation of authority and responsibility from the owners to the managers is practically nonexistent. Indians are reluctant to delegate and accept authority, fearful of making independent decisions, possessive toward their inferiors, and frequently submissive to their superiors. The government has made dramatic attempts to increase the role of professional managers in order to expedite the nation's management development. This requires a considerable change in the attitudes, working systems, strategy, human resources, and skills of Indian organizations.[29] Change is gradually taking place only in the few large organizations, whereas the remaining organizations continue under the auspices of owner-managers.

Management education remained substantially limited until the 1990s due to cultural factors favoring classical curricula in education and the lack of interest by organizations, managers, employees, society, and the government. The type of managerial education held by a small percentage of managers was haphazardly acquired on the job. Nevertheless, attempts were made to introduce modern management education. Consequently, management education is coming into its own in India. Training is being imparted by universities and specialized institutions, management and professional associations, and even industrial and commercial undertakings.[30] Today more than 200 universities have been established that offer both undergraduate and graduate management courses. Management education is traditionally seen as a means to facilitate learning of job-related behaviors in order to improve performance, whereas the human values component of management education continues to be an ignored domain of investigation.[31] Furthermore, the quality of instruction and instructors is not competitive, and it has become vital to improve other education streams by including commerce education and management orientation in professional courses like accounting and secretarial studies.[32] Many of the 2,000 or so management schools recognized by the All India Council for Technical Education have minimal faculty, most of whom have little practical experience in management and who undertake little research of decent quality.[33] There are strong indications that employers are not satisfied with the management education their managers receive and blame their managers for not learning the correct management principles and practices being taught in the institutions where they study. Managers appear to rebut the accusations by blaming their employers for not understanding advanced management theories and practices.

Because of the weakness of labor unions and the corporate form of business, Indian management is authoritarian. Management's view toward change and development is either very limited or nonexistent, and developmental changes are very difficult to implement. Paternalism prevails in the relationship between the owners and the managers in small and large Indian organizations. Paternalism has its roots in the millennia-old Indian culture which includes organizations. In reality, organizations are microcosms of the Indian society. Indian historians support the idea that paternalism was founded in the formative stage of the Indian society as a legacy of norms and practices, and was used by rulers, kings, and emperors to control their large numbers of subjects. Management authority is mostly expressed in the element of paternalism.

The paternal attitudes are based on the traditional relationships of a feudal agrarian society. In a village, the chief landowner is not only the employer of most of the people in the village, but also their friend, guide, and philosopher. He looks after their social needs, and they consult and obey him even in personal matters. There are two aspects to such paternalism. First, there is benevolence, which means that managers are responsible for their employees in the same manner as fathers are responsible for their children. Second, there is despotism, which denotes that managers expect their employees to obey them immediately in the same way as fathers expect their children to obey.

Due to the poor economic conditions prevailing in India, managers control their employees at the lowest echelon of Maslow's Hierarchy of

Needs: physiological, safety, and security. Resultant industrialization and scientific applications in agriculture have given rise to growth in the gross national product, but have not translated into better economic conditions for the masses. Unemployment has increased, and the gap of distribution of both land and income has become more noticeable.[34]

Indian employees can be easily dismissed, since they are generally unskilled and can be automatically replaced by others. There is very little employees can do to oppose management in a country where the per capita income is one of the smallest in the world. Indian employees cannot afford to lose their jobs in a nation where widespread unemployment and underemployment of labor is a notable feature of the economy.

Indian subordinates have been traditionally humble because their attitude towards authority is based upon the old agricultural family structure. In industry, new workers from a village are often grateful to the management for giving them a job, for they view it as a favor and exhibit their gratitude by an excess demonstration of humility and loyalty. As subordinates continue in industrial work, they soon obtain a certain independence of spirit and have new views as to what is expected of management. They rarely meet any of the management team except for their first-line supervisor, and they have no sense of belonging to the firm until they take an interest in labor unions. It is with labor unions that subordinates first experience any authority in which they may share. The union may collectively demonstrate some power over management, though this power is usually weak and uncoordinated because of the multiplicity of unions in one single firm and the political and governmental forces that keep labor unions substantially weak.

New management approaches to employee control have been introduced to India, including one where employees participate in groups in the decision-making process. This has been called industrial democracy, and the participating employees have been referred to as autonomous or self-managing groups. Such an approach emphasizes group work rather than individual work.[35] In most cases, the introduction and implementation of new management techniques, mostly of foreign origin, has generally resulted in limited economic benefits and, consequently, limited management improvement. However, Indians are continuously working to improve the management of their organizations. There is an increasing dependence on the Internet, as it gives them unique opportunities to improve their efficiency, but organizations that operate on the Internet are essentially those that provide services.[36]

Today, Indian management is a complex matrix of procedures, customs, and habits. The influence of the sociocultural dynamics of the Indian family system on the organizational practice is very strong. The organizational context has to be seen within the situation and mores of Indian sociocultural life. Any management practice taken out of the context of Indian culture, whether based on Western, Japanese or traditional Indian experience and however efficient it is projected to be, would only add to the existing confusion in Indian management today.[37]

Due to the negative impact of labor unions and the corporate form of business as well as the indirect negative impact of cultural factors, management authority and employee control are very autocratic. Management philosophy is very conservative, and management's views toward change and development are either nonexistent or excessively limited and impossible to implement. Attempts are currently being made to improve employee control.

References

Baixas, L. "Christopher Candland, Labor, Democratization and Development in India and Pakistan," review of *Labor, Democratization and Development in India and Pakistan*, by Christopher Candland. *South Asia Multidisciplinary Academic Journal* (2007): paras. 8-12. http://samaj.revues.org/index832.html

Bandyopadhyay, R. "O.R. Applications in Industry and Problems of Industrialization of a Developing Economy with Special Reference to India." *Journal of Operational Research Society* (September 1980): 770.

Budhwar, P., and J. Bhatnagar. *The Changing Face of People Management in India (Working in Asia)*. London, England: Rutledge Taylor & Frances, 2009.

Chibber, V. *Locked in Place: State-Building and Late Industrialization in India*. Princeton, NJ: Preston University Press, 2006.

Das, K. ed. *Indian Industrial Clusters*. Aldershot, England: Ashgate Publishing, 2005.

Datt, R., and K. P. M. Sundharam. *Indian Economy*. New Delhi, India: Niraj Prakashan, 1966.

Davis, H. J. *Management in India: Trends and Transition*. New Delhi, India: Response Books, 2009.

Directory of Education Online. http://www.directoryofeducation.net/colleges/worldwide/india/

Gopalakrishnan, R. "India and Tata National Development and the Corporation." *Innovations: Technology, Governance, Globalization* 3, 4. (Fall 2008): 3-13.

Hill, M. *International Business: Competing in the International Marketplace*, 8th ed. New York, NY: McGraw-Hill, 2011.

IndiaEducation.net "Management Education in India." Accessed March 25, 2010 from http://www.indiaeducation.net/management/Indian-Scenario.aspx

Indo-American Chamber of Commerce. *India: Business Opportunities*. Bombay: 1987.

Kanawaty, G., and E. Thorsrud. "Field Experiences With New Forms of Work Organization." *International Labour Review* (May-June 1981): 263.

Kar, A., and Bhattacharya. "E-recruitment and Customer Satisfaction: An Empirical Study in and around Kolkata." *The Icafaian Journal of Management Research* 8, 2. (2009): 34-53.

Krishnan, V. R. "Impact of MBA Education on Students' Values: Two Longitudinal Studies." *Journal of Business Ethics* 83, 233. (2008). doi:10.1007/s10551-007-9614-y

Morck, R. K. ed. *A History of Corporate Governance around the World*. Chicago, IL: University of Chicago Press, 2007.

Mukhopadhyay, K., and D. Chakraborty. "Environmental Impacts of Trade in India." *The International Trade Journal* 19, 2. (Summer 2005): 137. doi:10.1080/08853900590933116

Nandy, A. *Time Warps: Silent and Evasive Pasts in Indian Politics and Religion*. New Brunswick, NJ: Rutgers University Press, 2002.

NationMaster.com. "Trade union membership by country." Accessed October 1, 2010 from http://www.nationmaster.com/graph/lab_tra_uni_mem-labor-trade-union-membership

Nehru, Jawaharlal. *The Discovery of India*. Garden City, NY: Anchor, 1960.

Rao, S. L. "The Problem with Management Education in India." *Business Today*, October 18, 2009. http://proquest.umi.com/pqdweb?did=1878135741&sid=13&Fmt=3&clientld=11123&RQT=309&VName=PQD

Roberts, H. S., and P. F. Brissenden, eds. *The Challenge of Industrial Relations in the Pacific-Asian Countries*. Honolulu, HI: East West Center Press, 1965. doi:10.1177/002218566800800309

Rosen, G. *Democracy and Economic Change in India*. Los Angeles,

CA: University of California Press, 1966.

Sidhu, J. "A Tale of Two Indias." *Diverse Issues in Higher Education* 24, 15. (September 2007): 22. http://proquest.umi.com/pqdweb?did= 1375132161&sid=23&Fmt=3&clientId=11123&RQT=309&VName =PQD

Singh, A. *Fifty Years of Higher Education in India.* New Delhi, India: Sage Publications, 2004.

Terpstra, V. *The Cultural Environment of International Business.* Cincinnati, OH: South-Western Publishing, 1978.

Virmani, B. R. *The Challenge of Indian Management.* New Delhi, India: Response Books, 2007.

Wilcox, C., W. Weatherford, H. Hunder, and M. Bratz. *Economies of the World Today: Their Organization, Development, and Performance.* New York, NY: Harcourt, Brace & World, 1966.

Endnotes

1 R. Datt and K. P. M. Sundharam, *Indian Economy* (New Delhi, India: Niraj Prakashan, 1966).

2 K. Mukhopadhyay and D. Chakraborty, "Environmental Impacts of Trade in India," *The International Trade Journal* 19, 2. (Summer 2005): 137. doi:10.1080/08853900590933116

3 A. Nandy, *Time Warps: Silent and Evasive Pasts in Indian Politics and Religion* (New Brunswick, NJ: Rutgers University Press, 2002).

4 V. Terpstra, *The Cultural Environment of International Business* (Cincinnati, OH: South-Western Publishing, 1978).

5 Ibid.

6 A. Singh, *Fifty Years of Higher Education in India* (New Delhi, India: Sage Publications, 2004).

7 J. Sidhu, "A Tale of Two Indias," *Diverse Issues in Higher Education* 24, 15. (September 2007): 20.

8 Directory of Education Online. 2010. http://www.directoryofeducation.net/colleges/worldwide/india/

9 M. Hill, *International Business: Competing in the International Marketplace*, 8th ed. (New York, NY: McGraw-Hill, 2011).

10 C. Wilcox, W. Weatherford, H. Hunder, and M. Bratz, *Economies of the World Today: Their Organization, Development, and Performance* (New York, NY: Harcourt, Brace & World, 1966).

11 Datt and Sundharam, *Indian Economy*.

12 Jawaharlal Nehru, *The Discovery of India* (Garden City, NY:

Anchor, 1960), p.61.

13 G. Rosen, *Democracy and Economic Change in India* (Los Angeles: University of California Press, 1966).

14 R. Gopalakrishnan, "India and Tata National Development and the Corporation," *Innovations: Technology, Governance, Globalization* 3, 4. (Fall 2008): 6.

15 Datt and Sundharam, *Indian Economy*, p.161.

16 G. Rosen, *Democracy and Economic Change in India* (Los Angeles: University of California Press, 1966).

17 V. Chibber, *Locked in Place: State-Building and Late Industrialization in India* (Princeton, NJ: Preston University Press, 2006).

18 K. Das, ed., *Indian Industrial Clusters* (Aldershot, England: Ashgate Publishing, 2005).

19 H. S. Roberts and P. F. Brissenden, eds., *The Challenge of Industrial Relations in the Pacific-Asian Countries* (Honolulu, HI: East West Center Press, 1965). doi:10.1177/002218566800800309

20 L. Baixas, "Christopher Candland, Labor, Democratization and Development in India and Pakistan," review of *Labor, Democratization and Development in India and Pakistan*, by Christopher Candland, *South Asia Multidisciplinary Academic Journal* (2007): 3. http://samaj.revues.org/index832.html

21 B. R. Virmani, *The Challenge of Indian Management* (New Delhi, India: Response Books, 2007).

22 NationMaster.com. "Trade union membership by country." Accessed October 1, 2010 from http://www.nationmaster.com/graph/lab_tra_uni_mem-labor-trade-union-membership

23 Virmani, *The Challenge of Indian Management*.

24 R. K. Morck, ed., *A History of Corporate Governance around the World* (Chicago, IL: University of Chicago Press, 2007).

25 R. Gopalakrishnan, "India and Tata National Development and the Corporation," p.3.

26 H. J. Davis, *Management in India: Trends and Transition* (New Delhi, India: Response Books, 2009).

27 Morck, *A History of Corporate Governance around the World*.

28 Virmani, *The Challenge of Indian Management*.

29 P. Budhwar and J. Bhatnagar, *The Changing Face of People Management in India (Working in Asia)* (London: Rutledge Taylor & Frances, 2009).

30 IndiaEducation.net "Management Education in India." Accessed

March 25, 2010 from http://www.indiaeducation.net/management/
Indian-Scenario.aspx

31 V. R. Krishnan, "Impact of MBA Education on Students' Values:
Two Longitudinal Studies," *Journal of Business Ethics* 83, 233.
(2008). doi:10.1007/s10551-007-9614-y

32 S. L. Rao, "The Problem with Management Education in India."
Business Today, October 18, 2009. http://proquest.umi.com/pqdweb
?did=1878135741&sid=13&Fmt=3&clientId=11123&RQT=309&V
Name=PQD

33 Ibid.

34 R. Bandyopadhyay, "O.R. Applications in Industry and Problems
of Industrialization of a Developing Economy with Special Reference to India," *Journal of Operational Research Society* (September
1980): 770.

35 G. Kanawaty and E. Thorsrud, "Field Experiences With New Forms
of Work Organization," *International Labour Review* (May-June
1981): 263.

36 A. Kar and Bhattacharya, "E-recruitment and Customer Satisfaction:
An Empirical Study in and around Kolkata," *The Icafaian Journal
of Management Research* 8, 2. (2009): 34-53.

37 Virmani, *The Challenge of Indian Management.*

Chapter 3: Ecuador

Religion and Economic Development

Ecuador was a colonial possession of Spain and inherited practically all the characteristics of its conqueror. Ecuador inherited a feudal society which was dominated by the Roman Catholic Church, which had the great task of converting the native populations of the Americas to Christianity and indoctrinating them into Spanish culture and language. The position of the Church toward economic development had been inimical, as was the case in the Europe. Specifically, the ultimate goal of the Church was the salvation of people, and it made every effort to push the congregation in that direction.

During its formative period, the Roman Catholic Church incorporated parts of the philosophy of Plato and Aristotle, who viewed commerce and industry as necessary evils in society and manual work as demeaning. These concepts were transplanted into the Church's colonial domains, which were strongly controlled by the Catholic clergy. Descendants of the leading class (known as *peninsular* and *colonial* Spaniards) viewed work as a shameful activity and preferred to die from hunger than to engage in manual labor.[1]

Like the other Spanish possessions, Ecuador gained its independence in the early part of the 1800s. However, no socioeconomic changes took place, such as those in the United States after its independence from Great Britain. The Church continued its traditional negative attitude toward economic development. Furthermore, the absence of positive economic relations and cooperation among the people disallowed the formation of businesses that would lead to economic development.[2]

In the 1960s, the Roman Catholic Church started to change its attitude toward economic development. The change was first felt in Catholic Europe, then in Ecuador and the rest of the Latin American nations. The new position of the Church toward socioeconomic development received the name of *Iglesia Comprometida*—Compromised Church. The Ecuadorian Catholic Church officially announced its change toward economic and social development on April 23, 1963, with the promulgation of agrarian reform in the country.[3] This transformation of ideology in every Roman Catholic nation in the world was officially supported by the Vatican. In his Apostolic Letter commemorating the 80th anniversary of the *Rerum Novarum* Encyclical, Pope Paul VI clearly stated that to avoid misery and parasitism in the future of the human race, the Church must support governments' policies towards economic investments, the organization of production, the increase of commerce and industry, and in general, towards every aspect of improving the economy.[4]

Ecuadorian President Rafael Correa currently favors a socialist and macroeconomic model of economic development, whereas the private sector is supporting a microeconomic approach to reach that goal. Correa's economic plan for 2007 to 2010 proposed to achieve economic revitalization through social justice and freedom under the auspices of the government.[5] Ecuador's private sector favors a free-market approach with infrastructure predicated on the productivity, performance, and competitiveness of the country's private enterprises. Supporters of this approach claim that the economy based on the free-market system will be conducive to the development of all economic factors, especially the human one, because it provides and sustains freedom.[6]

Economic development has been progressing slowly and has relied on non-industrial products, mainly petroleum, agriculture, fishing, fruits, and related products since the country is rich with natural resources. Adequate economic development has not been realized yet and remains one of the most important goals in the country.[7]

The impact of religion upon economic development was negative from the beginning of the colonial period to the late 1960s. Although the Church changed its position and now favors economic development, the process is taking place slowly and has not produced sufficient results yet. Tremendous efforts are currently taking place to accelerate economic development, which still remains slow and anemic.

Religion and Education

The Church had total control over the education system in Ecuador from the beginning of the colonial period until the Liberal Revolution in the early 1900s. However, it continued to have substantial impact on education until the 1960s. The Church favored curricula in religion and classical studies and had no concern for curricula in economics, business, technology, and related areas. However, it should be carefully noted that while the Church ignored certain curricula, it also educated Ecuadorians and the rest of Latin America, and thus fostered most of the sense of scholarship in the New World. The Church contributed to the establishment of excellent universities, such as those in Santo Tomas de Aguino (1538), Santiago de la Paz (1540), Mexico City (1551), and Lima (1551).

By 1624 there were twenty-six universities in Latin America. However, the Church wielded great influence, not only in the spiritual sector, but also in educational, political, societal, and intellectual pursuits. Hence, the traditional hostile disposition of the Church and society towards curricula in economics, business, finance, marketing, and management education remained unchanged until the latter part of the 1990s.[8]

The emergence of Fidel Castro and the Marxist/Leninist philosophies of the Soviet Union regarding economic management of a national economy provided not only a socioeconomic alternative to the status quo, but also a challenge to the process of economic development and the attainment of a mass market. These changes necessitated a commensurate education system. An important appeal of the Soviet Union in Latin America was the temporary success of the Soviet economic development at that time. Many Latin American intellectuals and political leaders were profoundly concerned with discovering the magic of economic growth and the appeal of the communist economic model was widespread. The new Cuban values were abundantly applied in Latin America, and Fidel Castro promised that the decade of plenty was beginning.[9]

In the late 1980s and early 1990s, the driving forces of globalization, constant change, and evolving international standards of competitiveness required Ecuadorian organizations and the government to re-examine both the structural and operational aspects of how to create and sustain a competitive advantage. A key issue was to employ individuals who demonstrated the attitudes and skills necessary for success in this area.

A small number of countries in Latin America began to establish business schools in the 1960s. However, several powerful barriers retarded the growth of business education, such as limited government and private investment in academic and practical management education. Latin Americans who had studied management in North America or Europe were either underemployed or unable to find suitable positions at home; as a result, many of them returned to the nations where they had studied in search of productive employment.[10] However, the field of management education was not completely obliterated in Latin America. Ecuadorian universities started to offer limited education programs commensurate to preparing students to meet the needs of a modern economic system. The 1980s and 1990s was a period of differentiation of private sector competition. This process reflected the loss of central control over higher education expansion that resulted in the proliferation of state universities, one of which was the technical State University of Quevedo.[11] There are currently thirty-seven universities in the country;[12] however, recent statistics indicate that less than 18 percent of people twenty-four years old and older are formally attending universities or have taken classes in universities.[13] One important deficiency in university education is the preparation of the teaching faculty. As is the case in all Latin America, most university professors in Ecuador have only an undergraduate degree, especially those who teach in the area of business administration, and fewer than 4 percent of them have a doctoral degree which, in most cases, is not related to business curricula.[14]

From the beginning of the colonial period until the early part of the 1960s, the Roman Catholic Church had full control over the education system of the country, which was based on religious and classical studies. In the 1960s, the Church officially changed its position and started to support curricula in economics, business, technology and related areas commensurate to a modern economy. Ecuador slowly began to offer such curricula in existing and newly established universities. Deficiencies in higher education still exist today; one major issue is the insufficient preparation of professors, especially in the areas of economics, business, management, and related fields.

Religion and Social Structure

Prior to the arrival of the Spaniards, the geographic area that is now Ecuador was controlled by the Incas, who were ruthless oppressors of the indigenous people. The Incas created a hierarchal society that exploited indigenous groups, who were used for manual and inferior types of work. The subjugated populations were forced to give blind obedience and loyalty to the Incas, and disobedience was punished by death.

The conquest of the Americas by the Spaniards created well-planned political administrative units. In the northern part of South America, the region was under the Vice Royalty of New Granada, which became Gran Colombia after the War of Independence, and was subsequently divided into three parts that resulted in the formation of Venezuela, Colombia, and Ecuador. All three countries have basically the same national flag, with minimal variations, which personifies their common origin.

The arrival of the Spaniards introduced a rigid hierarchal structure from Spain. The social structure was dominated by the nobility of the Vice Royalty, the Spanish army, and the Spanish population. Initially, the upper class was from Spain (*peninsulares*) and it was inherited by the Spanish people born in Ecuador (*criollos*). The descendants of the

Spaniards acquired immense areas of land, dominated the economy, and provided work for the lower classes. Shortly after the arrival of the Spaniards, a new race appeared in Latin America, the *mestizos*, people of both Spanish and indigenous blood who became the second dominant social stratification in both Equador and the entire Latin American region. For the ruling class, ownership of land was the major characteristic of wealth, while the mestizos and purely indigenous populations worked as their servants.

This rigid social structure dominated the colonial period and lasted for another hundred years after the independence of the nation. It was adamantly supported by the Catholic Church, which claimed that such structure was blessed and supported by God and that the lower classes had to work for their superiors for minimal subsistence wages.[15] The lower classes had no opportunity for any type of improvement in their living conditions.

In the first decade of the 1900s, the Liberal Revolution took place in the country that limited, to some extent, the impact of the Church upon social, economic and political affairs. After the 1980s, social conditions continued to improve; nevertheless, overall improvement was modest and unevenly distributed, and Ecuadorian social development remained neglected in spite of dramatic basic needs deprivations and striking social disparities.[16]

The social structure in Ecuador remains inflexible and social mobility is still limited. However, strong attempts are being made by many responsible citizens of all professions to create a better social structure and improve mobility. Today the country is witnessing a revolution from below, a popular awakening that is challenging the traditional political parties and demanding a new system of governance that responds to the interests and needs of the popular classes.[17]

The social structure in Ecuador was rigid and hierarchal from the beginning of the colonial period up to the 1960s. Numerous efforts were made (and are still being made) with some success to change the class rigidity and increase mobility in the social structure, but no substantial improvements have yet taken place.

Extent of Industrialization

Slow economic development, an archaic education system, and a rigid social structure had a negative impact upon industrialization, which remained substantially limited until the end of the third quarter of the twentieth century. Industrialization was late, limited, low-tech, labor-intensive, and closely tied to resource extraction or agriculture.[18] The major industrial sectors of production were food and textiles. Textile production dates back to the 1900s; prior to that period, textiles were produced under the auspices of the domestic system. Petroleum became the most important product in the second half of the twentieth century and provided substantial revenues that mainly benefited the leading class. Thus the fate of industrialization followed that of the revenues from petroleum exports. Furthermore, industrial firms were small in size and mainly proprietorships or partnerships that were owned and operated by family members. Only a very small number of large industrial firms existed and still exist in the country—corporations that were formed for the benefit of a small group of people.[19] Currently, industrial organizations of all sizes constitute only 8.7 percent of total production in the nation.[20]

The government of Ecuador has supplied insufficient funds and relatively incorrect directions to the country's industrial sector, thus making it one of the weakest among its counterparts in the rest of Latin America. The negative characteristics of the industrial sector today include low-level of usage existing capacity, heavy centralization, low technology, and low utilization of manpower. Furthermore, it is mainly an assembly industry, and it does not have a focal point that can be used for industrial development.[21]

Industrialization was not supported by sufficient economic development, a modern education system, or a dynamic social structure; consequently, its development remains relatively slow. The government has been making efforts to develop industrialization, but such efforts have suffered from insufficient funds and incorrect directions. Nevertheless, industrialization is one of the most important goals in the Ecuadorian economy today.

Labor Unions

Because of the limited presence of industrialization, labor unions have been weak, powerless, and disorganized throughout the history of the nation. Labor unions appeared in the first quarter of the twentieth century, but were only officially recognized by the Labor Code of 1938. In the same year, the first labor union was founded—CEDOC (Central Ecuatoriana de Organizaciones Clasistas). Internecine arguments among labor unions and strong opposition from government and employers have placed unions in a disadvantageous position since their formation. Ecuadorian employers always have had a very negative attitude toward labor unions and for this particular reason, labor unions aligned themselves with political parties that assist and support them.[22]

Currently, four trade unions are active in the country: Confederación Ecuatoriana de Organizaciones Clasistas Unitarias de Trabajadores; Confederación de Trabajadores del Ecuador; Ecuador Confederation of Free Trade Union Organizations; and Frente Unitario de los Trabajadores.[23] Today, it is the Frente Unida de Trabajadores that dominates the arena of labor unions. There are also guilds whose membership includes artisans. Finally, middle class professionals and employees belong to professional associations known as *camaras*, whose membership includes influential persons who make socioeconomic decisions in the country. These associations positively interact with the government for mutual benefit.

The government does not enforce labor codes effectively or efficiently. Labor codes were modified twice toward the end of the twentieth century; their purpose is to regulate the formal labor element and the role of the government. It must be noted that the informal labor element is sizeable but powerless, and it is in this element that labor codes are frequently violated. However, Ecuadorians believe that business organizations must contribute to the well-being of workers by recognizing their right to share the benefits produced by the economy, and businesses need to consider that it is their responsibility to create jobs and to provide work for the people.[24]

The limited presence of industrialization in the country has resulted in weak and disorganized labor unions. Both employers and the government view unions negatively and there is ongoing antagonism among the labor unions that exist in the nation today.

The Corporation

Because of limited industrialization, the corporate form of business has played a very limited role in the society and economy of the nation. The Ecuadorian economy is composed of a large number of small private organizations, which are either proprietorships or partnerships and are owned and operated by family members. Small- and medium-size enterprises constitute 97 percent of all enterprises in the country.[25] The private sector is characterized by enterprises that typically employ small numbers of family members who function as both managers and employees. The average number of persons employed per business enterprise is three.[26] The small size and proliferation of family owned and managed enterprises have impeded the creation of private corporations and, consequently, the development of management.

In order to increase the presence of corporations, it is necessary for mergers to take place.[27] Larger-size organizations can lead to the formation of the corporate form of business, with the necessary factors of production, while the internal growth of proprietorships and partnerships is substantially difficult to attain under the present economic conditions. Ample organizational size is the first element necessary for the formation of corporations that possess the required factors of production.[28] Ecuadorian law does not restrict mergers; consequently, small- and medium-size organizations have the opportunity to merge easily. From 1998 to 2008, over 370 mergers of large corporations took place.[29] Mergers in large Ecuadorian enterprises have resulted in great advantages in all factors of production and have contributed to managerial development, and these enterprises are competing effectively and efficiently on an international basis.[30] Proposals from national and international economists and management consultants leading to the creation of more corporations through mergers are being seriously considered.[31]

Ecuadorian management consultant Carlos Lopez Cerdan Ripoll has been experimenting with a substantially different way of creating economies of scale for PYMES (*Pequenas y Medias Empresas*) an Spanish acronym for small- and medium-size business. He has articulated and integrated a small number of PYMES, mainly on a vertical basis, thus creating pseudo-vertical mergers or very small strategic alliances that have somehow resulted in more profits for the participating organizations. This temporary success has no solid foundations, and consequently, the participating organizations are not creating internal infrastructures for their growth and development.

Since industrialization has played a minor role in the economy of the country, the corporate form of business has not been developed, with the exception of a few large corporations. Approximately 97 percent of business organizations are proprietorships and partnerships of limited size, a situation that does not allow organizational growth and the development of the corporate form of business.

Management in Ecuador

The overwhelming majority of Ecuadorian managers work in small organizations that are owned and operated by family members. In other words, Ecuadorian managers manage small proprietorships and partnerships that belong to them, to their relatives and, in some cases, to their close friends. The selection of managers is simple because practically all of them are family members. Many small business owners have apparently reached the conclusion that non-family members cannot be trusted.[32]

The small organizational size and the proliferation of family owned and managed enterprises have impeded the development of management. Delegation is limited due to the Latin American social and business culture that favors centralization of control; all decisions are centralized, thus impeding delegation.[33] Ecuadorian organizations are opposed to changes that can lead to the development of management.[34] The majority of enterprises have only the top managerial level that consists of the owners, while the middle and lower operational levels are absent.[35] Departmentalization is nonexistent in the majority of private organizations and departments that exist in some organizations are limited to a very small number of large enterprises, while the remaining enterprises have no established departments.[36] The absence of departmentalization has caught the attention of some researchers in Ecuador, who claim that departments need to be formed in order to provide sufficient impetus for the development of Ecuadorian enterprises.[37]

Entrepreneurs who form a business organization or manage it do not identify themselves with the organization, do not strive for its success, and do not link their interests with those of the organization.[38] The ownership and management of PYMES are accustomed to operating using obsolete methods and controls, and they are not cognizant of the hidden costs that permeate in their organizations due to undetected diseconomies of scale.[39]

Ecuadorian management is authoritarian and paternalistic. Employees are dominated by managers, a cultural norm in Ecuadorian society.[40] Because of the poor conditions that prevail, Ecuadorian employees are controlled by exploiting their physiological, safety, and security needs. Ecuadorian employees are not protected by strong labor unions and are left at the mercy of their employers. However, many citizens in responsible positions want to change the working conditions of the people, and they support the idea that it is necessary to make the human element the number one priority of development.[41] A definitive characteristic of the labor market is the fact that there are a very small number of women employed. The inferior position of women in the labor market stems from their restricted access to resources and responsibility and their lack of autonomy in the workplace.[42]

Ecuadorians who have studied in North America and Europe, who are teaching management and other business administration curricula in higher education, or who are consulting in those same areas are pressing for developmental changes. In order for Ecuadorian business enterprises to survive and develop, the ownership and management must make substantial and fundamental changes in their business models and their organizing principles. Briefly stated, Ecuador's business owners and managers need to redefine themselves and implement the organization's strategy in the upper organizational level and delegate responsibility to lower levels that do not currently exist.[43] The ultimate goal of developmental changes is to make the organization more open and adaptive through increases in capability and potential so it can continue to make such planned change efforts on an action orientation basis.[44]

Ecuadorian managers do not have commensurate management education.[45] Even today, business owners have a negative view of management education and of management and business research. Curricula dedicated to educating managers are limited. Most educated managers have non-commensurate degrees, like law and engineering.[46] Law schools in the second part of the twentieth century were the first institutions to incorporate basic curricula in economics for those who wanted to be managers. Furthermore, managers are also responsible for resisting management education for cultural and economic reasons.[47] Lamentably, government support in management education remains limited.[48] Ecuadorian owners and managers need to change their business culture and receive commensurate management education, which will be conducive to the effective and efficient operation of their enterprises, and subsequently, to the development of managerial practices in their respective organizations.[49] The study of management education needs to become a lifelong study in order to assist the management of private enterprise to attain the required mission, goals, and objectives.[50] There are precedents of success in the development of management in the country. For example, a handful of large business organizations whose managers were educated in North America and Europe in commensurate management curricula made significant contributions to the economic development of Ecuador during more than seventy years of operation.[51]

Managers of smaller organizations can follow the successful steps of those large organizations and attain equal or even better success. This can be accomplished through changing Ecuador's managerial culture, increasing government assistance, and cooperating better with national and international universities that operate in the country. This involves increased and more vigorous management curricula and a synergistic rapport between educational institutions and business organizations.[52] To reiterate, there is profound need for advanced education in the areas of management and organizational development for both managers and owners in order to prepare them to implement the advanced managerial and organizational practices needed by newly formed and emerging enterprises.[53] Furthermore, it is necessary to increase the esteem of managers within the Ecuadorian society.[54]

Due to the negative impact of labor unions and the corporation, Ecuadorian management has not been developed. Business organizations are small and managed by individuals who are related to the owners. Due to the culture of the country, managers use paternalistic approaches to control their employees through their physiological, safety, and security needs. Employees are not protected by strong labor unions. Finally, managers do not have the necessary management education.

References

Acosta, A. *Breve Historia Económica del Ecuador*. Quito, Ecuador: Corporación Editorial Nacional, 2006.

Anderson, J. "The New Battle of Puebla." *Business México* 7, 2. (1997): 36-39.

Arosemena-Arosemena, G. "Las Empresas Apuntan a Fusiones." *Expreso de Guayaquil* 30, 14-15 (2007).

Arosemena-Arosemena, G. "Hacia la Superación Gerencial." *Industrias* 13, 20. (September 2008).

Burbach, R. "Ecuador's Popular Revolt: Forging a New Nation. *NACLA Report on the Americas* 40, 5. (September-October 2007): para. 32-37. http://proquest.umi.com/pqdweb?did=1405207071&sid=2&Fmt=3&clientld=11123&RQT=309&VName=PQD

Busch, E. T. "Small Business Hurdles in Ecuador." *Journal of Small Business Management* 71, January 1989.

Colegio de Economistas de Pichincha. *Realidad Economica y Social Del Ecuador*. Quito, Ecuador: Colegio de Economistas de Pichincha, 2004.

Correa, S. "Benchmarking: en Busca de las Mejores Prácticas." *Industrias* 13, 11. (November 2008): 36.

Crespo Merchan, M. "Formamos Gerentes Estrategas o Profesionales Administrativos? El Emprendedor." *Editorial Santiago Solano Gal-*

legos (December 2008): 16-24.

Directory of Education Online. http://www.directoryofeducation.net/colleges/worldwide/Ecuador

Franklin, G., and E. Mai. "The Role of State and Market in the Economic Development of Ecuador." *Journal of Economic Issues* (Association for Evolutionary Economics) 2, 72. (June 1993): 444.

Fualkner, A. H., and V. A. Lawson. "Employment versus Empowerment: A Case Study of the Nature of Women's Work in Ecuador." *The Journal of Development Studies* 27, 4. (July 1991): 24.

Haar, Jerry, and John Price. *Can Latin America Compete?: Confronting the Challenges of Globalization.* New York, NY: Palgrave McMillan, 2008.

Hassaurek, F. *Cuatro Anos entre los Ecuatorianos.* Quito, Ecuador: Abya Yala, 1997.

Hurtado, O. *El Poder Politico en Ecuador.* Quito, Ecuador: Editorial Planet del Ecuador, 1977.

Hurtado, O. *Las Constumbres De Los Ecuatorianos.* Quito, Ecuador: Editorial Ecuadora F.B.T.Cia., 2007.

Jameson, P. K. "Higher Education in a Vacuum: Stress and Reform in Ecuador." *Higher Education* 33, 1997: 272.

Kwok, C. "A Global Survey of International Business." *Journal of International Business* 9, 3 (1997): 132-135.

Lopez Cerdan Ripolli, C. "Aspectos Conceptuales De La Asociatividad Y Cooperación Empresarial De Las Pymes." *Taller de Capacitación Sobre Estrategias Taller Estrategias De Cooperación Empresarial Para El Mejoramiento De La Competitividad En Pymes.* Quito, Ecuador: IBERPYME, 2004.

Luna-Osorio, L. *Proyección del Ecuador al Mundo: 2007-2010.* Quito, Ecuador: Pudeleco Editores, 2007.

Lucio-Paredes, P. *En Busca de la Constitución Perdida.* Quito, Ecuador: TRAMA Ediciones, 2008.

Murillo-Moncayo, V., and M. Méndez Prado. "La Fusión de Empresas en el Ecuador como Opción de Crecimiento: Un Análisis de Casos." *Revista Tecnológica ESPOL* 20, 2008. Guayaquil, Ecuador.

NationMaster.com. "Trade Union Membership by Country." Accessed October 1, 2010. http://www.nationmaster.com/graph/lab_tra_uni_mem-labor-trade-union-membership

Ospina Peralta, P. *Nuestro Ecuador: Manual de Realidad Nacional.* Quito, Ecuador: Universidad Andina Simón Bolívar, 2007.

Panchana Pita, V., and C. Yong Paraga. "Estudio De Fusiones Y Adquisiciones Y Sus Efectos En Retornos Del Accionista: Caso Interbrew-Ambev." *Escuela Superior Politécnica Litoral*, 2006. Guayaquil, Ecuador.

Rigail, A. "La Educación, la Tecnología y la Productividad Laboral y Empresarial." *Arco Consutores* 2, 2006: 1-4.

Rigail, A. "El Rol de los Gerentes Generales para la Transformación de las Pymes." *Arco Consultores* 3, 2007: 36.

Rigail, A. "La Mentalidad de la Abundancia." *Arco Consultores* 5, 2008: 4-8.

Roberts, K. "Social Inequalities without Class Cleavages in Latin America's Neoliberal Era." *Studies in Comparative International Development* 36, 4. (2002): 5.

Schalb, M., R. Grosse, and E. Romero Simpson. "Developing Entrepreneurs in Developing Countries: The PEG Program in Peru." *Journal of Management Development* 4, 1998: 31-40.

Striffler, S. "Class Formation in Latin America: One Family's Enduring Journey between Country and City." *International Labor and Working Class History* 65, April 2004: 2. http://proquest.umi.com/pqdweb?did=1516220631&sid=3&Fmt=3&clientld=11123&RQT=309&VName=PQD

Superintendencia de Companias. *Las 1000 Mas Grandes Companias de Ecuador*. Quito, Ecuador: Superintendencia de Companias, 2008.

Theodore, John D. *The Development of Managerial Practices in Selected Nations in the World*. Edina, MN: Alpha Editions, 1991.

Theodore, John D. "The Impact of Religious, Social, and Economic Forces upon the Development of Management Education in Latin America." *Journal of Third World Studies* 16, 2. (1999): 133-139.

Theodore, John D. "Organization Development: Target Areas and Goals for Planned Change Interventions." *New Zealand Institute of Management*, March-April 2002: 52-65.

Theodore, John D. "Holistic Management." *EAN* 47, January-April 2003: 122-136.

Theodore, John D. "Desarrollo de Organizaciones: una Apuesta a la Eficiencia." *Ekos*, June 2004: 125-130.

Theodore, John D. "Organizational Size: A Key Element in the Development of Private Enterprises in the Less Developed Countries: The Case of Ecuador." *International Journal of Business & Economics Research* 8, 7. (July 2009): 45-49.

Theodore, John D. "Management Education: A Key Element for the Development of Private Enterprises in Latin America: The Case of Ecuador." *International Business & Economics Research Journal* 9, 2. (2010).

Theodore, John D. "Mergers of Private Enterprises: A Powerful Force for the Development of Private Business Organizations in Latin America: The Case of Ecuador." *International Business & Economics Research Journal* 10, 1. (January, 2011).

Tiffin, S., ed. *Entrepreneurship in Latin America*. Westport, CT: Praeger, 2004.

Uggen, J. "The Emergence of Multinational Enterprise in Ecuador: The Case of the Ecuadorian Corporation." *Business and Economic History Online* 6, 2008: 3-8.

Vásquez, L., and N. Santos. *Ecuador: Su Realidad*. Quito, Ecuador: Fundación de Investigación y Promoción Social "José Peralta", 2008.

Endnotes

1   F. Hassaurek, *Cuatro Anos entre los Ecuatorianos* (Quito, Ecuador: Abya Yala, 1997).

2   O. Hurtado, *Las Constumbres De Los Ecuatorianos* (Quito, Ecuador: Editorial Ecuadora F.B.T.Cia., 2007).

3   O. Hurtado, *El Poder Politico en Ecuador* (Quito, Ecuador: Editorial Planet del Ecuador, 1977).

4   John D. Theodore, *The Development of Managerial Practices in Selected Nations in the World* (Edina, MN: Alpha Editions, 1991).

5   L. Luna-Osorio, *Proyección del Ecuador al Mundo: 2007-2010* (Quito, Ecuador: Pudeleco Editores, 2007).

6   P. Lucio-Paredes, *En Busca de la Constitución Perdida* (Quito, Ecuador: TRAMA Ediciones, 2008).

7   Luna-Osorio, *Proyección del Ecuador al Mundo: 2007-2010*.

8   John D. Theodore, *The Development of Managerial Practices in Selected Nations in the World*.

9   Ibid.

10 M. Schalb, R. Grosse, and E. Romero Simpson, "Developing Entrepreneurs in Developing Countries: The PEG Program in Peru," *Journal of Management Development* 4, 1998: 31-40.

11 P. K. Jameson, "Higher Education in a Vacuum: Stress and Reform in Ecuador," *Higher Education* 33, 1997: 272.

12 Directory of Education Online. http://www.directoryofeducation.net/

colleges/worldwide/Ecuador

13 P. Ospina Peralta, *Nuestro Ecuador: Manual de Realidad Nacional* (Quito, Ecuador: Universidad Andina Simón Bolívar, 2007).

14 Jerry Haar and John Price, *Can Latin America Compete?: Confronting the Challenges of Globalization* (New York, NY: Palgrave McMillan, 2008).

15 Hurtado, *El Poder Politico en Ecuador*.

16 G. Franklin and E. Mai, "The Role of State and Market in the Economic Development of Ecuador," *Journal of Economic Issues* (Association for Evolutionary Economics) 2, 72 (June 1993): 444.

17 R. Burbach, "Ecuador's Popular Revolt: Forging a New Nation, *NACLA Report on the Americas* 40, 5 (September-October 2007): para. 32-37. http://proquest.umi.com/pqdweb?did=1405207071&sid=2&Fmt=3&clientld=11123&RQT=309&VName=PQD

18 S. Striffler, "Class Formation in Latin America: One Family's Enduring Journey between Country and City," *International Labor and Working Class History* 65, April 2004: 2. http://proquest.umi.com/pqdweb?did=1516220631&sid=3&Fmt=3&clientld=11123&RQT=309&VName=PQD

19 A. Acosta, *Breve Historia Económica del Ecuador* (Quito, Ecuador: Corporación Editorial Nacional, 2006).

20 Luna-Osorio, *Proyección del Ecuador al Mundo: 2007-2010*.

21 L.Vásquez and N. Santos, *Ecuador: Su Realidad* (Quito, Ecuador: Fundación de Investigación y Promoción Social "José Peralta", 2008).

22 K. Roberts, "Social Inequalities without Class Cleavages in Latin America's Neoliberal Era," *Studies in Comparative International Development* 36, 4 (2002): 5.

23 NationMaster.com. "Trade union membership by country."

24 Hurtado, *El Poder Politico en Ecuador*.

25 Vásquez and Santos, *Ecuador: Su Realidad*.

26 Hurtado, *Las Constumbres De Los Ecuatorianos*.

27 G. Arosemena-Arosemena, "Las Empresas Apuntan a Fusiones," *Expreso de Guayaquil* 30, 14-15 (2007).

28 John D. Theodore, "Holistic Management," *EAN* 47, January-April 2003: 122-136.

29 Superintendencia de Companias, *Las 1000 Mas Grandes Companias de Ecuador* (Quito, Ecuador: Superintendencia de Companias, 2008).

30 V. Murillo-Moncayo and M. Méndez Prado, "La Fusión de Empresas en el Ecuador como Opción de Crecimiento: Un Análisis de Casos," *Revista Tecnológica ESPOL* 20, 2008.

31 V. Panchana Pita and C. Yong Paraga, "Estudio De Fusiones Y Adquisiciones Y Sus Efectos En Retornos Del Accionista: Caso Interbrew-Ambev," *Escuela Superior Politécnica Litoral*, 2006.

32 E. T. Busch, "Small Business Hurdles in Ecuador," *Journal of Small Business Management* 71, January 1989.

33 Hurtado, *Las Constumbres De Los Ecuatorianos*.

34 C. Kwok, "A Global Survey of International Business," *Journal of International Business* 9, 3 (1997): 132-135.

35 Vásquez and Santos, *Ecuador: Su Realidad*.

36 Luna-Osorio, *Proyección del Ecuador al Mundo: 2007-2010*.

37 S. Correa, "Benchmarking: en Busca de las Mejores Prácticas," *Industrias* 13, 11 (November 2008): 36.

38 Hurtado, *Las Constumbres De Los Ecuatorianos*.

39 G. Arosemena-Arosemena, "Hacia la Superación Gerencial," *Industrias* 13, 20 (September 2008).

40 Hurtado, *El Poder Politico en Ecuador*.

41 Colegio de Economistas de Pichincha. *Realidad Economica y Social Del Ecuador*. (Quito, Ecuador: Colegio de Economistas de Pichincha, 2004).

42 A. H. Fualkner and V.A. Lawson, "Employment versus Empowerment: A Case Study of the Nature of Women's Work in Ecuador," *The Journal of Development Studies* 27, 4 (July 1991): 24.

43 Arosemena-Arosemena, "Hacia la Superación Gerencial."

44 John D. Theodore, "Organization Development: Target Areas and Goals for Planned Change Interventions," *New Zealand Institute of Management*, March-April 2002: 52-65.

45 John D. Theodore, "Management Education: A Key Element for the Development of Private Enterprises in Latin America: The Case of Ecuador," *International Business & Economics Research Journal* 9, 2 (2010).

46 A. Rigail, "La Mentalidad de la Abundancia," *Arco Consultores* 5, 2008: 4-8.

47 Arosemena-Arosemena, "Las Empresas Apuntan a Fusiones."

48 A. Rigail, "La Educación, la Tecnología y la Productividad Laboral y Empresarial," *Arco Consutores* 2, 2006: 1-4.

49 Ibid.

50 M. Crespo Merchan, "Formamos Gerentes Estrategas o Profesion-
     ales Administrativos? El Emprendedor," *Editorial Santiago Solano
     Gallegos* (December 2008): 16-24.
51 J. Uggen, "The Emergence of Multinational Enterprise in Ecuador:
     The Case of the Ecuadorian Corporation," *Business and Economic
     History Online* 6, 2008: 3-8.
52 Ibid.
53 John D. Theodore, "Mergers of Private Enterprises: A Powerful
     Force for the Development of Private Business Organizations in
     Latin America: The Case of Ecuador," *International Business &
     Economics Research Journal* 10 (January, 2011).
54 S. Tiffin, ed., *Entrepreneurship in Latin America* (Westport, CT:
     Praeger, 2004).

Chapter 4: Brazil

Religion and Economic Development

The Byzantine Empire, which occupied the lower part of Southeastern Europe and all of Asia Minor during its eleventh century existence, had strong commercial and diplomatic relations with the Far East. This empire had sea lanes to Asia, China, and modern Vietnam, where it procured spices, sandalwoods, silk, and other useful products. Overland trade with Asia used the Silk Road, which linked Constantinople with various Far Eastern cities.

During the twelfth century, internal strife broke out among the various Turko-Mongolic tribes in Central Asia, which resulted in population movements that blocked the Silk Road and severed overland trade between Europe and Asia. For this reason, the advanced European states of Portugal and Spain decided to reach Asia in a different manner: by sea.

Portugal, a nation on the Atlantic as opposed to the Mediterranean, became the first new maritime power and explorer. Portuguese ships sailed due south of the country, reaching every part of continental West Africa and the nearby islands where Portugal established its first colonies. Portuguese sailors reached the tip of South Africa, where they established a brilliant new city, Cape Town (O Cabo da Boa Esperanca), and then continued due east, establishing new colonies in the Indian Ocean, India, China, and several Pacific Islands.

The Spaniards followed the Portuguese, but in a different direction. In 1492, a Spanish expedition under the leadership of Christopher Columbus sailed westward and reached a group of islands off the Florida coast. As both advanced nations continued their expansion, signs of conflict appeared concerning the ownership of the new lands. In 1494, under the auspices of the Pope, Spain and Portugal signed the Treaty of Tordesillas, which clearly divided the new lands. All lands located east of the 50th meridian west became the property of the King of Portugal, with one exception—the bulge of Brazil, which was discovered by the Portuguese explorer Pedro Alvares Cabral in 1500. Most historians believe that the discovery of Brazil was accidental, but others argue that it was done on purpose in order for Portugal to acquire territories under the jurisdiction of Spain in the Americas. Brazil was a Portuguese colony from 1530 to 1822, characterized by slave labor. Slaves were imported from Africa or were descendants of Africans; the rest of the slaves were indigenous people. Offspring of mixed Portuguese and indigenous blood were called *mamelucos* and played a very important role in the socioeconomic structure of early Brazil.

The position of the European Roman Catholic Church toward economic development was inimical. Specifically, the ultimate goal of the Church was the salvation of people, and it made every effort to direct its congregation toward that goal. However, the role of the Portuguese Catholic Church in Brazil was much broader because the clergy also had to function as strong defenders of the lands occupied by Portugal. The Church of Brazil, controlled and assisted by the Portuguese government, started to build missions in the occupied territories to convert the native population and the African slaves to Christianity and to teach them the Portuguese culture and language. These missions also served as military outposts and centers of economic activity. The Church received extremely expensive gifts from the business people engaged in the various economic activities and industries in the colony. For all practical purposes, the Church accepted economic development.

Economic development started in Brazil shortly after it became a colony. The first industry to appear was brazilwood, which had dye-making qualities and was mainly exported to Portugal. The cattle industry appeared in the northern part of the colony, followed by additional agricultural products of great importance: coffee, cotton, and rubber.[1] Sugar was abundantly cultivated in the tropical, humid areas of the northern part of the Brazilian colony. Sugar was first cultivated in the sixteenth century south of Recife, in the wetter Mata Umida. In the twentieth century, sugar production had extended north of Recife into the dryer, flatter coastal tablelands of the Mata Seca.[2] Eventually, large areas for producing sugar were formed called *latifundias*, which operated under the best economies of scale and thus allowed Brazil to become the most important exporter of sugar in the world.

The Portuguese government and economic sector were not fully satisfied with the immense wealth agricultural industries generated for the mother country. Instead, both entities were constantly looking for gold, desiring to find gold as the Spaniards had on the other side of the continent. Gold was finally found in what is now known as Minas Gerais and Mato Grosso. The discovery of gold attracted a large number of Portuguese and colonials to those areas of the colony. Shortly after the discovery of gold, diamonds were discovered. Brazil was the only colony in the Portuguese Empire that provided high returns on investment for the mother country. For this reason, Portugal continued to invest abundantly in Brazil.

Brazil was under the mercantile auspices of Portugal until 1822, when it won its independence in a relatively bloodless revolt. However, the economy continued to depend on the same familiar products (which continued to created substantial wealth) until the 1930s, when vigorous attempts were made to modernize the Brazilian economy and create a strong industrial infrastructure. After World War II, the country embarked on a new economic challenge to assist its industries to grow and eventually replace all imports, especially consumer goods. This was known as the famous *import substitution period*, which was very successful and created a strong industrial infrastructure in the country under very modern conditions.

Over the last century, Brazil has developed extensive manufacturing and scientific infrastructures; however, the interactions between them have been historically weak. The same situation continues today with a tendency for short-lived collaborations between academia and industry, low private sector investment in research and development, and the concentration of research in exclusively academic settings.[3] On one hand, Brazil has the tenth largest economy in the world and has been classified as a country with a medium degree of human development. On the other hand, Brazil has a high degree of income inequality that compels millions of people to live under the harsh conditions of poverty.[4]

Lamentably, as was the case in all Latin American countries, a macro-economic approach to economic development was introduced by socialist administrations in the government with disastrous results. Subsequently, the country applied a second import substitution policy that developed and exported manufactured goods.[5]

While the idea of Brazil as an emerging power is largely welcomed by native foreign policy makers and an increasing number of foreign commentators, it is doubtful that the country's economy can sustain this status.[6] Brazil is the leader in South American integration (initiated by the continental integration movement with the 2000 Brazilian summit of South American presidents), but it is unwilling to assume the costs necessary to develop the project.[7]

The impact of religion upon economic development was neutral, but in several periods it showed a rather positive influence, as economic development became viewed as a way of supporting the clergy. In turn, the clergy protected Portuguese (and eventually Brazilian) territories while converting African slaves and indigenous people to Christianity and teaching them Portuguese language and culture. The economy of Brazil started with agricultural products during the colonial period and then entered its industrial era in the 1930s. The economy of Brazil personifies a strong cyclical fluctuation, but in the long run the country is having problems with economic development.

Religion and Education

The Catholic Church controlled the colonial educational system in Brazil, but its control diminished after the country's independence from Portugal. The current education system in Brazil is the result of the 1988 Constitution, which specified that everyone in the country has the right to receive an education. The Federal Government controls all aspects of national education, but it also allows the Brazilian states to participate in the educational process in matters that relate to them. The educational system of Brazil had experienced serious problems in the past that arose at various levels. For this reason, it now needs to analyze education models that promote an effective and efficient educational system.[8]

The Brazilian educational system has three levels: primary or fundamental education, the secondary or intermediate education, and higher education. Primary school is compulsory between the ages of seven and fourteen, and studies include language (Portuguese), history, geography, biology, physics, and mathematics.

Secondary education consists of four years of studies. Those who attend secondary education usually strive to apply for admission to universities, which have stringent entrance examinations. However, there are serious concerns about the deficient quality of primary and secondary level education, which is failing to provide the minimum literacy and mathematical skills necessary for active citizenship.[9]

Higher education in Brazil was started by the Jesuits, whose purpose was to educate barbarian men in a barbarian country.[10] The Jesuits started the educational system under Manoel da Nobrega in 1549, and ceded their control in 1759 under the presidency of the Jesuit Antonio Viera. Many well-known universities were established during the colonial period: Rio de Janeiro (1638), Sao Paulo (1708), Olinda (1607), Recife (1721), Maranao (1709), and Para (1695). The universities offered degrees in civil law, philosophy, and theology. Everyone was able to attend the universities, regardless of race or place of birth, because all were subjects of the King of Portugal. The fact that one was born in Portugal was not a criterion.[11]

As was the case in Ecuador and other Latin American nations, Brazil was influenced by the temporary success of Soviet economic development in the early 1960s. Many Latin American intellectuals and political leaders were profoundly concerned with discovering the magic of economic growth, and the communist economic model had widespread appeal. The policies of communist Cuba were applied all over Latin America as Fidel Castro promised the beginning of the decade of plenty. As a result, Brazil was one of the first countries in Latin America to establish business schools in the 1960s.

During an expansion of the production of industrial goods and a massive increase in exports in the late 1980s and early 1990s, the driving forces of globalization, constant change, and evolving international standards of competitiveness required Brazilian organizations and the Brazilian government to re-examine both the structural and operational aspects of how to create and sustain a competitive advantage. A key issue was the employment of individuals who demonstrated the attitudes and skills necessary for success in this area.

However, several powerful barriers retarded the growth of business education, such as a limited amount of government and private investment in academic and practical management education. Also, Brazilians who had studied management in North America and Europe were either underemployed or unable to find suitable positions at home, and as a result, many of them returned to the nations where they were educated in search of productive employment.[12]

Higher education in Brazil today offers a wide variety of degrees and curricula, and consists of both public and private universities and colleges. Public institutions receive generous subsidies from the government and therefore provide quality education with well-prepared professors and modern buildings and laboratories. Recently, private universities have been improving their quality of instruction. Undergraduate programs last for four years, culminating in a degree known as *bacharelado*. With this degree, students may apply for entrance into graduate school (*pos-graduacao*), which usually consists of two more years of intensive studies. In most cases, a thesis is required for entrance. Brazilian doctoral programs are relatively difficult to complete and consist of four years of full-time studies followed by a doctoral dissertation. There are 151 colleges and universities in Brazil.[13] The clear majority of them offer curricula in economics, business, and management.

The Catholic Church controlled education in Brazil during the colonial period and for 150 years after independence, and supported curricula in law, philosophy, theology, and related areas. However, after the 1960s, it became necessary for the country to adopt curricula in business, management, and economics. The Church did not oppose this adaptation because it was necessary for the survival of the country; furthermore, the old curricula remained intact. Brazil has a relatively good educational system, but serious problems exist at the elementary and secondary levels. The nation's higher education system offers all types of curricula at the undergraduate, graduate, and doctoral levels. Business, economics, and management curricula are widely available.

Religion and Social Structure

During the first part of the colonial period, the social structure of Brazil was divided into two groups: those who used slaves and those who did not. The first group consisted of the aristocracy, owners of large estates who were exceedingly powerful. The aristocracy could be only challenged by the business world, which provided the necessary finances for the operation of large aristocratic estates that used slave labor. The estate owners and business people were opposing forces that frequently clashed. The only impact the Roman Catholic Church of Brazil had upon the structure of the Brazilian society was its inimical position against slavery. However, it accepted generous gifts from wealthy business persons, especially those who opposed the owners of large estates with slaves.[14]

There was another heterogeneous group of people that had no social structure—poor whites from Portugal, native Brazilians, free African slaves, free indigenous tribes, and *mamelucos*.[15] Finally, there was a social distinction between the inhabitants of the coastal areas and the interior parts of Brazil. Inhabitants of coastal areas have always been considered more learned and cultured than those in the interior parts of the nation, according to the Southern European tradition. The Brazilian Roman Catholic Church had practically no impact upon the formation and sustenance of those social structures.

After Brazil won its independence, social stratification began, consisting of a small elite class at the top of the social pyramid, a large middle class of free people of every color and origin, and a large lower class of slaves at the bottom. Brazil abolished slavery in 1886 without any conflict or confrontation.

After the Second World War, Brazilian social stratification in urban areas consisted of a large lower class of unskilled workers without regular employment who did manual work on the streets. Above them were manual workers with established professions, such as street cleaners, ditch diggers, and garbage collectors. Above the manual workers was a small class of professionals and government officials with limited education and salaries. At the top was a very small upper class with high-compensating jobs and that controlled the wealth of country.[16]

During the famous import substitution period and the second import substitution policy, forced labor mobility occurred on a national scale that deformed the existing social structure and formed a new labor market in every region of the country. A heterogeneous proletariat was created that included workers with access to markets that offered higher wages and salaries. Another proletariat group was established that consisted of highly skilled, well-educated workers mostly employed in cities.[17]

The social structure in Brazil has become dynamic and flexible and serves the interests of its members in procuring commensurate employment and ascending to professional echelons. In some cases, race plays a role in the social stratification and social mobility in the country; people of African descent often have fewer opportunities in Brazilian society. The modern labor market in Brazil consists of people who are employed, unemployed people seeking work, and people unemployed due to the lack of a demand for their labor.[18]

Brazilian society has suffered from a number of problems which still prevail to a lesser extent. For example, in the 1990s, an entire segment of Brazilian society became dehumanized in the eyes of the entire population. The overloaded and corrupt justice system would not address the problem, and most people were either too scared or too detached to do anything about the judicial situation.[19] The World Bank wants Brazil to continue on a reform agenda, and the long list of desired reforms includes improving primary and secondary education, reducing inequities through social transfer programs, reducing bureaucratic red tape, increasing foreign trade, reforming the social security system, and maintaining fiscal balance.[20]

The Catholic Church did not have an impact upon the social structure and social mobility of the country, which depended upon the economic conditions that prevailed in each period and was influenced by economic cyclical fluctuation. The social structure in early Brazil was vaguely defined and had more than one structure. In the 1940s, Brazilian society started to change and became more flexible. The subsequent industrialization of the economy played an important role in creating a flexible and dynamic society that is yet still affected by race issues.

Extent of Industrialization

Economic development in Brazil played a positive role in the development of industrialization, but industry did not have the support of the educational system and social structure until after the Second World War. Industry first appeared in Brazil in the nineteenth century with the creation of small-size industries that produced consumer products to compete with similar imported goods. This era of industrialization was the progenitor of the import substitution policy. It is important to note that initially industrialization was not supported by the government because many Brazilian politicians were under the influence of more industrialized nations of Europe and the United States, who wanted Brazil to buy their industrial products. At that time, there was no strong industrial class in the country to oppose the anti-industrialization sentiments of the politicians.[21]

The small industrialists persisted and grew substantially; industrialization gained sufficient ground, but in an uncoordinated way because the government did not organize or interfere in the process. Once it became evident to government officials that industrialization did not pose a threat to the agricultural sector of the economy, the Brazilian government started to support industrialization through investments in capital goods, educated manpower, and existing technology. By 1960, the city of Sao Paulo and its suburbs had become the largest industrial park in the developing nation at that time. One major problem in instituting the industrialization process was the lack of education and discipline of workers from agricultural and impoverished urban areas.

One important factor in the industrial sector of modern Brazil points to strong signs of deindustrialization similar to those that occurred in Russia and Greece in the 1990s. The substitution of agricultural commodity exports for fuel exports and Embraer airplane sales for MiG fighters demonstrates the underlying risk of Brazil's current commodity export boom.[2]

Today Brazil is a highly industrialized nation, although its economy is not equitably developed throughout the country. The gross domestic product grew from 235 billion US dollars in 1980 to 798 billion in 2005. In 2008, the industrial sector accounted for 38 percent of all economic activities, whereas agriculture accounted for 8 percent and services for

54 percent.[23]

The economic development of the country provided substantial assistance to the creation, sustenance, and development of industrialization. However, the educational system and social structure did not offer significant support for industrialization until recently.

Labor Unions

As a result of the growing importance of industrialization, labor unions have developed, and they provide sufficient support for their members in most cases. The first labor unions in the country appeared in the early 1880s in the industrial areas, such as the railroad and shipyards.[24]

These unions were managed by people who were not accepted by the majority of society: anarchists. The anarchists were opposed by socialists, who had a better view of syndicalism from a European perspective. During this time, great tides of European immigrants who were familiar with labor unionism came to Brazil. However, the large numbers of immigrants flooded the labor market, making it difficult for the average worker to acquire employment. European immigrant workers gradually convinced their employers that adequately paid and well-treated employees also act as consumers and contribute to the growth and development of the economy.

Brazilian labor unions were vehemently opposed by both the government and the owners and management of enterprises; consequently, unions have endured many turbulent periods. There have been incidents of brutal clashes between police officers and labor union members that resulted in multiple deaths and property destruction. In 1937, the labor provision of the Estado Novo specified that labor is a social duty, and that intellectual, technical, and manual labor has the right to protection by the state.[25] Until 1980, these organizations were dominated by confederations under the auspices of the government; each profession had its own confederation. After 1980, several confederations merged into larger ones. The largest confederations today are the Central Única dos Trabalhadores and the Confederação Geral dos Trabalhadores.[26]

Like Ecuador, the Brazilian government does not enforce labor codes effectively and efficiently. Labor codes were modified after 1980 to regulate the formal labor element and the role of the government. However, male and female employees were not treated equally in the country's labor unions; furthermore, women were largely ignored by rural trade unions in the 1980s.[27] The informal labor sector is sizeable but powerless, and it is here that the labor codes are frequently violated. Under President Lula, the government launched an innovative program to grant limited benefits to employees in the informal sector, but the program received a strong negative reaction from labor unions fearing attenuation of workers representation and collective powers.[28]

Modern Brazilian labor unions are strong and provide sufficient support for their members; however, they are also centers of political activity that frequently causes counterproductive results. While trade unions can work to improve local work conditions and pay rates, wage rates naturally gravitate toward the national minimum wage across the country.[29]

The Corporation

The corporate form of business did not originally play a role in the early Brazilian economy; it appeared later as the result of industrialization. However, corporations initially appeared as government-owned and operated entities. The first important government corporation was the National Steel Company, built in 1942; it was the first large-scale iron and steel-producing plant in Brazil.[30]

At that time, President Getúlio Vargas wanted to implement the concept of corporatism, which involved the adoption of modern capitalist ideas while avoiding the extremes of laissez-faire permissiveness on the one hand and total state direction on the other. This was accomplished by establishing syndicates representing specific economic sectors.[31]

In 1990, President Fernando Collor de Mello introduced a bold privatization plan that transferred a large number of state-owned corporations to the private sector. President Fernando Henrique Cardoso continued the privatization process.[32] However, Brazil still has the largest government relative to GDP among large middle-income economies, and it has a larger government than other economies in the high-income category.[33] This means that a substantially large number of corporations still remain under government ownership and control. Opening corporations to the public in Brazil is popularly associated with an expropriation of dispersed shareholders, as the controlling entity lowers firm performance and share prices and then gradually buys back shares, thus reducing liquidity and further depressing share prices.[34] Private corporations are also not viewed positively by the public due to their lack of ethical standards. The social responsibility of corporations is not a topic that preoccupies Brazilian society. Indicators such as government transparency and anti-corruption measures, supplier relations, and consumer and customer relations each were mentioned in less than 5 percent of the news stories in the Brazilian press.[35] The proportion of companies with an ethics statement is higher among listed companies and large transactional and holding companies than among family businesses, companies with a low degree of internationalization, and small companies.[36] The majority of Brazilian firms studied (77 percent) have some kind of written ethics document. The most common documents are codes of ethics, codes of conduct, and company vision or company mission statements.[37]

Industrialization supported the creation and sustenance of corporations in the country, but the majority were owned and operated by the government. Therefore, private professional management in the corporate sector was absent. Recent presidents started privatizing corporations, but even today the government sector is substantially active in the corporate area.

Management in Brazil

Most managers in Brazil work in small organizations owned and operated by family members. Managers operate small proprietorships and partnerships that belong to them, to their relatives and, in some cases, to their close friends. The selection of managers is simple because practically all of them are family members.

The 2005 Investment Climate Survey of Brazil by the World Bank indicated that micro firms (up to 19 employees) constitute 20 percent of the economy; small firms (20-99 employees), 52 percent; medium-size firms (100-499 employees), 23 percent; and large firms (more than 500 employees), 5 percent.[38]

Since most Brazilian business organizations are small in size, they do not have the capability to develop and become competitive. Larger firms are more able and more likely to respond effectively to increasing competitive pressure.[39] Medium- and large-size firms have the necessary size to develop the principles of organization and advanced management practices, provided that the management and employees are qualified and have the necessary education and training in management and organization. Although micro and small business organizations have the ability and agility to generate some economic activity and their importance is recognized,[40] these enterprises do not operate under economies of scale, for their small size prohibits them from using principles of organization and advance management practices. As a result, their role is very limited in the Mercosul association.[41]

Most corporate managers come from high social stratifications and are appointed by government officials in the government-owned and operated corporate entities. The 2003 Investment Climate Survey of Brazil by the World Bank indicated that 10.9 percent of the managers had graduate degrees and 16.8 percent had undergraduate degrees. In small firms, 42 percent had graduate degrees and 53.8 percent had undergraduate degrees; in medium-size firms, 32.9 percent and 25.8 percent; and in large firms, 14.2 percent and 3.6 percent.[42] It is evident that a large percentage of Brazilian managers are educated; however, in most cases they do not have commensurate management education. In the 1960s, Brazil established *A Univeridade do Trabalho* for the purpose of creating active, practical business people, ready to work in a technical profession and seek high returns on their investments.[43]

The small size of organizations and the perpetuation of family owned and managed enterprises have impeded the development of management in most Brazilian organizations. Delegation is limited due to a Latin American social and business culture that favors centralization of control. The middle organizational level is absent in the majority of enterprises; the top managerial level consists of the owners. Departmentalization is embryonic in the majority of private organizations, and departments that exist in some organizations are limited to a very small number of large enterprises.

Due to Brazilian culture, management is authoritarian and paternalistic. Additionally, due to Brazil's uneven economic conditions, many employees are controlled by exploiting their physiological, safety, and security needs. However, labor unions are constantly aiming at increasing wages and salaries for their members. Progress has been made in the area of human resource management. Human resource management centers on the HR professional, who is seen as an advocate for employees rather than strictly an agent of the organization.[44]

Women are playing a limited role in the management of private organizations. The absence of women in the hierarchy can only be explained by the lack of women in certain fields or occupations. This phenomenon seems to be related to organizational size and culture, and to the absence of human resources policies that encourage women to get involved in the organization.[45]

Even today, business owners have a negative view of management education and research and of business management in general. Curricula dedicated to educating managers are abundantly available, but only a small number of managers take advantage of this opportunity. Managers of small organizations resist management education for cultural and economic reasons.

The organizational and managerial culture of Brazil is depicted by plasticity and formalism. Plasticity has its roots in the country's colonization process, and manifests in the easy assimilation of foreign practices and customers, including managerial practices imported from abroad that have not been examined in order to determine if they can be correctly used by Brazilian managers. In many cases it leads to lip-service behaviors, where organizations appear to adopt a new managerial technique while the operation continues to be managed as before. Formalism relates to attachment to laws and rules, albeit ambiguous, as such attachment is frequently shown in façade behaviors.[46]

As the direct result of the increase in information, curricula and courses in competitive intelligence in Brazil, universities are expanding and are being used as tools for strategic decision making.[47] Brazil leads Latin America in terms of the number of universities with courses on entrepreneurship. As to support for technical entrepreneurship, Brazil overwhelms the rest of Latin America in investments in business incubators.[48] A life-long study of management education is needed in order to assist the management of private enterprises to attain their mission, goals, and objectives.[49]

The software of human capital management came to improve the management of Brazilian human resources, enabling a more agile dissemination process. For small, medium, and large Brazilian organizations, software providers need to exhibit flexibility in order to rapidly adopt to the needs of their clients and to provide precise, effective, and efficient information.[50] The integrative philosophy of Total Quality Management is highly visible in medium- and large-size Brazilian organizations.[51]

The development of management in Brazil has been delayed by government ownership and control of the corporate form of business, the small size of most Brazilian business organizations, and the non-commensurate education of managers. However, the country continues to privatize corporations; it has instituted academic and professional curricula in business and management in many institutions of higher learning, and it is providing informal managerial training programs for owners and managers of small business organizations. Serious efforts should be made to merge small business organizations in order to create more and better economies of scale. Emphasis should also be placed on changing the static mentality of owners and managers of private organizations in order to promote dynamic management and development of their organizations from both a short- and long-term perspective.

References

Albuquerque, M. M. *Pequena Historia de la Formacao Social Brasileira*. Rio de Janeiro: Graal, 1981.

Arraes, Virgílio Caixeta. "The Brazilian Business World: The Difficult Adaptation to Globalization." *Revista Brasileira de Política Internacional* 53, 2 (2010): 198-216. http://search.ebscohost.com/login.aspx?direct=true&db=a9h&AN=57264707 &site=ehost-live

Barbosa, A., T. Narciso, and M. Biancalana. "Brazil in Africa: Another Emerging Power in the Continent?" *Politikon* 36, 1. (2009): 59-86. doi: 10.1080/02589340903155401

Basso, M. *Mercosul*. Sao Paulo, Brazil: Editora Atlas S.A., 2007.

Becker, Bertha K., and Claudio A. G. Egler. *Brazil: A New Regional Power in the World-Economy*. Cambridge, England: Cambridge University Press, 1992.

Burges, S. W. "Bounded by the Reality of Trade: Practical Limits to a South American Region." *Cambridge Review of International Affairs* 18, 3. (2005): 437- 454. doi: 10.1080/09557570500238076

Corrêa, A. M. C., and J. De Castro. "Brasil: Cinco Séculos de Riqueza, Desigualdade e Pobreza." *Impulso* 12, 27. (2000): 127-141. http://search.ebscohost.com/login.aspx?direct=true&db=a9h&AN=33336306 &site=ehost-live

Cason, J. "Searching for a New Formula: Brazilian Political Economy in Reform." *Latin American Research Review* 42, 2. (2007): 212-224. http://search.ebscohost.com/login.aspx?direct=true&db=mh&AN=25268070 &site=ehost-live

Coelho, G., H. Dou, L. Quoniam, and C. Henrique Da Silva. "Ensino e Pesquisa no Campo da Inteligencia Competitiva no Brasile a Cooperacao Franco-Braileira." *PUZZLE: Revista Hispana de la Inteligencia Competitiva* 5, 23. (2006): 12-19. http://search.ebscohost.com/login.aspx?direct=true&db=a9h&AN=22188087 &site=ehost-live

Dalfovo, O., and D. Dias. "Do Capital Humano: Comparação na Localização de Software de Gestao do Capital Humano Entre os Países Brasil, Argentina e México." *Revista Brasileira de Gestao de Negócios* 11, 33. (2009): 333-350. http://search.ebscohost.com/login.aspx?direct=true&db=bth&AN=47332597 &site=ehost-live

Donaires, O. S., M. G. Pinheiro, L. Cezarino, L. O. Ostanel, and D. P.

Martinelli. "Systemic Model for Diagnosis of the Micro, Small and Medium Enterprises from Two Cities from the Countryside of the State of São Paulo in Brazil." *Systemic Practice & Action Research* 23, 3. (2010): 221-236. doi:10.1007/s11213-009-9157-5

Directory of Education Online. http://www.directoryofeducation.net/colleges/worldwide/brazil/

Elvira, M. M., and A. Davila. "Emergent Directions for Human Resource Management Research in Latin America." *International Journal of Human Resource Management* 16, 12. (2005): 2265-2282. doi: 10.1080/09585190500358703

Endres, A. *Melhoria De Desempenho Em P&D-O Modo Juran*. Rio de Janeiro: Editora Bookmark Ltda, 1997.

Ferreira, T. L. *Historia Da Educacao Lusobrasileira*. Sao Paulo, Brazil: Edicao Saraiva, 1966.

Ferreira, T. L. and M. R. Ferreira. *Historia Da Civilizaco Brasileira*. Sao Paulo, Brazil: Grafica Biblos, 1960.

Filho, M. R. *Organizacao e Administracao Escolar*. Sao Paulo, Brazil: Edicoes Melhoramentos, 1967.

Franco, M. S. C. *Homens Liveres na Ordem Social Escravocrata*. Sao Paulo, Brazil: Atica, 1974.

French, J. D. *Labor Law and Brazilian Political Culture*. Chapel Hill: University of North Carolina Press, 2004.

Fontes Filho, J. R., and G. S. A. Nunes. "O Estrategista da Micro, Pequena e Média Empresa Privada Brasileira." *Revista Brasileira de Gestão de Negócios* 12, 36. (2010): 271-288. http://search.ebscohost.com/login.aspx?direct=true&db=bth&AN=54490625 &site=ehost-live

Grande, Humberto. *A Universidade do Trabalho e o Desajustamento Entre Massas e Classes Dirigentes*. Rio de Janeiro: Departamento De Imprensa Nacional, 1965.

Haar, J., and J. Price. *Can Latin America Compete?* New York, NY: Palgrave McMillan, 2008.

Kumar, A. and M. Francisco. *Enterprise Size, Financing Patterns, and Credit Constraints in Brazil*. Washington, D.C.: The World Bank, 2005. http://search.ebscohost.com/login.aspx?direct=true&db=a9h& AN=22188087 &site=ehost-live

Mele, D., P. Debeljuh, and M. Arruda. "Corporate Ethical Policies in Large Corporations in Argentina, Brazil and Spain." *Journal of Business Ethics* 63, 1. (2006): 21-38. doi: 10.1007/s10551-005-7100-y

Nenova, T. "Control Values and Changes in Corporate Law in Brazil." *Latin American Business Review* 6, 3. (2005): 1-37. doi: 10.1300/ J140v06n03_01

Porter, G., C. Dabat, and H. R. de Souza. "Local Labour Markets and the Reconfiguration of the Sugar Industry in Northeast Brazil. *Antipode* 33, 5. (2001): 826-854. http://search.ebscohost.com/login.aspx? direct=true&db=a9h&AN=5854562& site=e host=live

Rangel, I. M. *Economia Brasileira Contemporanea*. Sao Paulo, Brazil: Bienal, 1987.

Ribeiro, E. P. "Fluxo de Empregos, Fluxo de Trabalhadores e Fluxo de Postos de Trabalho no Brasil." *Revista de Economia Politica* 30, 3. (2010): 401-419. doi: 10.1590/S0101-31572010000300003

Rodriguez, Alberto, Carl Dahlman, and Jamil Salmi. *Brazil: Knowledge and Innovation for Competitiveness in Brazil*. Washington, D.C.: The World Bank, 2008.

Sá, Creso. "Research Policy in Emerging Economies: Brazil's Sector Funds." *Minerva: A Review of Science, Learning & Policy* 43, 3. (2005): 245-263. doi: 10.1007/s11024-005-6474-4

Saravia, E., and R. C. Gomes. "Public Management in South America: What Happened in the Last Ten Years?" *Public Management Review* 10, 4. (2008): 493-504. doi: 10.1080/14719030802263939

Selwyn, B. "Trade Unions and Women's Empowerment in North East Brazil." *Gender & Development* 17, 2. (2009): 189-201. doi: 10.1080/13552070903009734

Selwyn, B. "Gender Wage Work and Development in North East Brazil." *Bulletin of Latin American Research* 29, 1. (2010): 51-70. doi: 10.1111/j.1470- 9856.2009.00311.x

Skidmore, Thomas E. *Brazil: Five Centuries of Change*. 2nd ed. Oxford, England: Oxford University Press, 2010.

Stewart, J. "Portrait of Brazil: A Society Out of Control." *Harvard International Review* 14, 1. (1991): 47. http://search.ebscohost.com/ login.aspx?direct=true&db=a9h&AN=9701272984&site=ehost-live

Summerhill, William R, III. *Order Against Progress: Government, Foreign Investment, and Railroads in Brazil (1854-1913)*. Stanford, CA: Stanford University Press, 2003.

Suzigan, W. *Industria Brasileira: Origem e Desenvolvimento*. Sao Paulo, Brazil: Brasiliense, 1986.

Tavares, M. C. *De Substitucao de Importacao ao Capitalism Financieiro*. Rio de Janeiro: Zahar, 1987.

Tiffin, S., ed. *Entrepreneurship in Latin America*. Westport, CT: Praeger, 2004.

Vazquez, J. L. *Comercio Exterior Brazileiro*. Sao Paulo, Brazil: Editora Atlas S.A., 2007.

Vivarta, V., and G. Canela. "Corporate Social Responsibility in Brazil: The Role of the Press as Watchdog." *Journal of Corporate Citizenship* 21 (2006): 95-106. http://search.ebscohost.com/login.aspx?direct=true&db=bth&AN=20025830 &site=ehost-live

Wood , T., and A. de Paula. "Pop-Management Literature: Popular Business Press and Management Culture in Brazil." *Canadian Journal of Administrative Sciences* 25, 3. (2008): 185-200. doi: 10.1002/CJAS.71

Endnotes

1 M. C. Tavares, *De Substitucao de Importacao ao Capitalism Financieiro* (Rio de Janeiro: Zahar, 1987).

2 G. Porter, C. Dabat, and H. R. de Souza, "Local Labour Markets and the Reconfiguration of the Sugar Industry in Northeast Brazil," *Antipode* 33, 5 (2001): 830. http://search.ebscohost.com/login.aspx?direct=true&db=a9h&AN=5854562& site=e host=live

3 Creso Sá, "Research Policy in Emerging Economies: Brazil's Sector Funds," *Minerva: A Review of Science, Learning & Policy* 43, 3 (2005): 207. doi: 10.1007/s11024-005-6474-4

4 A. M. C. Corrêa and J. De Castro, "Brasil: Cinco Séculos de Riqueza, Desigualdade e Pobreza," *Impulso* 12, 27 (2000): 140. http://search.ebscohost.com/login.aspx?direct=true&db=a9h&AN=33336306 &site=ehost-live

5 I. M. Rangel, *Economia Brasileira Contemporanea* (Sao Paulo, Brazil: Bienal, 1987).

6 A. Barbosa, T. Narciso, and M. Biancalana, "Brazil in Africa: Another Emerging Power in the Continent?" *Politikon* 36, 1 (2009): 83. doi: 10.1080/02589340903155401

7 S. W. Burges, "Bounded by the Reality of Trade: Practical Limits to a South American Region," *Cambridge Review of International Affairs* 18, 3 (2005): 451. doi: 10.1080/09557570500238076

8 M. R. Filho, *Organizacao e Administracao Escolar* (Sao Paulo, Brazil: Edicoes Melhoramentos, 1967).

9 Alberto Rodriguez, Carl Dahlman, and Jamil Salmi, *Brazil: Knowledge and Innovation for Competitiveness in Brazil* (Washington,

D.C.: The World Bank, 2008).

10 T. L. Ferreira and M. R. Ferreira, *Historia Da Civilizaco Brasileira* (Sao Paulo, Brazil: Grafica Biblos, 1960).

11 T. L. Ferreira, *Historia Da Educacao Lusobrasileira* (Sao Paulo, Brazil: Edicao Saraiva, 1966).

12 M. Schalb, R. Grosse, and E. Romero Simpson, "Developing Entrepreneurs in Developing Countries: The PEG Program in Peru," *Journal of Management Development* 4 (1998), 31-40.

13 Directory of Education Online. http://www.directoryofeducation.net/colleges/worldwide/brazil/

14 M. M. Albuquerque, *Pequena Historia de la Formacao Social Brasileira* (Rio de Janeiro: Graal, 1981).

15 M. S. C. Franco, *Homens Liveres na Ordem Social Escravocrata* (Sao Paulo, Brazil: Atica, 1974).

16 E. P. Ribeiro, "Fluxo de Empregos, Fluxo de Trabalhadores e Fluxo de Postos de Trabalho no Brasil," *Revista de Economia Politica* 30, 3 (2010): 404. doi: 10.1590/S0101-31572010000300003

17 J. Stewart, "Portrait of Brazil: A Society Out of Control," *Harvard International Review* 14, 1 (1991): 47. http://search.ebscohost.com/login.aspx?direct=true&db=a9h&AN=9701272984&site=ehost-live

18 Ribeiro, "Fluxo de Empregos, Fluxo de Trabalhadores e Fluxo de Postos de Trabalho no Brasil," 404.

19 Stewart, "Portrait of Brazil: A Society Out of Control," 3.

20 J. Cason, "Searching for a New Formula: Brazilian Political Economy in Reform," *Latin American Research Review* 42, 2 (2007): 220. http://search.ebscohost.com/login.aspx?direct=true&db=mh&AN=25268070 &site=ehost-live

21 W. Suzigan, *Industria Brasileira: Origem e Desenvolvimento* (Sao Paulo, Brazil: Brasilienese, 1986).

22 Rodriguez, Dahlman, and Salmi, *Brazil: Knowledge and Innovation for Competitiveness in Brazil.*

23 Ibid.

24 William R. Summerhill, III, *Order Against Progress: Government, Foreign Investment, and Railroads in Brazil (1854-1913)* (Stanford, CA: Stanford University Press, 2003).

25 J. D. French, *Labor Law and Brazilian Political Culture* (Chapel Hill: University of North Carolina Press, 2004).

26 NationMaster.com. "Trade union membership by country."

27 B. Selwyn, "Gender Wage Work and Development in North East

Brazil," *Bulletin of Latin American Research* 29, 1 (2010): 51-70. doi: 10.1111/j.1470- 9856.2009.00311.x

28   J. Haar and J. Price, *Can Latin America Compete?* (New York, NY: Palgrave McMillan, 2008).

29   B. Selwyn, "Trade Unions and Women's Empowerment in North East Brazil," *Gender & Development* 17, 2 (2009): 189-201. doi: 10.1080/13552070903009734

30   Bertha K. Becker and Claudio A. G. Egler, *Brazil: A New Regional Power in the World-Economy* (Cambridge, England: Cambridge University Press, 1992).

31   Thomas E. Skidmore, *Brazil: Five Centuries of Change*, 2nd ed. (Oxford: Oxford University Press, 2010).

32   E. Saravia and R. C. Gomes, "Public Management in South America: What Happened in the Last Ten Years?" *Public Management Review* 10, 4 (2008): 497. doi: 10.1080/14719030802263939

33   Rodriguez, Thomas, and Salmi, *Brazil: Knowledge and Innovation for Competitiveness in Brazil.*

34   T. Nenova, "Control Values and Changes in Corporate Law in Brazil," *Latin American Business Review* 6, 3 (2005): 13. doi: 10.1300/J140v06n03_01

35   V. Vivarta and G. Canela, "Corporate Social Responsibility in Brazil: The Role of the Press as Watchdog," *Journal of Corporate Citizenship* 21 (2006): 102. http://search.ebscohost.com/login.aspx?direct=true&db=bth&AN=20025830 &site=ehost-live

36   D. Mele, P. Debeljuh, and M. Arruda, "Corporate Ethical Policies in Large Corporations in Argentina, Brazil and Spain," *Journal of Business Ethics* 63, 1 (2006): 2. doi: 10.1007/s10551-005-7100-y

37   Ibid., 23.

38   A. Kumar and M. Francisco, *Enterprise Size, Financing Patterns, and Credit Constraints in Brazil* (Washington, D.C.: The World Bank, 2005). http://search.ebscohost.com/login.aspx?direct=true&db=a9h&AN=22188087 &site=ehost-live

39   Rodriguez, Dahlman, and Salmi, *Brazil: Knowledge and Innovation for Competitiveness in Brazil.*

40   M. Basso, *Mercosul* (Sao Paulo, Brazil: Editora Atlas S.A., 2007).

41   J. L. Vazquez, *Comercio Exterior Brazileiro* (Sao Paulo, Brazil: Editora Atlas S.A., 2007).

42   Kumar and Francisco, *Enterprise Size, Financing Patterns, and Credit Constraints in Brazil.*

43 Humberto Grande, *A Universidade do Trabalho e o Desajustamento Entre Massas e Classes Dirigentes* (Rio de Janeiro: Departamento De Imprensa Nacional, 1965).

45 M. M. Elvira and A. Davila, "Emergent Directions for Human Resource Management Research in Latin America," *International Journal of Human Resource Management* 16, 12 (2005): 2265. doi: 10.1080/09585190500358703

44 Elvira and Davila, "Emergent Directions for Human Resource Management Research in Latin America," 2270.

46 T. Wood and A. de Paula, "Pop-Management Literature: Popular Business Press and Management Culture in Brazil," *Canadian Journal of Administrative Sciences* 25, 3 (2008): 196. doi: 10.1002/CJAS.71

47 G. Coelho, H. Dou, L. Quoniam, and C. Henrique Da Silva, "Ensino e Pesquisa no Campo da Inteligencia Competitiva no Brasile a Cooperacao Franco-Braileira," *PUZZLE: Revista Hispana de la Inteligencia Competitiva* 5, 23 (2006): 18. http://search.ebscohost.com/login.aspx?direct=true&db=a9h&AN=22188087 &site=ehost-live

48 Tiffin, *Entrepreneurship in Latin America*.

49 Mele, Debeljuh, and Arruda, "Corporate Ethical Policies in Large Corporations in Argentina, Brazil and Spain," 2.

50 O. Dalfovo and D. Dias, "Do Capital Humano: Comparação na Localização de Software de Gestao do Capital Humano Entre os Países Brasil, Argentina e México," Revista Brasileira de Gestao de Negócios 11, 33 (2009): 246. http://search.ebscohost.com/login.aspx?direct=true&db=bth&AN=47332597 &site=ehost-live

51 A. Endres, *Melhoria De Desempenho Em P&D-O Modo Juran* (Rio de Janeiro: Editora Bookmark Ltda, 1997).

Chapter 5: Russia

Religion and Economic Development

The traditional religion of the Russian people is the Russian Orthodox Church. Prior to the Communist Revolution, the customs and beliefs of the Russians about economic development were similar to those that prevailed in the Greek and Latin world because Byzantium—the Medieval Greek Empire—was responsible for the Christianization of most of the Slavs. The Russian Orthodox Church prior to the Communist Revolution did not favor economic development because it distracted the people from dedicating their time to religious practices.[1] The imperial government of Russia confronted the Church about its negative stance and paved the way toward economic development. The desire for economic development and industrialization during the latter portion of the Czarist era began to direct the Russian society and education system toward rapid economic development and industrialization.[2] It is highly important to show that under the Czars, the Russian economic developments displayed basic similarities with European developments.[3]

Russia became a part of the Soviet Union and followed the rules dictated by communism for three generations. Communism, which in many ways took the place of religion in Russia, had convinced the people that the future of this political, social, and economic system was based—among other things—on economic development, industrialization and industrial prosperity.[4] However, the economic development of the Soviet Union was substantially different than that of the Western nations because it was totalitarian, centralized, and favored military production. After the fall of the Soviet Union, Russia started making tremendous efforts to redevelop itself in capitalist terms. Changes have been made conducive to capitalist development, but notable results are not yet visible. Today, Russian business organizations face challenges involving research, development, capital widening, technological progress, and diffusion, and they seek an optimal rate of economic growth which depends on scientific and technological progress and entrepreneurship.[5] Lamentably, such prerequisites to Russian economic development are not yet sufficient, although great efforts are being made to develop them.

The Russian Orthodox Church did not favor economic development, but the imperial government of Russia placed great emphasis upon development during the last two centuries of its regime. The Communist Revolution that followed the imperial era fervently precipitated economic development under a centralized and totalitarian basis. After the fall of the Soviet Union, Russia has made tremendous efforts to create economic development under capitalist terms.

Religion and Education

Education in Russia under the Soviet Union was primarily a tool of the regime for the maintenance and furtherance of the communist society. The role of Soviet education was to help build the communist society, to shape the materialist world outlook of the students, to equip them with a good grounding in the different fields of knowledge, and to prepare them for socially useful work.[6]

The Soviet society demanded political awareness from the Soviet citizenry, and education was used as an instrument for indoctrinating the political attitudes of the Communist Party and the ideological beliefs of Marx and Lenin. The Soviet social credo supported the belief that education must function according to the needs of society. According to communist ideology, a socialist society supported communism aided by a strong educational infrastructure. Literacy and the development of higher education were thus regarded as political necessities for the government and as a social duty for the individual. Soviet schools strived to impart universal competence in the basic skills and to motivate the youth toward general education.

Soviet children received an elementary education by attending the *Eight-Year School*. This school was divided into two stages: elementary, comprising the first four grades; and secondary, consisting of the last four grades. The majority of Soviet children received a type of secondary education that placed a great emphasis on the physical sciences and engineering but neglected the social sciences. Curricula in economics and related fields were limited. Higher education was available only to a fraction of those who sought it because party affiliation played an important role in being admitted to an institution of higher learning. Because the Soviet society needed a vast number of persons to fill an expanding skilled labor force, vocational training and guidance were extended. Those schools were known as trade schools and offered an education and specialization in a particular trade. General subjects were limited to approximately 15-20 percent of school time, the remainder being spent in the field or the workshop.

College and university graduates were assigned to different enterprises, not according to their needs but according to the opinions of the Communist Party decision-makers. When a large labor turnover took place in a particular sector, the regime established labor exchange offices for the redistribution of employees. To take care of the workers who would be placed on different jobs, the government announced the formation of a chain of labor exchanges to help with the redistribution of jobs; offices opened in every city with a population of more than 100,000 inhabitants.[7]

Since the fall of the Soviet Union, Russian education has been fighting for identity and recognition. While much has recently changed in Russian education, the institution is still forging a new identity and attempting to find direction in an erratically evolving political and economic milieu.[8] The new Russian education system started a long process of change in order to serve the new economic and social system of the country. Elementary education is compulsory for children ages six to ten. This is followed by the basic general secondary education for children ages ten to fifteen. This is then followed by two years of the upper secondary school. Upon the completion of this program, students receive a completion certificate. Vocational schools have four-year programs and include students between the ages of fifteen to nineteen.

The modern Russian higher education system can be regarded as a mixture of both Soviet and post-Soviet traditions because a lot of the Soviet past is still present within Russian universities.[9] However, notable progress has been made in the present education system, and Russian higher education institutions—both public and private—have benefited from massive retraining. A whole range of new disciplines emerged almost simultaneously;[10] however, Russian higher education continues to emphasize mathematics instead of liberal arts.[11] There are currently 218 colleges and universities in the country.[12]

Under the Soviet Union, education in Russia was strongly influenced by communist doctrine and served as an instrument of communism. The extent of education was satisfactory and available to all citizens up to the completion of secondary studies. Currently, the Russian education system is undergoing drastic and rapid developments in order to serve a free society. The education system in Russia is not yet ready to provide the necessary education for the new socioeconomic system that is gradually developing in the country.

Religion and Social Structure
The Orthodox Church had played a supreme role in Russian society since

its introduction to the country by the Greeks from Constantinople. The Russian Patriarch had almost the same power as the Czar. For thousands of years before the Russian Revolution, social structure was rigid and controlled by a small number of persons at the top echelon, while the peasant population was enslaved and had no civil rights at all. After the fall of the imperial family and the establishment of the Soviet Union, three major philosophies emanated from the communist doctrine and prevailed in Russia: the elimination of private property; the end of transmission of economic power and status from one generation to another; and the equality of opportunity in education and employment.

Although some of the former distinctions of class had been eliminated, other social distinctions persisted and tended to become more incisive. The first distinction was based on power, because power was concentrated in the hands of the ruling class, and power generated influence and privilege. Although the people in power could not amass wealth, their power was such that it enabled them to acquire more material goods and privileges than those who had less power.

The second basis of distinction was the prestige and income accorded to various occupations and professions. Occupations were distinguished from one another by privilege, by prestige, and by the differences between civilians and the military. Responsible managerial positions were mainly staffed by members of the top social echelon and appointed by the state.

The Soviet government itself had acknowledged that there were occupational strata, although it concealed the fact that there was class distinction per se. In the late 1950s and early 1960s, the Soviet government condemned the idea that labor was degrading and asked for education reforms to stop the tendency of those with some education to treat menial work as demeaning. Because of the continuing delineation of social and occupational classes, there was less opportunity to rise from subordinate to favored classes unless the aspirants for ascension were members of the Communist Party or were sponsored by such members.[13] Because the social structure was formed by the Communist Party, the top echelon was comprised of party members who occupied important positions in all socioeconomic and military posts, including managerial positions in the state-controlled and managed enterprises. Consequently, social mobility and change were profoundly limited.

Russian society has been undergoing dramatic changes since the fall of the Soviet Union. The big transition of Russian society from communism to democracy began in the mid-1990s, but the changes were met with resistance because emphasis was placed on elements unknown to the population, such as the formation of basic democratic values, personal responsibility, individualism, and community responsibility. Ideology as a criterion in the social structure of the nation no longer existed. The social transformation of the 1990s was approached by former social power groups from the individual perspective. Systemic, structural changes are interpreted as coming about via individual-level changes, which is why education is so crucial for success.[14] The challenges for the Russian elite that emerged in the post-Soviet period are mainly based on three dimensions: socio-political democratization, economic deregulation, and state decentralization.[15]

The ensuing power struggle revealed the fragility of Russian society, leaving the nation divided in the midst of great disarray and uncertainty about the future.[16] Members of the intelligentsia have found a way to obtain professional gains in civic activity that promote their interests, help themselves, and seek social change. In turn, civic activity has produced new social hierarchies and inequities by offering the educated class a chance to achieve social mobility, power, and resources.[17]

Russia's current society is based on wealth and privilege. The majority of those who possess wealth and have privileges today are former Communist officials and their descendents. A Soviet-era middle class that is growing smaller and insecure—even as elements of a post-Soviet entrepreneurial class are being established—is most unlikely to serve as the social foundation for stable political democracy in a country where neither the institutions nor the values of democracy have taken root.[18]

Russian society was influenced by the Orthodox Church; it was a rigid society ruled by a small number of people at the top, while the lower classes were oppressed and enslaved. The introduction of communism in the country created a society that was based on the tenets of communism, with communists at the top of the social hierarchy and less-privileged layers below. The fall of the Communist regime in 1990 upset the social stratification and created great turmoil in the country. A new Russian society has not yet crystallized.

Extent of Industrialization

Under the Soviet Union, the economy, social structure, and education system supported industrialization, but its purpose was to serve the communist regime, not the general population of the country. Russia under the Soviet Union was one of the most industrialized nations in the world, but Soviet industrialization was different than that in the West because it diverted a higher proportion of its output to non-consumption uses than did non-communist economies, and it shaped its investment activities toward state rather than household ends. Soviet industrialization did not result in the emergence and growth of independently owned and operated industrial and commercial enterprises. Instead, the government created entities that were operated by individuals appointed by the state. However, attempts to change this situation are slowly taking place. The key to accelerating development was the conversion of the national economy to intensive methods of growth, and the only alternative was to switch to intensive development rooted in increased efficiency in the public sector.[19]

Since the fall of the Soviet Union, Russia's industrialization has been growing. However, it is not receiving the necessary support from the economy, social structure, and education system because these three elements are still undergoing changes and are not yet stable. Industry experienced a notable upswing in the late 1990s, but appeared to be on a rather slow growth path. There is strong evidence indicating that Russia's industry has stepped onto a path to sustainable development motivated by the possibility of improvement in production, set through technological progress and improvements in technological efficiency.[20] Industry occupies close to 35 percent of total economic activities.

After the fall of the Soviet Union, industrialization had not sufficiently increased because it was not receiving the necessary support from the economy, social structure, and education system, since these three elements have not reached a state of stability. All three factors are still undergoing changes as the economy moves from a state-controlled system to a democratic system.

Labor Unions

In Russia under the Soviet Union, the impact of industrialization created labor unions that followed communist philosophy and modus operandi. Unlike their Western European and North American counterparts, Russian labor unions included both managers and workers. Their structure commenced at the Central Council of Trade Unions through the republic, regional, and local agencies. The government controlled the trade unions, and the element of democracy was totally absent. One of the most effective tools trade unions use in the West—the strike—was missing because the state exercised ultimate control in regard to strikes. The absence of strikes in Russia was undoubtedly a plus factor in terms of managerial effectiveness; however, informal restrictive practices on the part of industrial employees were quite pervasive under the Soviet industrial system.[21]

Unionism in Russia passed through a stage of lack of discipline and low productivity of workers, a stage of dictatorial oppression by the regime, and a stage of embryonic constitutionalism in the 1960s. The Communist Committee on Trade Unions acknowledged that the level of work of trade unions obviously lagged behind the demands of life.[22] Labor unions were not formed in order to promote better compensation or more safety and strength for their members, but for the purpose of government control.

After the fall of the Soviet Union, Russia allowed the formation of labor unions as the people now had the right to free association. The people received the right to form, regulate, restructure, and dissolve labor unions. Specifically, Russian citizens are now allowed to join trade unions at the age of fourteen. Currently, there are three trade union federations in the country: the All-Russian Confederation of Labor, the Confederation of Labor of Russia, and the Federation of Independent Trade Unions of Russia.[23]

Russian labor unions have been dysfunctional since their establishment, having been infiltrated with opportunistic and greedy leaders interested in gaining wealth and power for themselves, not for the members of their organizations. Economic forces are undermining organized labor's capacity to act as a unified political and economic force. Organized labor stumbles not for what it is done but for what is has failed to do.[24] The all-inclusive membership of the union—its membership includes employers, employees and health care officials—impedes the formation of collective identity on the basis of common professional or employee interests.[25]

Labor unions in Russia under the Soviet Union were instruments of the Communist Party and included both managers and employees. After the fall of the Soviet Union, Russian law allowed its citizens to form and participate in labor unions. Today's labor unions are unstable, and have been infiltrated with leaders who are looking out for their own benefit, not that of members.

The Corporation

There were no private corporations in Russia during the Soviet period. After the fall of the Soviet Union, Russia started a rigorous process of privatizing government corporations. The process was initiated with state-owned and operated organizations because such entities were already in existence. Their metamorphosis into private organization was a strong exhibition of a fundamental economic change from communism to the free enterprise system. However, selling shares to the public was not very successful due to a lack of private funds and public suspicion toward the new system. Millions of people formally became owners of public assets, but the actual control remained firmly in the hands of top managers, who as a group captured control of firms that was much greater than the share of ownership they gained.[26] It is difficult for Russian enterprises to liberate themselves entirely from any social experience gained under the Soviet regime. The credibility of few business values is threatened further by the fact that the entrepreneurship culture is seen by a considerable part of Russians as the continuation and development of the same dishonest practices that existed in the Soviet days.[27] In addition, privatization is not enough; it also matters who the owners are, what constraints in their operations they face, and the business climate they operate in. The government's second best choice may be to privatize selected firms with strong profits and reputedly honest managers, and then watch these firms carefully once they are privatized, while building the legal and market institutions to control self-dealing.[28]

Under the Soviet regime, there were no private corporations in Russia. After the fall of communism, a strong privatization process of the government-controlled organizations has been taking place. For all practical purposes, the private corporate form of business has not stabilized yet and exists in continuous turmoil. Consequently, the private corporate form of business has not impacted the development of management in private organizations in the country.

Management in Russia

Management was limited by the Communist regime of the Soviet Union and functioned as a microcosm of the totalitarian socioeconomic system of the state. Neither labor unions nor corporations played any role in impacting management, managers, and employees. Labor unions were instruments of the totalitarian system, and private corporations were totally nonexistent.

There were no private or professional managers in Russia under the Soviet Union because managers were appointed by the state. In order for Soviet citizens to become managers in state-owned organizations, they had to be members of the Communist Party. The managers of the Soviet Union contrasted sharply with the managerial group of modern industry elsewhere in the world because of the stress on political reliability.[29] Until the 1960s, Soviet managers were under great pressure by the state. They had subordinate legal rights, their children were discriminated against in higher education, they did not enjoy equal access with workers to housing, and they were considered inferior.[30] Management remained a rather closed profession to many because managers emanated from the top social echelon and were members of the Communist Party. They were most restrictive in the selection of candidates for the training program from the point of view of loyalty, party standing, past performance, etc.[31]

During the 1960s, the prerequisites for entrance into the managerial field changed as a result of less rigidity in the government and better understanding of the necessary managerial qualifications. The Soviet regime encouraged capable, intelligent persons to pursue managerial careers by providing basic salaries well above the national average, and by providing those who reach the top rungs of the managerial ladder with fringe benefits, such as a company car and favored housing.[32]

Unlike Western managers, most Soviet managers were not individuals who had specialized management knowledge. Instead, Soviet industrial enterprises were managed primarily by engineers with no concept of cost. They were given materials, labor, and markets. All they worried about was input. In fact, there was much evidence that the nation was suffering from the overemphasis and the specialization in scientific engineering and advanced training in excess of the requirements of the industry.[33]

After the end of the Soviet Union, Russia made tremendous efforts to move its economy and management from a totalitarian infrastructure to a free one. In 1992, a commission of Russian and Western experts concluded that millions of adults needed to change their occupations. For the post-Soviet Union managers, neither the knowledge acquired under Soviet control nor the experience accumulated in Soviet enterprises has been adequate to function effectively and efficiently under the new system. As a result, many of them had to leave business, while others have learned to function in accordance with the rules of the market game as it had taken shape in Russia.[34] The task of training millions of managers to perform adequately in a new economic and social environment was needed.[35]

Currently, the development of Russian managers has entered a new and challenging era. In 1997, the Russian government launched a massive retraining initiative designed primarily for mid-career managers in industry.[36] Human resource management has gained ground recently, and even though human resources and management of human resources are widely recognized as being problematic, small enterprises do not seem to have any alternative other than considering it to be the most important strength of the organization.[37] Russian entrepreneurs and their managers are the product of a social system under transformation and that has an influence on the stability of their psychological cosmos. The transition to qualitative new social, economic, and political foundations in society inevitably leads to changes in individual perception of position within in the social hierarchy.[38]

Management education as it is known in the West did not exist in the Soviet Union. In the 1970s, several management training centers were created. For example, the Plekhanov Institute of the National Economy organized an industrial production division whose faculty consisted of well-known management professors and practitioners in the country. In the 1980s, two organizations were providing training and retraining with the cooperation of the government: the Higher Commercial Management School and Inforcom.[39] American management techniques and concepts were introduced in the 1990s.

Management education is omnipresent in Russia today. More than 200 business schools have opened in Russia over the last seven years, and their graduates are now filling key roles once occupied by American and European expatriates or launching their own companies.[40] Management studies are very important in all business schools in post-Soviet Russia; management became the second most popular major after accounting in the new business schools.[41] Russian business schools have also entered into partnerships with Western counterparts.

Under the Soviet Union, Russian managers were very authoritarian, and their authority was derived from the Communist Party. It was also necessary to severely restrict the authority and autonomy of managers in order to coordinate the literally billions of interdependent and interrelated decisions and activities that were made throughout the economy.[42] Another characteristic of this absolute authority was the constant managerial pressure upon employees. One of the most striking characteristics of Russian management was the extreme stress that was placed on the application of incessant pressure from superior to subordinate.[43] Employees accordingly viewed their managers as oppressors rather than as friends, thus widening the gap between those two components. Soviet employees had a remarkably low level of expectations and ambition partly because they did not live in a competitive society; their frame of mind was that of the Russian peasant.[44] Moreover, management in Russia was not oriented toward providing employee motivation, adequate involvement, or interest in the job.

The control of the Russian employee was based on the element of cooperation with the Communist Party. Management used monetary incentives to control employees because additional pay was the only valid instrument for motivating the average employee, who was primarily concerned with the satisfaction of their physiological and safety needs. Even rewards for managers provided little incentive to achieve success because salary structures in Russia were relatively flat by Western standards. The general lack of direct incentives at all levels in the organizational hierarchy was reflected in low labor productivity, which was one of the endemic problems of the system.[45] The most common type of monetary incentive was the bonus given to employees who produced on the basis of piecework, and determined by higher productivity and the reduction of waste in raw materials and semi-finished products. Incentives were bestowed either individually or collectively; Russian authorities disagreed which policy was better for the worker. Nevertheless, incentives in one form or another seemed to be consistently reduced because the standards for performance were constantly being raised. As far as psychological incentives for the employees were concerned, there was a plethora of motivation for those workers who earnestly believed that by exerting their optimum effort, they were contributing to the welfare of the state and their society.

Employee groups were not allowed to form unless they were relevant to affairs specified by the management of the enterprise or the regime. Therefore, possible motivation through groups—one of the essential tools for motivation in the West —did not exist in Russia. Furthermore, the relationship between management and employees per se was not on amicable terms because there was frequently jealousy between them. However, toward the end of the Soviet Union, there were indications that changes had started to take place in the development of management, and there was a new trend in the relations of production workers with management, which meant the increased active participation of workers in management.[46]

Even after the fall of the Soviet Union, Russian organizations continued to view employees as an expense rather than a resource because Russian managers tend to place greater emphasis on quantitative gains. In addition, while Russia has had a well-developed and demanding education system, relatively little attention was paid to skill development once the Russian was employed in a firm.[47] Currently, the need for good human resource management is of paramount importance in all organizations, especially for assisting in phasing out the old culture and replacing it with a new one. However, for many Russians, the concept of human resource management is new.[48]

Management was dictated by the centrally controlled system that characterized the Soviet Union and reflected the totalitarian socioeconomic system of the state. Neither labor unions nor corporations had any impact upon management, managers, and employees. Labor unions were instruments of the totalitarian system and corporations were totally nonexistent. Because of the impact of the cultural factors, management authority and employee control were autocratic, and management's view toward change and development did not exist.

Since the fall of the Soviet Union, management, managers, and employees in the newly established private organizations are going through dramatic changes, and currently remain in a stage of turmoil which is gradually phasing out.

References

Aganbegyan, A. G. "The New Economic Strategy of the USSR and its Social Dimensions." *International Labor Review*, January-February 1987: 96-97.

Bernard, B., R. Krakkman, and A. Tarassova. "Russian Privatization and Corporate Governance: What Went Wrong?" *Stanford Law Review* 52, 6. (July 2000): 1733-1734. http://find.galegroup.com.prx01.lirn. net/gps/infomark.do?&contentSet=IACDocuments&type=retrieve&ta bID=T002&prodId=IPS&docId=A67330821&source=gale&srcprod= ITOF&userGroupName=lirn_wu&version=1.0

Baykov, A. *The Development of the Soviet Economic System*. New York, NY: McMillan, 1974.

Black, G. "All that Glitters is not Glasnost." *Business Marketing*, July 1989: 80.

Brown, E. "Interests and Rights of Soviet Industrial Workers and the Resolution of Conflicts." *Industrial Labor Review*, January 1963: 252.

Dewitt, N. *Soviet Professional Manpower*. Washington, DC: National Science Foundation, 1958.

Directory of Education Online. http://www.directoryofeducation.net/

colleges/worldwide/russia/

Eaton, J. S. "Russia: The State of Education at the Turn of the Century." *Social Education* 65, 2. (March 2001): 102. http://find.galegroup. comprx01.lirn.net/ps/infomark.do?&contentSet=IACDocument&type =retrieve&tabID=T001&prodId=IPS&docId=A72265851&source=g ale&srcprod=ITOF&userGroupName=lirn_wu&version=1.0

Fey, C., P. Engstrom, and I. Bjorkman. "Doing Business in Russia: Effective Human Resource Management Practices for Foreign Firms in Russia." *Organizational Dynamics*, Autumn 1999: 69.

Fainsold, M. *How Russia is Ruled.* Cambridge, MA: Harvard University Press, 1958.

Gel'man, V., and A. Steen, eds. *Elites and Democratic Development in Russia.* London, England: Routledge Taylor & Francis, 2003.

Gerschenkron, A. "Social Attitudes, Entrepreneurship and Economic Development." *Explorations in Entrepreneurial History* 6, 1954: 1-19.

Golenkova, Z. T., and E. D. Igitkhanian. "Certain Aspects of the Russian Entrepreneur's Life Today." *Sociological Research*, 47, 2. (March-April 2008): 66-81. doi:10.2753/SOR1061-0154470203

Granick, D. *Management of the Industrial Firm in the U.S.S.R.* New York, NY: Columbia University Press, 1954.

Heckinger, F. M. *The Big Red Schoolhouse.* Gloucester, MA: Peter Smith, 1968.

Information U.S.S.R. New York, NY: MacMillan, 1972.

International Labour Review. "Bridging the Gap Between Yesterday's Skills and Tomorrow's Needs in the Russian Federation." *International Labour Review* 133, 2. (1994): paragraph 7.

Jumpponen, J., M. Ikävalko, and T. Pihkala. "Management and Change in Turbulent Times: How Do Russian Small Business Managers Perceive the Development of their Business Environment?" *Journal of Business Economics and Management* 9, 2. (March 2007): 120. doi:10.3846/1611-1699,2008.9.115-122

Kortunov, A. "Russian Higher Education." *Social Research* 76, 1. (Spring 2009): 209. http://find.galegroup.prx01.lirn.net/gps/infomark. do?&contentSet=IACDocuments&type=retrieve&tabID=T002&prod Id=IPS&docId=A203482043&sourcce=gale&srcprod=ITOF&userGr oupName=lirn_wu&version=1.0

Kubicek, Paul J. *Organized Labor in Post-Communist States.* Pittsburgh, PA: University of Pittsburgh Press, 2004.

Kuznetsov, A. *Russian Corporations: The Strategies of Survival and Development*. New York, NY: International Business Press, 2002.

Leinster, C. "We Need Yuppies in Moscow." *Fortune*, November 20, 1989: 155.

Lynch. A. *How Russia is not Ruled: Reflections on Russian Political Development*. Cambridge, MA: Cambridge University Press, 2005.

Matthews, O., and A. Nemtsova. "Pistols Out, Paper In: Business Degrees are Trumping Bulletproof Vests as the New Must-Have Accessory for Russian Executives." *Newsweek* (International Edition), June 2007.

Mechitov, A. I., and H. M. Moshkovich. "Russian Business Schools in a Time of Transition." *Journal of Education for Business* 81, 4. (March-April 2006): 225-229. http://find.galegroup.com.prx01.lirn. net/pgs/infomark.do?&contentSet=IACDocuments&type=retrieve&ta bID=T002&prodId=IPS&docId=A145156441&source=gale&srcprod =ITOF&userGroupName=lirn_wu&version=1.0

Moore, B. *Terror and Progress U.S.S.R.* Cambridge, MA: Harvard University Press, 1989.

NationMaster.com. "Trade Union Membership by Country." Accessed October 1, 2010 from http://www.nationmaster.com/graph/lab_tra_uni_mem-labor-trade-union-membership

Richman, B. *Soviet Management with Significant American Comparisons*. Englewood Cliffs, NJ: Prentice-Hall, 1965.

Rosefielde, S. *The Russian Economy: From Lenin to Putin*. Malden, MA: Blackwell Publishing, 2007.

"Russia: Getting More Output from Fewer Comrades." *Business Week*, November 1, 1969: 38-39.

Saari, S. *Promoting Democracy and Human Rights in Russia*. London, England: Routledge Curzon, 2009.

Salmennienemi, S. *Democratization and Gender in Contemporary Russia*. London, England: Routledge Curzon, 2008.

Schalb, M, R. Grosse, and E. Romero Simpson. "Developing Entrepreneurs in Developing Countries: The PEG Program in Peru." *Journal of Management Development* 4 (1998), 31-40.

"The Grid Goes to Russia." *Training*, January 1990: 80.

Voigt, P., and H. Hockmann. "Russia's Transition Process in the Light of Rising Economy: Economic Trajectories in Russia's Industry and Agriculture." *European Journal of Comparative Economics* 5, 2. (December 2008): 251-267. http://find.galegroup.com.prx-01.lirn.net/

gps/infomark.do?&contentSet=IACDocuments&type=retrieve&tabl
D=Too2&prodId=IPS&docId=A200907161&source=gale&srcprod=
AONE&userGroupName=lirn_wu&version=1.0

Yelyutin, V. P. *Higher Education in U.S.S.R.* English Language Publication, U.S.S.R. Government, 1969.

Zaslavskaia, T. I. "The Vanguard of the Russian Business Community: M. E. Sharpe, Inc." *Sociological Research* 46, 5. (September-October 2007): 6-7. doi:10.2753/SOR1061-0154460501

Endnotes

1   A. Gerschenkron, "Social Attitudes, Entrepreneurship and Economic Development," *Explorations in Entrepreneurial History* 6, 1954: 1-19.

2   F. M. Heckinger, *The Big Red Schoolhouse* (Gloucester, MA: Peter Smith, 1968).

3   A. Gershen Gerschenkron, "Social Attitudes, Entrepreneurship and Economic Development," 1-19.

4   *Information U.S.S.R.* (New York, NY: MacMillan, 1972).

5   S. Rosefielde, *The Russian Economy: From Lenin to Putin* (Malden, MA: Blackwell Publishing, 2007).

6   V. P. Yelyutin, *Higher Education in U.S.S.R* (English Language Publication, U.S.S.R. Government, 1969), 41.

7   "Russia: Getting More Output from Fewer Comrades," *Business Week*, November 1, 1969: 38-39.

8   J. S. Eaton, "Russia: The State of Education at the Turn of the Century," *Social Education* 65, 2 (March 2001): 102. http://find. galegroup.comprx01.lirn.net/ps/infomark.do?&contentSet=IAC Document&type=retrieve&tabID=T001&prodId=IPS&docId=A 72265851&source=gale&srcprod=ITOF&userGroupName=lirn_ wu&version=1.0

9   A. Kortunov, "Russian Higher Education," *Social Research* 76, 1 (Spring 2009): 209. http://find.galegroup.prx01.lirn.net/gps/info-mark.do?&contentSet=IACDocuments&type=retrieve&tabID=T00 2&prodId=IPS&docId=A203482043&sourcce=gale&srcprod=ITOF &userGroupName=lirn_wu&version=1.0

10   Kortunov, "Russian Higher Education," 209.

11   A. I. Mechitov and H. M. Moshkovich, "Russian Business Schools in a Time of Transition," *Journal of Education for Business* 81, 4 (March-April 2006): 225-229. http://find.galegroup.com.prx01.lirn.

net/pgs/infomark.do?&contentSet=IACDocuments&type=retrieve&
tabID=T002&prodId=IPS&docId=A145156441&source=gale&srcp
rod=ITOF&userGroupName=lirn_wu&version=1.0

12 Directory of Education Online. http://www.directoryofeducation.net/
colleges/worldwide/russia/

13 Heckinger, *The Big Red Schoolhouse*.

14 S. Salmennienemi, *Democratization and Gender in Contemporary
Russia* (London, England: Routledge Curzon, 2008).

15 V. Gel'man and A. Steen, eds., *Elites and Democratic Development
in Russia* (London, England: Routledge Taylor & Francis, 2003).

16 S. Saari, *Promoting Democracy and Human Rights in Russia*
(London, England: Routledge Curzon, 2009).

17 Salmennienemi, *Democratization and Gender in Contemporary
Russia*.

18 A. Lynch, *How Russia is not Ruled: Reflections on Russian Political
Development* (Cambridge, MA: Cambridge University Press, 2005).

19 A. G. Aganbegyan, "The New Economic Strategy of the USSR
and its Social Dimensions," *International Labor Review*, January-
February 1987: 96-97.

20 P. Voigt and H. Hockmann, "Russia's Transition Process in the Light
of Rising Economy: Economic Trajectories in Russia's Industry and
Agriculture," *European Journal of Comparative Economics* 5, 2
(December 2008): 251-267. http://find.galegroup.com.prx-01.lirn.
net/gps/infomark.do?&contentSet=IACDocuments&type=retrieve&
tabID=Too2&prodId=IPS&docId=A200907161&source=gale&srcp
rod=AONE&userGroupName=lirn_wu&version=1.0

21 E. Brown, "Interests and Rights of Soviet Industrial Workers and the
Resolution of Conflicts," *Industrial Labor Review*, January 1963:
252.

22 Ibid.

23 NationMaster.com. "Trade union membership by country."

24 Paul J. Kubicek, *Organized Labor in Post-Communist States* (Pittsburgh, PA: University of Pittsburgh Press, 2004).

25 Salmennienemi, *Democratization and Gender in Contemporary
Russia*.

26 A. Kuznetsov, *Russian Corporations: The Strategies of Survival and
Development* (New York, NY: International Business Press, 2002).

27 Ibid.

28 B. Bernard, R. Krakkman, and A. Tarassova, "Russian Privatiza-

tion and Corporate Governance: What Went Wrong?" *Stanford Law Review* 52, 6 (July 2000): 1733-1734. http://find.galegroup.com. prx01.lirn.net/gps/infomark.do?&contentSet=IACDocuments&type =retrieve&tabID=T002&prodId=IPS&docId=A67330821&source= gale&srcprod=ITOF&userGroupName=lirn_wu&version=1.0

29   D. Granick, *Management of the Industrial Firm in the U.S.S.R.* (New York, NY: Columbia University Press, 1954).

30   A. Baykov, *The Development of the Soviet Economic System* (New York, NY: McMillan, 1974).

31   N. Dewitt, *Soviet Professional Manpower* (Washington, DC: National Science Foundation, 1958).

32   B. Richman, *Soviet Management with Significant American Comparisons* (Englewood Cliffs, NJ: Prentice-Hall, 1965).

33   C. Leinster, "We Need Yuppies in Moscow," *Fortune*, November 20, 1989: 155.

34   T. I. Zaslavskaia, "The Vanguard of the Russian Business Community: M.E. Sharpe, Inc.," *Sociological Research* 46, 5 (September-October 2007): 6-7. doi:10.2753/SOR1061-0154460501

35   International Labour Review, "Bridging the Gap Between Yesterday's Skills and Tomorrow's Needs in the Russian Federation," *International Labour Review* 133, 2 (1994): paragraph 7.

36   Saari, *Promoting Democracy and Human Rights in Russia.*

37   J. Jumpponen, M. Ikävalko, and T. Pihkala, "Management and Change in Turbulent Times: How Do Russian Small Business Managers Perceive the Development of their Business Environment?" *Journal of Business Economics and Management* 9, 2 (March 2007): 120. doi:10.3846/1611-1699,2008.9.115-122

38   Z. T. Golenkova and E. D. Igitkhanian, "Certain Aspects of the Russian Entrepreneur's Life Today," *Sociological Research*, 47, 2 (March-April 2008): 75. doi:10.2753/SOR1061-0154470203

39   G. Black, "All that Glitters is not Glasnost," *Business Marketing*, July 1989: 80.

40   O. Matthews and A. Nemtsova, "Pistols Out, Paper In: Business Degrees are Trumping Bulletproof Vests as the New Must-Have Accessory for Russian Executives," *Newsweek* (International Edition), June 2007.

41   Mechitov and Moshkovich, "Russian Business Schools in a Time of Transition," 225-229.

42   M. Fainsold, *How Russia is Ruled* (Cambridge, MA: Harvard

University Press, 1958).

43 Richman, *Soviet Management with Significant American Comparisons*.

44 Ibid.

45 Granick, *Management of the Industrial Firm in the U.S.S.R.*

46 B. Moore, *Terror and Progress U.S.S.R* (Cambridge, MA: Harvard University Press, 1989).

47 C. Fey, P. Engstrom, and I. Bjorkman, "Doing Business in Russia: Effective Human Resource Management Practices for Foreign Firms in Russia," *Organizational Dynamics*, Autumn 1999: 69.

48 Ibid.

Chapter 6: Japan

Religion and Economic Development

In feudal Japan—as in India at the present time—there existed a disparity between religious views and governmental attitudes toward economic development. This disparity had been obscured by the giant shadow of strong economic development. The Buddhist and Confucian philosophies—the major religious dogmas in that nation—were definitely opposed to economic development based on industrial prosperity and leaned toward an agricultural society. Also, Confucian-inspired business ideology de-emphasized profit as the central goal of business, stressing that the primary motivation of business was to promote the welfare of society rather than personal material gain.[1] Profit, the primary motivational factor, had traditionally been regarded as degrading. The leading class had traditionally been restrained by the low social status associated with commercial and industrial prosperity and the low morale in which the pursuit of profit and personal aggrandizement were held.[2]

The negative impact of religion was superseded by the strong desire of the Japanese government to attain economic development for the glorification of the nation. The Japanese military undertook the task of leading the nation toward the accomplishment of this goal. The army formed an alliance with the authoritarian *Meiji* oligarchy and placed themselves on the top of the social echelon. Together they established an education system that propagated their interests and the glorification of both the Emperor and the nation, and they constructed an industrial network under governmental control primarily for military purposes. The people always had a deep sense of obligation toward the Emperor—the ultimate source of what it means to be Japanese.[3] Consequently, the motivation of Japanese industrialization and economic development was for the glorification of the Emperor and the nation rather than the prosperity of the individual. Similarly, Japanese employees glorified, and are still glorifying, their place of employment in every aspect of their life, and it is evident in their culture that the people are likely to be defined by the organization for which they work.[4]

The negative impact of religion upon economic development in Japan was superseded by government and military desire to glorify both the Emperor and the nation. The military, with the help of the Meiji oligarchy, placed themselves at the top of the social echelon and created economic development through a powerful industrial network under governmental control.

Religion and Education

Due to the country's strong religious character, education in Japan in the past leaned toward religion and the fine arts. However, religion came under the pressure of new power centers, which demanded an education system able to assist in the economic development of the country. The education system was affected by the turmoil of continuous internal conflicts and foreign wars. Finally, on November 3, 1946, Japan adopted a new constitution which guaranteed the right of all people to receive an education commensurate with their ability. The constitution allowed the law to develop basic policies into such specific principles as equal opportunity, compulsory education, co-education, public education, and social education, as well as the prohibition of improper control, partisan political teaching, or sectarian religious instruction in public schools.

The enactment of the Fundamental Law, which was dedicated to educational improvements and changes, was followed by the adoption of a series of statutes that brought about the decentralization of public education and the establishment of the 6-3-3-4 school system. This system includes six years of elementary school, three years of lower high school, three years of upper high school, and four years of higher education. Under the law, the first nine years are compulsory for children between the ages of six to fifteen. Since 1946, with the enactment of the nine-year compulsory education law, the literacy rate has been consistently rising. Furthermore, the Educational Law of 1908 was reinforced, stating that Japanese employees must generally have nine years of schooling.

The organization of the junior high school in Japan is based on the American junior high school. Graduates of this school complete the time of compulsory education and are then given a graduate certificate, making them eligible to apply for admission to upper secondary schools and teaching colleges, and to obtain employment.

Attendance in the upper secondary school is optional and offers academic courses, specialized vocational courses, and a combination of the two. However, there were not adequate facilities for all applicants until the 1980s; therefore, admission was usually very selective and competitive, restricting the opportunity for all young Japanese to pursue a free education at the upper secondary school and the university level.

Vocational-technical education provides a five-year continuous program with special emphasis on producing medium-level technicians for specialized fields of industry. The greatest need for such technicians has been in the mechanical engineering and electrical engineering fields. Admissions to the program are highly competitive, and selection is made through examinations.

University undergraduate programs include four years of study, with 124 credit hours required for a bachelor's degree. Courses are classified as general education, foreign language, health and physical education, and professional subjects. Students must acquire the prescribed number of credits in each group of subjects. The curriculum is independently made by each university with due reference to the regulations of the Ministry of Education. Admission to a university is usually quite competitive, as it requires twelve years of elementary and secondary education, pursuing prescribed academic admission requirements, and passing the university's entrance examinations. Japanese general and specialized education is adequate and available to all up to the termination of secondary studies. Higher education has been available to a small percentage of the population; only the intellectually gifted were chosen and, after completing their university studies, these graduates assumed important positions in society.[5] The idea of Japanese distinctiveness in the process of status attainment can be found in the thesis of *educational credentialism*, which states that the value of the person is based on the fame of the university they graduated from.[6]

Modern Japan has an excellent education system, especially in higher education, but it also has its shortcomings. Japan's education system is succeeding because it produces the largest and most capable, cultured, compatible, and self-assured people on earth; however, it is failing because it imposes on men and women a suffocating, nationalist, single-track concept of what the ideal Japanese worker should be.[7] There are currently 570 colleges and universities in the country.[8] The structure of Japan's universities is changing, with national universities becoming much more independent of government regulation, and with a striking shift to faculty business ventures and to university-business joint efforts.[9]

After the end of World War II, Japan started developing an excellent education system, parts of which were modeled after the American system. Today, Japan has an education system that serves the needs of the citizens and provides the type of education needed for the high socioeconomic demands of the new century.

Religion and Social Structure

Japanese society, under Buddhist and Confucian influence, originated from an excessively rigid system known as the *four-tier system*, with the samurai warriors at the top. Eventually the samurai lost power when the island nation started to have a period of peace and tranquility. The samurai then pursued other professions, a situation similar to the former communist elites in Russia today. A very important change in the economic development of the country occurred when merchants gained importance and were no longer viewed as outcasts in the oncoming era of industrialization. The merchants formed a new class, the *chonin*, which became responsible for the nation's initial movement toward social mobility, change, and economic prosperity.

In the 1870s, a new class consisting of the formal military of the country was established and occupied the top of the national social structure. The military class formed an alliance with the oligarchic and authoritarian Meiji elite for the purpose of attaining economic development and industrialization for the glorification of the nation. Consequently, both the military and the Meiji occupied the top social echelon. The social structure was rigid; the upper class was very small, while the lower class was excessively large. The upper class had the benefits of education, social status, honor, and political power; a wide gulf separated that class from the other classes.[10] Occupants of the top echelon of society were appointed to responsible managerial positions in government-controlled enterprises and large private enterprises under indirect government control.

The American occupation of Japan in 1945 altered the rigidity of the social structure to some degree, but the occupation was principally concerned with causing change in the political sphere, known as the democratization of Japan.[11] Some believed that the eradication of the ancient social structure had already gone terribly far. However, if one lived among the people for a while, one saw how little they were affected by the intelligentsia and how little impact social tradition had upon their lives.[12]

Social mobility had been stagnant in the past, and social mobility was still slow in the 1990s, for only those who belonged to prominent families occupied the upper echelons. In the Japanese socioeconomic system, rigid class structure and barriers to individual mobility caused growing concern in the country, although changes in the system were evolving very gradually.[13]

The social changes which took place were involuntary in the sense that they did not originate with the people. Some experts believe that they were not changes but rather assimilation, as the Japanese assimilated foreign industrialization philosophies while still retaining much of its old culture.[14] Japan went through a period of cultural metamorphosis after 1945 because of a massive infusion of Western ideas, which led to the coexistence of the old and the new cultures in the country, as tradition dies hard and it would take generations to change the basic thinking of the Japanese.[15] The top social echelon still has some of the descendants of the pre-World War II ruling class who now work in many important professions, including that of the professional manager.

The country is now enjoying exceptional economic and social health by virtually all measures.[16] In the 21st century, Japan has moved steadily toward a class society, with the weight of family background bearing considerably upon aspirations to management or factory ownership.[17] Japan has now a mature society and a mature economy, and has seen truly extraordinary change in the economy in the past half-century, from poverty to wealth with all manner of periodical crises.[18] On the other hand, some experts believe that there are still tendencies toward a militaristic solution of Japan's difficulties.[19] However, from the Japanese social structure's point of view, the militarist solution is not the only possible one, for Japan is more apt to accentuate such tendencies than change them.[20]

Initially, Japanese society and its social structure were influenced by the Buddhist and Confucian religions, which had created a rigid social network serving religious interests more than the people. Subsequently, new internal power players appeared who changed the social structure. Japanese society today is more democratic than ever before and has a higher social mobility rate than in the past.

Extent of Industrialization

Japan is one of the most industrialized countries in the modern world. Japanese industries began to develop during the early part of the twentieth century under the strict control of the military and the Meiji oligarchy. Starting in the 1930s, a rapid transition of heavy industries began to gather momentum, accelerated by the demands of war. The economy, the education system and the social structure were coerced to assist an industrialization process that benefited the war machine of the country, not the population. However, when the war ended in August of 1945, most of Japan's industrial plants had been destroyed.

Since 1945, industrialization has received the necessary support from

the economy, social structure, and education system of the country. Industrial development over the past four decades has fallen into four broad
stages. The first stage, known as the period of reconstruction, was implemented from 1945 to 1952, during which industrial capacity was rapidly
rebuilt so that by 1953, the demand for postwar reconstruction had been
virtually fulfilled. The second stage, known as the period of consolida-
tion, continued into early 1959. The third stage of Japan's postwar economic development ended in 1973. During that period, industries were
organized and expanded, and the basis for the nation's industrial structure shifted decisively to heavy industries. After the completion of the
third stage, Japan entered into the stage of qualitative improvement and
international dominance in commercial and industrial sectors. The industrial sector accounts for almost 22 percent of economic activities, the
agriculture sector, less than 2 percent, and the service sector, 75 percent.
Industries are continuously developing, and have had a top position in
innovative capacity over the last ten years.[21]

The post-World War II industrialization of Japan received substantial
support from the economy, the social stratification, and the education system of the country. Today, Japan is one of the most industrialized nations
in the world.

Labor Unions

The impact of post-World War II industrialization formed labor unions
that were deeply imbedded in the culture of the country, with a profound
emphasis upon paternalism. Unionism in Japan had traditionally been
viewed as an association and belongingness issue rather than as an employee weapon to countervail management. Each union is made up of the
employees of only one company and includes all employees up to supervisory ranks, a situation that substantially differs from labor unionism
in the West and that inhibits employees' democratic participation in the
firm.[22] Mostly at the request of the Japanese government, management
and labor unions met frequently and developed a strong cooperation.
However, labor unions were weak and easily controlled by management
and the government, and for this reason Japan had fewer strikes than other industrialized nations. Some movement toward national unionism had
taken place in the past, but localism and the rule of the particular situation
managed to prevail, partially attributed to the traditional paternalistic attitude of management toward employees. Japanese labor unions have not
been able to strengthen the employees' position when interacting with

management due to their modus operandi, the fact that they have been controlled by both the government and management, and because of the strong cultural emphasis placed upon superior-subordinate relationships.

Although Japanese employees often appeared hostile toward opportunistic union leaders, it would have been a mistake for the average Japanese employee to overtly display strong anti-union sentiments for employees were generally reluctant to undertake actions which could have endangered their job security.[23] The structure of labor unions in each enterprise follows the structural changes of the enterprise as they have no choice but to reconsider their own organizational structure every time a corporation restructures.[24] Consequently, the *enterprise union* in Japan has not disappeared but remains the dominant form of union organization, and still has about a fifth of the workforce in their membership.[25] Currently, there are four trade unions in the country: the Japan Teachers Union, RENGO, Sohyo, and the National Union of General Workers.[26]

Each organization formed its own labor union which included all the stakeholders in the enterprise; labor unions are a power center, much like the rest of the stakeholders—government, employer, and others. Confrontations between labor unions and management are limited because the protection of the employees and their strength in the organization emanates from the stakeholders, not from the union itself.

The Corporation

At first, Japanese corporations enjoyed a large degree of autonomy in their management practices and corporate decisions, but during World War II, Japan de facto nationalized many major corporations, subordinating them to central planners. Government decrees abolished corporate boards' rights to appoint managers in 1943, reassigning them to a government agency.[27] Until the end of World War II, small- and medium-size corporations, which constituted the overwhelming majority of this legal entity, played a limited role in the development of management. This occurred because the majority of these corporations were family-owned and operated, and because there was no separation between management and ownership. Furthermore, very little was done to create new corporations that included the philosophy of the separation of management from ownership. Many characteristics of this situation continued through the 1960s and 1970s, resulting in small-size organizations. One could easily see the dichotomy between the large-scale sector of the industry, where control was strongly concentrated, and the sector composed of small-

and medium-size highly competitive firms.[28] Until the 1970s, even large Japanese corporations did not separate management from ownership because many characteristics were still present from the former *Zaibatsu* system. The Zaibatsu system, which was based on the fusion of ownership and management, had been an integral force that provided impetus to the Westernization of Japan, but was no longer viable once the country attained industrial maturity. After 1945, attempts were made to totally eradicate the existence of the Zaibatsu system; however, the elements and the principles of this system still remain hidden under the façade of the modern Japanese corporation. The dissolution made the industrial and mining companies of the former Zaibatsu important industries, and the former Zaibatsu insurance companies and banks, though weakened, remained the chief financial institutions of the country.[29]

Private companies in Japan, known as the *kaisha*, brilliantly adopted Western technology and put that technology to use in organizations based entirely on Japanese cultural values.[30] Today, the Japanese corporation *kaisha* plays a paramount role in the Japanese economy and society; it is a social organization and a community, not a collection of physical and financial assets, and the primary stakeholders are the employees. Despite the recent downfall of the Japanese economy, there are indications that corporations are regaining their past strength and discovering new swagger amid structural changes taking place in the global economy.[31]

After World War II, the well-balanced industrialization of Japan contributed to the creation of more private corporations and precipitated the separation of ownership from management, thus paving the way for management development under the distinct cultural auspices of the nation.

Management in Japan

The impact of labor unions upon management is an event that takes place in each organization individually, and it is influenced by the idiosyncrasies of the stakeholders in each firm. The Japanese corporation *kaisha* plays a paramount role in the Japanese development of management within the limits of each corporate entity. The role and impact of the Japanese corporation upon management is substantially different than that in Western corporations. The Japanese corporation is a social organization and a community, and the primary stakeholders are its members. Employees identify with the company they are working for rather than with the skill category in which they work.[32]

The selection of Japanese managers has been based on the idea of creating a cohesive force. To be hired, the candidate must display moderate views and a personality that interacts harmoniously within the managerial spectrum. Job competence is important, but applicants may be eliminated during the selection process if they arouse suspicion that they cannot get along with people, possess radical views, or come from unfavorable home environments.[33] Since most business organizations were small in the past, most managers were owner-managers; in larger organizations, many professionals were former government bureaucrats. It was quite common in Japan for high-ranking bureaucrats to retire and move into top management positions in private enterprises.[34] This practice started to change in the 1970s, when many managers were replaced by successors who were promoted at a younger age and often had more technical training; consequently, this trend undermined traditional perceptions.[35]

Because most of the professional managers emanated from the upper social echelon, they were highly educated and enlightened. More than 90 percent of top executives were graduates of such institutions as Tokyo, Kyoto, Keio, or Waseda universities, the most prestigious schools in the country, while only about 3 percent of top executives were educated abroad.[36]

During the last twenty years, tremendous changes have taken place in the background and origin of Japanese managers. Managers now come from all socioeconomic backgrounds, and they have the opportunity to attain the status of the professional manager in most Japanese enterprises. They work their way up from the bottom, spending time in several sections and departments and solidifying relationships with superiors, peers, and subordinates.[37] The internal promotional system for general management careers in most Japanese organizations indicates that managers are moving from division to division.[38] These changes were part of even bigger changes in the Japanese economy that occurred during the last twenty years, a period in which Japan's industries restructured and redesigned themselves to deal with the requirements of a changing economic world.[39]

Management education is now offered by every university and specialized school in the country. During the 1980s and 1990s, Japanese management became the target of admiration, and many business schools in the West started imitating Japanese management methods and applications. Successful business management in the 1990s required the understanding of Japanese language, culture, and management.[40] Management education is considered to be elite, and Japanese business schools have adopted excellent training programs to support managerial training for all types of enterprises. The secret of the Japanese learning process is that the Japanese education system, its approach to training, and its approach to management work together in harmony,[41] and even include training programs for small- and medium-size enterprises.[42]

Japanese management education places heavy emphasis on research and development, and financial support emanates from both the private sector (mainly industry) and the government. Even during economic downturns, these two sources generously continue to provide financial assistance for research and development in management and other areas of business. Japan spends more on research and development in proportion to its economic size than any other nation in the world. Also, the most exciting new development in research and development is the changing and quickly-expanding role of the universities, and increased university-industry collaboration.[43]

Until the 1980s, employee control was based mainly on the satisfaction of the employees' lower echelon needs, and on appealing to the individual's dedication to the organization and its glorification. Up until the 1980s, the average Japanese employee was fighting for their basic necessities, and Japanese organizations showed disregard for the physical and mental health of their employees, such as canceling scheduled days off and keeping unsafe equipment in operation to keep production quotas up.[44] At that time, the Japanese people did not have the level of economic prosperity they currently enjoy. One Japanese high official stated that as a country they were the third greatest power, but when it came to private individuals, their poverty ranked them at about the same level as Venezuela.[45]

Another major characteristic of employee control was based on paternalism, an innate ideal of Japanese society that dates back to the historical roots of the nation. Under this system, Japanese employees did exactly what their managers told them to do and had no voice of their own.[46] The patron-client relationship was (and still is to a lesser degree) the relationship between the superior and the subordinate in any Japanese organization. A *patron* was a person who was regarded as a protector, a guide, and a model to copy, and as someone or something else more powerful than oneself. Profound patriotism and dedication to the glorification of Japan through one's place of employment has been traditionally emphasized, and it would be correct to link Japan's success to the coercive, regimented side of its society, which Americans would hardly want to emulate.[47]

Another basis for Japanese paternalism was that those employees who obeyed the paternalistic injunctions of their employers were granted life-time employment. Since business firms were committed to lifetime em-ployment for their workers, the need for job security was satisfied.[48] A good example of long-term job security is the case of the *Kogai*, a young man who joins an organization immediately after graduation and stays with it, one whose wholehearted loyalty was assured.[49] Another charac-teristic of security-oriented Japanese employees was that they developed a strong loyalty to the company.[50] The Japanese employee was more con-cerned with job security than promotion or advancement. However, this practice started to drastically change toward the end of the 1980s, for as Japanese companies diversified, they increasingly hired skilled mid-career people away from other companies.[51]

Until the 1980s, the Japanese acquired their jobs through referrals by their relatives and friends rather than through the human resources de-partments, which only existed in large organizations. Concern for the employee as a total person was implemented by the enterprise, which is synonymous with the family and thus is the home of most of the employ-ees. Japanese management claimed that the employees are interested in their place of employment because they feel that their work is contribut-ing to accomplishing the goals of the enterprise.[52]

The group sense of responsibility for work and the success of the or-ganization in Japan serves as the foundation for the relationship between management and employees. This Japanese value illustrates the belief that teamwork is responsible for success. The origin of the Japanese em-phasis on groups has been attributed mainly to Japan's history as a rice culture, which necessitated centuries of interdependence and cooperation among farmers and communities.[53] Furthermore, the Japanese have neat-ly mutated communal traditions into the modern industrial workplace, succeeding in balancing individual and communal interests.[54] Japanese managers also put little emphasis on rewarding individual effort or in singling out individuals for special recognition.[55] Each person is merely a part of the group, thus eliminating individualism, whereas in the West, it is the individual who cooperates with others to form a harmonious group. If a talented person behaved in a highly individualistic manner and tried to aggressively demonstrate their talents, it is likely that they would not be promoted. In fact, they would probably be regarded as a very un-cooperative person by the organization.[56] However, there was evidence that the elimination of the individual's importance had detrimental re-sults. Many employees took advantage of the situation and did only their specified work; if there was no more work to do, they slept on the job, read magazines, and took interminable tea-breaks. Some even indulged in *saburu*, a word coined from sabotage, which was their term for gross slacking on the job.[57]

Group decision-making as it exists in the West did not and does not exist in Japan. So-called decision-making meetings in Japan were used to nurture a sense of corporate identity and build consensus rather than to make decisions.[58] The authoritarian attitude of Japanese managers, according to the Japanese philosophy, demonstrated that power depended on excessively autocratic authority. If a manager was strong, the vertically and hierarchically oriented organizational structure would yield to his authoritarian and autocratic control. But if the manager was not strong, the indirect nature of his control over the group tended to weaken his power and constrain his freedom.[59] Nowhere was authoritarianism and paternalism more pervasive than in Japanese enterprises; in both small and large firms,[60] managers were men who applied managerial despotism.[61] Of course, this meant that both lower levels of management and employees could neither function nor respect their superiors unless they exercised power in an autocratic manner. Specifically, force and an authoritarian attitude were imperative in order to achieve results in the Japanese management process, and Japanese management appeared to be a peace-time extension of the old military system, where uniforms were simply exchanged for dark blue business suits.[62]

As Japan's management style was starting to be questioned at home, it was really being put to the test as it moved offshore, where it just fell apart.[63] Some organizations in Western Europe and North America attempted to adopt Japanese management practices in the 1980s and 1990s. However, Japanese managerial practices could not be easily transplanted into the Western world (unless they were technical in nature) because they evolved under the unique influence of Japanese cultural factors. Japanese management was a product of historical development and could not be smoothly transplanted to countries with different historical backgrounds.[64]

As the result of economic prosperity and the difficult economic times that followed during the last thirty years, Japanese organizations underwent substantial restructuring that affected their management. Currently, a major characteristic in Japanese management is the social contact between firm and employee, a commitment to work as a community to achieve economic security for all members of the workforce. Japan's economic success is due to the genius of building a management system based on its own culture, and any move away from that base can be taken only with very great risk.[65]

The impact of labor unions and corporations upon the development of management has taken place under the distinct auspices of Japanese culture. Both labor unions and corporations influenced the development of management in a substantially different way than their counterparts in the West, and created a unique type of management development that faithfully reflects the cultural factors of the country.

References

Abegglen, J. C. *21st-Century Japanese Management: New Systems, Lasting Values*. New York, NY: Palgrave McMillan, 2006.

Adams, T. F. M., and N. Kodayashi. *The World of Japanese Business*. Tokyo, Japan: Kodansha International, 1959.

Allen, G. C. *Japan's Economic Expansion*. Oxford, England: Oxford University Press, 1965.

Benedict, R. *The Chrysanthemum and the Sword*. Boston, MA: Houghton Mifflin, 2006.

Benent, J., and I. Ishino. *Paternalism in the Japanese Economy*. Minneapolis, MN: University of Minnesota Press, 1963.

Business Week. "When in Japan, Put a Japanese at the Top." November 18, 1972.

Cook, A. *Japanese Trade Unions*. Ithaca, NY: Cornell University Press, 1966.

Cross, L. R. "Educational Leadership: A Strategic Co-Operative Japanese Corporate Model." *Leadership & Organization Development Journal* 14, 3. (1993): 4. http://proquest.umi.com/pqdweb?did=81666 &sid=15&Fmt=3&clientId=11123&RQT=309&VName=PQD

Cutts, R. L., and C. Johnson. *An Empire of Schools: Japan's Universities and the Molding of a National Power Elite*. Armonk, NY: M. E. Sharpe, 1997.

Davis, K., and R. Blomstrom. *Business and its Environments*. New York, NY: McGraw-Hill, 1966.

De Mente, B. L. *Kata: The Key to Understanding and Dealing with the Japanese*. Boston, MA: Tuttle Publishing, 2003.

Directory of Education Online. http://www.directoryofeducation.net/ colleges/worldwide/japan/

Drucker, P. F. *The Age of Discontinuity*. New York, NY: Harper & Row,

1969.

Economist. "The Five Ages of Man(agement)." May 1983.

Halberstram, D. "Reflections on Japan, Inc." *Business Monthly*, February 1989.

Hasegawa, Y. *Rediscovering Japanese Business Leadership: 15 Japanese Managers and the Companies they are Leading to New Growth.* Singapore: John Wiley and Sons, Asia, 2010.

Hayes, L. D. "Higher Education in Japan." *Social Science Journal* 34, 3. (July 1997): paragraphs 2-3. http://find.galegroup.com.prx01.lirn.net/gtx/infomark.do?&contentSet=IAC-Documents&type=retrieve&tabID=T002&prodId=ITOF&docId=A19909452&source=gale&srcprod=ITOF&userGroupName=lirn_wu&version=1.0

Imai, M. "The Ingredients of Executives Selection in Japan." *Personnel*, July-August 1969.

International Management. "Younger Blood Rising to the Top in Japanese Companies." July 1983.

Ishida, H. *Social Mobility in Contemporary Japan: Educational Credentials, Class and Labour Market in a Cross-National Perspective.* Stanford, CA: Stanford University Press, 1993.

Japanese Economic Journal. "Community gets Priority," January 1987.

Kamat, S. *Japan in the Passing Lane.* New York, NY: Pantheon, 1983.

Kaynak, E. and Y. Sai. *The Eight Core Values of the Japanese Businessman: Toward an Understanding of Japanese Management.* Binghampton, NY: International Business Press, 1999.

Keiichiro, Nakagawa. "Japanese Management: An Interdisciplinary Approach." Japan Foundation, Office for the Japanese Studies Center, August 1983: 1-5.

Keys, J. B., and T. R. Miller. "The Japanese Management Theory Jungle." *Academy of Management Review*, 1984.

Levy, M. J. "Some Implications of Japanese Social Structure." *American Sociologist* 31, 2. (Summer 2000): 3-5.

Lorriman, J. "Lifelong Learning in Japan." *Journal of European Industrial Training* 9, 2. (1995): 8-15. http://proquest.umi.com/pqdweb?did=8988438&sid=3&Fmt=3&clientId=1123&RQT=309&VName=PQD

Modic, S. J. "Myths about Japanese Management." *Industry Week*, October 1987.

Morck, R. K., ed. *A History of Corporate Governance around the World.* Chicago, IL: University of Chicago Press, 2007.

NationMaster.com. "Trade Union Membership by Country." Accessed October 1, 2010 from http://www.nationmaster.com/graph/lab_tra_uni_mem-labor-trade-union-membership

Ouchi, Dr. William. *Theory Z: How American Business can Meet the Japanese Challenges*. Reading, MA: Addison-Wesley, 1981.

Pascale, R. T., and A. G. Athos. *The Art of Japanese Management*. New York, NY: Warner Books, 1981.

Pekkanen, R. "After the Development State: Civil Society in Japan. *Journal of East Asian Studies* 4, 3. (September-December 2004): 4-7.

Runciman, W. G. *Social Science and Political Theory*. Cambridge: Cambridge University Press, 1963.

Sako, M. *Shifting Boundaries of the Firm: Japanese Company—Japanese Labor*. Oxford, England: Oxford University Press, 2008.

Scalpino, R. *Democracy and Party Movement in Prewar Japan*. Berkeley, CA: University of California Press, 1961.

Smith, J. M. "The Japan Syndrome: Demystifying Japanese Management." *Management Decision* 25, March 1983.

Stewart, P., ed. *Beyond Japanese Management: The End of Modern Times?* London, England: Frank Cass, 2001.

Storey, D. J. "Exploring the Link, Among Small Firms, Between Management Training and Firm Performance: A Comparison between the UK and other OECD Countries." *International Journal of Human Resource Management* 15, 1. (February 2004): 119. doi:10.1080/0958519032000157375

Toshiki, S. "Is Japan a 'Classless' Society?" *Japan Quarterly* 48, 2. (April-June 2001): 25-30. http://proquest.umi.com/pqdweb?did=72460583&sid=3&Fmt=4&clientId=11123&RQT=309&VName=PQD

Training and Development Journal. "Eastern and Western Management: Different World." August 1982.

Whenmouth, E. "Is Japan's Corporate Style Changing?" *Industry Week*, October 1989.

Yoshino, M. Y. *Japan's Managerial System*. Cambridge, MA: M.I.T. Press, 1968.

Endnotes

1   M. Y. Yoshino, *Japan's Managerial System* (Cambridge, MA: M.I.T. Press, 1968).

2   Ibid.

3   R. Benedict, *The Chrysanthemum and the Sword* (Boston, MA.

Houghton Mifflin, 2006).

4 R. T. Pascale and A. G. Athos, *The Art of Japanese Management* (New York, NY: Warner Books, 1981).

5 L. D. Hayes, "Higher Education in Japan," *Social Science Journal* 34, 3 (July 1997): paragraphs 2-3. http://find.galegroup.com.prx01. lirn.net/gtx/infomark.do?&contentSet=IAC-Documents&type=retri eve&tabID=T002&prodId=ITOF&docId=A19909452&source=gale &srcprod=ITOF&userGroupName=lirn_wu&version=1.0

6 H. Ishida, *Social Mobility in Contemporary Japan: Educational Credentials, Class and Labour Market in a Cross-National Perspective* (Stanford, CA: Stanford University Press, 1993).

7 R. L. Cutts and C. Johnson, *An Empire of Schools: Japan's Universities and the Molding of a National Power Elite* (Armonk, NY: M.E. Sharpe, 1997).

8 Directory of Education Online. http://www.directoryofeducation.net/ colleges/worldwide/japan/

9 J. C. Abegglen, *21st-Century Japanese Management: New Systems, Lasting Values* (New York, NY: Palgrave McMillan, 2006).

10 R. Scalpino, *Democracy and Party Movement in Prewar Japan* (Berkeley: University of California Press, 1961).

11 P. F. Drucker, *The Age of Discontinuity* (New York, NY: Harper & Row, 1969).

12 Scalpino, *Democracy and Party Movement in Prewar Japan.*

13 *Business Week*, "When in Japan, Put a Japanese at the Top," November 18, 1972, p.41.

14 K. Davis and R. Blomstrom, *Business and Its Environments* (New York, NY: McGraw-Hill, 1966).

15 *Japanese Economic Journal*, "Community gets Priority," January 1987: 7.

16 Abegglen, *21st-Century Japanese Management: New Systems, Lasting Values.*

17 S. Toshiki, "Is Japan a 'Classless' Society?" *Japan Quarterly* 48, 2 (April-June 2001): 25-30. http://proquest.umi.com/pqdweb?did=724 60583&sid=3&Fmt=4&clientId=11123&RQT=309&VName=PQD

18 Abegglen, *21st-Century Japanese Management: New Systems, Lasting Values.*

19 R. Pekkanen, "After the Development State: Civil Society in Japan," *Journal of East Asian Studies* 4, 3 (September-December 2004): 5.

20 M. J. Levy, "Some Implications of Japanese Social Structure,"

American Sociologist 31, 2 (Summer 2000): 4.

21 Abegglen, *21st-Century Japanese Management: New Systems, Lasting Values.*

22 P. Stewart, ed., *Beyond Japanese Management: The End of Modern Times?* (London, England: Frank Cass, 2001).

23 A. Cook, *Japanese Trade Unions* (Ithaca, NY: Cornell University Press, 1966).

24 M. Sako, *Shifting Boundaries of the Firm: Japanese Company—Japanese Labor* (Oxford, England: Oxford University Press, 2008).

25 Stewart, *Beyond Japanese Management: The End of Modern Times?*

26 NationMaster.com. "Trade union membership by country."

27 Morck, *A History of Corporate Governance around the World.*

28 G. C. Allen, *Japan's Economic Expansion* (Oxford, England: Oxford University Press, 1965).

29 Ibid.

30 Abegglen, *21st-Century Japanese Management: New Systems, Lasting Values.*

31 Y. Hasegawa, *Rediscovering Japanese Business Leadership: 15 Japanese Managers and the Companies they are Leading to New Growth* (Singapore: John Wiley and Sons, Asia, 2010).

32 Morck, *A History of Corporate Governance around the World.*

33 M. Imai, "The Ingredients of Executives Selection in Japan," *Personnel*, July-August 1969, p.25.

34 Ibid.

35 *International Management*, "Younger Blood Rising to the Top in Japanese Companies," July 1983: 16.

36 Yoshino, *Japan's Managerial System.*

37 B. L. De Mente, *Kata: The Key to Understanding and Dealing with the Japanese* (Boston, MA: Tuttle Publishing, 2003).

38 Sako, *Shifting Boundaries of the Firm: Japanese Company—Japanese Labor.*

39 Abegglen, *21st-Century Japanese Management: New Systems, Lasting Values.*

40 L. R. Cross, "Educational Leadership: A Strategic Co-Operative Japanese Corporate Model," *Leadership & Organization Development Journal* 14, 3 (1993): 4. http://proquest.umi.com/pqdweb?did=81666&sid=15&Fmt=3&clientId=11123&RQT=309&VName=PQD

41 J. Lorriman, "Lifelong Learning in Japan," *Journal of European*

Industrial Training 9, 2 (1995): 10. http://proquest.umi.com/pqdweb
?did=8988438&sid=3&Fmt=3&clientld=1123&RQT=309&VName
=PQD

42 D. J. Storey, "Exploring the Link, Among Small Firms, Between
Management Training and Firm Performance: A Comparison
between the UK and other OECD Countries," *International Journal
of Human Resource Management* 15, 1 (February 2004): 119.
doi:10.1080/0958519032000157375

43 Abegglen, *21st-Century Japanese Management: New Systems,
Lasting Values.*

44 S. Kamat, *Japan in the Passing Lane* (New York, NY: Pantheon,
1983).

45 Ibid.

46 J. Benent and I. Ishino, *Paternalism in the Japanese Economy*
(Minneapolis, MN: University of Minnesota Press, 1963).

47 J. B. Keys and T.R. Miller, "The Japanese Management Theory
Jungle," *Academy of Management Review*, 1984.

48 *Training and Development Journal*, "Eastern and Western Management: Different World," August 1982: 11.

49 Imai, "The Ingredients of Executives Selection in Japan."

50 Ibid.

51 E. Whenmouth, "Is Japan's Corporate Style Changing?" *Industry
Week*, October 1989: 33.

52 E. Kaynak and Y. Sai, *The Eight Core Values of the Japanese Businessman: Toward an Understanding of Japanese Management*
(Binghampton, NY: International Business Press, 1999).

53 Ibid.

54 D. Halberstram, "Reflections on Japan, Inc.," *Business Monthly*,
February 1989: 47.

55 Ouchi, *Theory Z: How American Business can Meet the Japanese
Challenges.*

56 *Japanese Economic Journal*, "Community gets Priority," January
1987: 7.

57 T. F. M. Adams and N. Kodayashi, *The World of Japanese Business*
(Tokyo, Japan: Kodansha International, 1959).

58 *Economist*, "The Five Ages of Man(agement)," May 1983: 72.

59 Adams and Kodayashi, *The World of Japanese Business.*

60 Benent and Ishino, *Paternalism in the Japanese Economy.*

61 Imai, "The Ingredients of Executives Selection in Japan."

62 J. M. Smith, "The Japan Syndrome: Demystifying Japanese Management," *Management Decision* 25, March 1983.

63 S. J. Modic, "Myths about Japanese Management," *Industry Week*, October 1987: 49.

64 Nakagawa Keiichiro, "Japanese Management: An Interdisciplinary Approach," Japan Foundation, Office for the Japanese Studies Center, August 1983: 1-5.

65 Abegglen, *21st-Century Japanese Management: New Systems, Lasting Values*.

Chapter 7: Greece

Religion and Economic Development

The ancient Greek world was under the politico-economic influence of Plato and Aristotle. Both men advocated an agrarian society which considered agriculture to be the noblest profession of all, followed by the military. Commerce and industry were regarded as necessary evils. Ironically, the Ionian Greeks favored not only commerce and industry, but also manual work, and they took the human hand as their emblem. However, the Ionians were overshadowed by the Athenians who, with the Spartans and Macedonians, represented the ancient Greek world, which consisted of various Greek states ranging from South Italy and Sicily to eastern Asia Minor. Aristotle, who followed Plato and in many ways overshadowed him, concurred with his mentor regarding trade and industry as inferior professions, and he also condemned the practice of usury and lending money.

Christianity was first introduced into the Greek world in Asia Minor, Cyprus, and Crete at the middle of the first century A.D. The Church acquired tremendous power to the point where the Greek Patriarch of Constantinople had equal power with the Greek Emperor of the Byzantine Empire, which included all the former Greek states and portions of the Roman Empire in the West. During its formation, the Church accepted Aristotle's philosophy vis-à-vis trade and commerce, and adopted most, if not all, of the Aristotelian ideology. Although the Church split in the eleventh century, Aristotelian ideas remained intact in both the Greek and Roman parts of the Church. The ultimate goal of the Church was the salvation of the human race, and accordingly every effort was made to direct the attention of the congregation to this end. Anything that might impede religious guidance toward salvation was considered evil. Therefore, it is logical to conclude that the Church was not hostile toward industry and commerce per se, but opposed the practices which detracted from full dedication to religious salvation.

Despite the Church's opposition, the Medieval Greeks contributed greatly to trade and industry. Up until the twelfth century, before Venice and Genoa appeared as commercial powers, and long before Marco Polo went to China, or the first Portuguese expeditions outside the Mediterranean took place, the Medieval Greeks had sea lanes to Asia, sub-Saharan Africa, and even to China and modern Vietnam, from where they procured spices, sandalwood, silk and other useful products. *Cosmas the Indicopleustes*, the Sailor of the Indies, described Ceylon as the Indian trade clearinghouse of the East, where the goods from China, Indo-China, and India were collected.[1] Greek overland trade with Asia used the Silk Road which linked Constantinople with various Central Asian and Chinese cities.

The negative attitude of the Orthodox Church toward economic development in the Modern Greek state started to change after World War II. It was necessary for the survival of the country—as was the case with the Roman Catholic Church's change of position in Latin Europe and Latin America. The Greek economy had remained agricultural and dependent upon the revenues from those working in the merchant marine and from Greeks living abroad. Economic development started in the 1960s, but the process was cachectic due to the fact that the country did not have qualified business people capable of supporting the developmental process. The government's role, in order to sustain economic development, pivoted around foreign investment and tourism. The latter proved to be a success that has been continuously creating substantial amounts of revenues for the country.

In 1981, Greece entered into the European Economic Community (EEC) and became subject to the EEC's economic and social regulations. This resulted in the removal of most protectionist policies and opened the road to trade liberalization. Consequently, Greece started an intensive and extensive commercial interaction with the EEC that proved to be astronomically beneficial. The private sector in the economy also began to gain ground, and the Greek economy started to become largely dependent on the private sector, resulting in more privatization, which had a positive influence on business in the country.[2] Furthermore, in the early 1990s, a strong privatization movement opened state enterprises to private access with great success. Tax reforms followed, and by the end of 2010, the country had impressive success in the areas of banking and financial services, service industries, textiles, food, tourism, and telecommunications, all despite the fact that recent problems in the fiscal sector of the economy present a different picture to the world. Capitalism is developed and dynamic; the economy ranks high in the world on the basis of gross domestic product and has achieved high growth rates, with some domestic industries ranking among the most powerful on the world market. Greek capital exports are increasing, and Greek magnates dominate international shipping.[3] Furthermore, since the 1990s, the Greek economy has combined relatively strong economic performance (rapid GDP growth rate and strong productive growth) with very weak performance on many other fronts, ranging from poor labor and product market institutions to low competitiveness and poor environmental protection.[4] In 2007, 12.4 percent of employed persons worked in agriculture, 22.4 percent in industry, and 65.2 percent in services.[5] Due to the fiscal problems of the Greek government, economic development in 2010 has slowed down, but it is expected to revive at the end of 2011 or the beginning of 2012.

The impact of the Orthodox Church upon economic development in Greece was initially negative, but it started to change after World War II, as was the case with the Roman Catholic Church in Latin Europe and Latin America. The country has attained substantial economic development, but inherent weaknesses still exist in the labor market, product competitiveness, and organizational effectiveness and efficiency.

Religion and Education

The Greek education system has been influenced by the Greek Orthodox Church since Byzantine times. The system traditionally leaned toward classical education, such as religion, art, law, medicine, and music, similar in nature to the Italian education system. Education in religion, the fine arts, music, and history continues to be emphasized. However, after the 1960s, the influence of the Church turned toward educational curricula that favor modern socioeconomic systems, including vocational, commercial, economic, and technical and technological curricula. Although the Greek education system tends to be sclerotic, inflexible, and resistant to change, the country has made great improvements in the general education level of its population in recent years.[6]

The Greek education system currently is under the auspices of religious and educational administrative offices and closely follows the education systems of Germany and France. Greek children must attend school from ages six to fifteen, and education is free and compulsory at that age. The time frame encompasses the entire six years of elementary education and six years of studies in *Gymnasium* (high school). Technical-vocational education was seriously lacking;[7] even as late as 2003, the country did not promote technical-vocational education and thus missed an opportunity to attain higher levels of economic development.[8] Young people are very interested in education; they seem to have internalized a way of thinking about education as a personal project for which social forces and other external factors play only a secondary role, if any.[9] Once students finish their gymnasium education and pass entrance examinations, they are eligible to enter into institutions of higher learning. Because the entrance examinations are highly competitive, only a small number of the applicants are accepted into universities. Higher education in Greece is provided exclusively by public institutions, namely technological institutions and universities. The main difference between them is that only universities have the authority to offer students post-graduate research-based courses, such as Ph.D.s.[10]

Greek universities have been underfunded and therefore have not offered graduate curricula until recently. They also had antiquated internal operations, which were eventually upgraded to more modern ones influenced by American, German, and French models. All Greek universities have been government institutions, but attempts to create private universities and import foreign private universities are beginning to bring some results. In 2010, the Papandreou government made great efforts to modernize the entire education system. Proposals are now being made to place universities under a Council of Administration for financing purposes, and the administration of each university will be under the deanship of every school. Proposals for changing the entrance criteria for universities are also being made. Furthermore, graduate curricula are being slowly added, some leading to master and doctoral degrees. There are currently thirty-eight colleges and universities in the country.[11] In 1997, the *Hellenic Open University* opened its doors and now offers both undergraduate and graduate curricula on a distance learning basis.[12] Lifelong education (which includes personal development classes, leisure activities, civic education, and cultural education) has appeared, but it is progressing slowly. It accounts for just 1.4 percent of education, while the average in the European Union is around 8.5 percent.[13] Teacher training programs are also being sponsored by the government with positive results.[14]

The Greek Orthodox Church favored classical education, such as religion, art, law, medicine, and music, but it changed its position in the 1960s and started to favor curricula in economics, business, technology, vocational education, and related areas commensurate to a modern socio-economic system.

Religion and Social Structure

The Olympian pantheon of deities and demigods played a very important role in the societies of all Greek states, ranging from South Italy and

Sicily all the way to the eastern part of Asia Minor; there was no unified Greek state during ancient times. The ancient Greek states were similar to the German states prior to their unification. Alexander the Great was the first Greek who attempted to create a single Greek state under Macedonian rule, an idea that was partially successful. The unification of all Greek states took place with the emergence of the Byzantine Empire, which inherited the remnants of the Roman Empire in the West and the Greek states in the East. The Byzantine Empire was a theocratic state in which the Patriarch and the Emperor had equal power. During its initial stage, the Church was responsible for the destruction of depictions of the classical part of the Greek world and society. The Church ordered the destruction of temples, statues and other objects of art and architecture; it outlawed many ancient customs, closed ancient academies and universities, and ended the Olympic Games. The Church had full control over the unified Greek societies under the Byzantine Empire.

In the eleventh century, the Church was divided between the Latin West that became the Roman Catholic Church and the Orthodox Churches of the East, each under jurisdiction of an Orthodox nation such as Bulgaria, Russia, Serbia, Romania, or the Ukraine. The Church continued to have the same influence after the Byzantine Empire was destroyed by Central Asian invaders, who eventually occupied all the Christian nations of South-Eastern Europe (the most advanced region of Europe during Byzantine times) and placed them under the rule of the Steppe. Thanks to the Spanish naval victory in Lepanto, South Greece, and the heroic resistance of the Austrians in Vienna, the rest of Europe remained free and began its brilliant supremacy, starting with the Italian Renaissance (highly influenced by refugees from the Byzantine Empire) and subsequently by the French Renaissance. The Church continued to influence Greek society even after the establishment of a maimed modern Greek state, which included and still includes a small fraction of the Greek world.

Unlike the Spanish Reconquista, which managed to expel foreign invaders from the Iberian Peninsula, the Greek world liberated most but not all of its European possessions. The remaining possessions in Asia Minor and the small European territories were lost, uprooting of millions of Ionian Greeks, Pontian Greeks, and Armenians from their homelands. A sizeable number of those expelled immigrated to the Greek state, where they became second-class citizens. The Modern Greek state witnessed a number of subsequent wars. World War II resulted in the occupation of the country by European Axis powers. The country was liberated in 1944 by Greek and British Armed Forces that had been stationed in the Middle East and Egypt from 1941 to 1944.

The liberation was followed by a communist guerilla invasion sponsored by Stalin, a period euphemistically known as the Greek Civil War. Communist-supported guerrillas ransacked the countryside and small cities for several years until their final defeat by the Greek Armed Forces assisted by generous foreign aid from the United States under the Truman-Marshal Plan. By 1949, the countryside and small cities were devastated, and children from these areas were taken from their parents by the guerillas and sent to neighboring communist nations for training and indoctrination. The social structure and society of the devastated areas were in turmoil, just like Germany after World War II.

In the large cities unaffected by the guerilla warfare, the social structure remained rigid, with the Ionian Greeks, Pontian Greeks, and Armenians occupying the lowest stratification. Industry did not employ enough people at that time to generate the rates of urban migration experienced in the country after the immediate post-war period.[15] Up until the 1960s, Greek society was characterized by a lack of mobility; it was very difficult for a person belonging to a lower social stratification to reach higher society levels because the society was deeply underdeveloped.[16] However, in the 1960s, the attitude of the Church toward social structure and mobility became positive and supportive, thus allowing for the creation of a modern socioeconomic system. The Church still remains a force in the social affairs of the country, and it has grown in political importance.[17] The Ionian Greeks, Pontian Greeks, and the Armenians are now fully integrated in the Modern Greek society and occupy high positions in every facet of the social, political, and economic sectors. The shifting of broad strata of the Greek population into economic activities brought about these changes.[18]

There has not been any population increase during the last twenty years on the part of the native element in the country. The percentage of older people is increasing, as is the case in Italy, France, and most of the other members of the European Union. The family still remains one of the most important elements in Greek society. Today, the social structure is relatively flexible and sufficiently mobile. Women have the opportunity to attend universities and other institutions of higher learning. They also have equal access to the professions, such as medicine, law, teaching, and recently have made impressive entrances in the political arena of the country. However, one of the major social problems is the welfare system. Welfare state provisions are perversely distributed on the basis on the political bargaining power of social groups and individual position in the clientele network, rather than on the basis of the needs of the people and their citizenship rights.[19]

There are a substantially large number of immigrants in the country, making up almost 10 percent of the total population. Most of them are from neighboring nations in the north, but there are immigrants from the Middle East, Africa, and Asia. Due to the economic competition between immigrants and the native population, some Greeks have taken an anti-immigrant stance, a situation similar to that of the other Western, Central, and Southern states of the European Union. There are few religious issues, since most of the immigrants are Christians entering a Christian country, but sporadic incidents from Islamic immigrants appear in large cities.

Social and economic reforms continue in the country. As in Italy, there are problems with the employment of young people. A weak labor market treats young people as outsiders, depriving them of security and optimism, and providing fertile ground for violent protests and riots.[20] Additionally, school-work programs are in an embryonic state. In the last few years, universities initiated a cooperative education program, which was launched by University Careers Offices and partially funded by the European Union.[21] The pressure for reform has been evident over the last decade, combining a domestic discourse on modernization with belief in the importance of Greece remaining a part of the core membership of the European Union.[22] Furthermore, Greece is in an era of significant technological and economic transformation. Public policy is being changed because the old corporatist policies have been rendered obsolete, and the paradigm of community policies often seems more applicable to modern political and economic realities.[23] In 2010, the Papandreou government initiated revolutionary changes that will profoundly and positively affect the future socioeconomic development of the nation.

Since Byzantine times, the Church has had a profound impact upon the societies of all Greek states as well as the Modern Greek state. Despite political turmoil, the Church maintained a rigid society; when the mentality of the Church changed in the 1960s, Greek society started to become flexible and allow social mobility. Greek society today is characterized by sufficient flexibility, mobility, and change. However, it is confronting issues with immigrants, an aging population, insufficient employment for the youth, and a defective welfare system.

Extent of Industrialization

Industrialization came late in the early 1960s, and was followed by a rapid shift to post-Fordism in the 1980s, well before a culture of contractual relationships and attendant modes of social solidarity were widely developed.[24] This event had a tremendous impact upon the lack of opportunity for merging small organizations into larger ones, thus creating the corporate form of business and leading to the formation of new and larger organizations in the corporate form. The Greek government supported the development of industrialization, and provided assistance in the form of tax breaks, tariffs, and investments in capital goods for industrial production purposes. It should be noted that investments in manufacturing from developed nations inside and outside Europe have been limited, and some experts indicate that the entrepreneurial inclination of the Greeks is toward commerce, not manufacturing.[25] It was during the rapid industrialization period that labor unions acquired the strength they have today. In 1963, out of three and a half million employed people, industry employed half a million.[26]

In 1992, a short revival in manufacturing took place that provided impetus for exports, and many industries were able to compete internationally because they had the protection of a cheap currency that was regularly devalued. However, the introduction of the euro brought an end to this policy, and companies based in Greece can now compete internationally only by becoming more innovative, keeping down their costs, and increasing their productivity.[27] Before the decline in manufacturing in 1991, this sector of the economy provided about 18 percent of the GDP; in 2006, industry accounted for 22 percent of the GDP. Currently, industry accounts for 22 percent of the GDP.[28] De-industrialization resulted in the reduction of the nation's GDP from around 20 percent in the mid 1970s to less than 13 percent in the late 1990s. This was a very hard blow for the economy, and it is imperative that the balance of manufacturing and service shares in the composition of Greek output should be fruitfully shifted in favor of manufacturing.[29] Other areas of industrial production include energy, private construction, public projects, mining, ship-building, and the military industry, which is owned and operated by the Greek government. Subsectors include the production of food, textiles, footwear, and transportation equipment. The employment structure reflects Greece's late industrialization and it is based on the importance of services, the disproportionate size of agriculture, the relatively low importance of industry, low rates of employment for women, and long-term structural unemployment.[30] Greek industrialization performance is hampered by low GDP per capita, the deep economic recession, and the unfavorable influence of the manufacturing trade. The preponderance of traditional, low-tech consumer goods sectors over high-tech industries also contributes to the declining share of manufacturing.[31]

Industrialization came late in the early 1960s and continued until the middle part of the 1990s. Subsequent deindustrialization that exists to this date has created an uneven economy that militates against the normal development of the country. This negative state of industrialization has not allowed the formation of new corporations or the mergers of existing small ones, a situation that has deterred the development of management.

Labor Unions

There are two general confederations of trade unions in Greece: The General Confederation of Greek Labor (GSEE) for employees of private organizations, and the Supreme Administration of Civil Servants (AD-EDY).[32] In 1950, an important trade union conference took place during which the structure and functions of the trade unions were defined and crystallized. Recently, both confederations have passed resolutions in favor of a future merger. Workers may then choose to join either a firm-level or a craft-based constituent union.[33] The Greek labor force can be distinguished by three main categories: public sector employees, private sector employees, and those working in public organizations and enterprises, including the banking sector.[34] In the GSEE, the union leader is a tenured private sector employee, predominantly male, middle-aged and exclusively Greek. In contrast, the typical worker is younger, employed by private firms, and insured with the general scheme in an increasingly feminized and multi-ethnic workforce.[35]

The General Confederation of Greek Labor increased in numbers and strength during the period of industrialization, but its membership decreased during the deindustrialization process. Briefly, the GSEE represents employees in the private sector under private law contracts. The aim of this Confederation is to remain free of government pressure and political involvement. Both confederations have ties with other European Union labor unions, especially in France. Like the rest of the EU labor unions, both confederations are strong and have been participating in strikes, a situation exacerbated in 2010 by the fiscal problems of the country, which led to lower compensation of government and private employees and the elimination of some fringe benefits. Collective bargaining in Greece provides for national general agreements, national agreements in single industry or occupation, regional agreements in a single industry or occupation, and enterprise agreements. From an international perspective, employment protection legislation in Greece is among the strictest.[36]

During the dynamic and short period of industrialization in Greece, labor unions found the opportunity to establish themselves as strong entities in the socioeconomic infrastructure. Today, they are power centers that impose their will upon the management of private and governmental organizations.

The Corporation

Greece went through a process of deindustrialization in the early 1980s that precipitated the decline of the formation of new corporations and the inability of existing ones to grow in size and strength. The economy has been traditionally composed of a very large number of small private organizations. Statistical data from the early 1960s indicated that in 1959, 52 percent of all enterprises employed fewer than nine people, 27 percent employed ten to nineteen people, 14 percent employed twenty to twenty-nine people, and only 0.7 percent employed more than fifty people.[37] The ownership of business organizations did not desire the increase in organizational size that is attained through the corporate form of business, fearing a loss of control and power. The same situation prevails today.

The structure of the economy is marked by very few large enterprises and very many micro firms and small firms.[38] The CEO in Greek enterprises is the father of the family, who has full control of the operation. The rest of the family members follow him faithfully.[39] Unfortunately, this situation has remained the same for the last decade. Most business organizations remain small and play a limited role in Greek economic life, whereas large-size enterprises, although comprising only 1 percent of the total number of firms in all sectors, play a vital role in the Greek economy mainly because of exports and the development of its stock market.[40] Traditional family businesses are still a big part of the Greek economy, as is self-employment in newer businesses. The entrepreneurial spirit runs high in Greece.[41]

Recent studies in Greece and in other Southern European countries indicate that the size of enterprises plays a very important role in organizational productivity. Large firms operating in Greece perform better than small firms, regardless of their profitability level and performance measure; moreover, the magnitude of the size effect on profitability is identical across firms.[42] In the 1960s, the government made great efforts to convince small business owners to enter into mergers, but these attempts were not very successful.[43] This movement was also supported by many academics in both Greece and abroad.[44]

In the 1960s, practically all small- and medium-size enterprises were managed by owners who were adamantly opposed to any type of mergers,[45] and the same situation still prevailed in the first decade of 2000. Business firms in Greece are mainly family-owned or controlled by a group of shareholders. Innovation is absent in private enterprises, and the country is lagging behind in the introduction and adoption of innovations and the development of business networks. One of the major elements needed to change this situation is to stimulate and improve management and entrepreneurship.[46] Today, in the overwhelming majority of Greek enterprises, there is no separation of ownership from management because such organizations do not have sufficient size to create the corporate form of business. Close corporations were reluctant to open in order to acquire more capital and develop themselves in all factors of production, including management.[47] In 1960, only 4 percent of the private organizations were open corporations in the country.[48]

In the late 1990s, the Greek government began the process of privatizing public companies. This decision was influenced by the change of political climate within Greece and driven externally by EU competition rules.[49] The majority of medium and small organizations (mostly family-owned companies) have adopted the minimum mandatory requirements and lack further efficient corporate governance mechanisms.[50] Lamentably, mergers have taken place only in a small number of business organizations.

The majority of Greek business organizations are small, thus preventing the formation of an infrastructure that leads to the development of management through the effective and efficient use of all factors of production. The ever-increasing evidence of the country's failure to be competitive rests upon the weakness of microeconomic development that pivots around the strength of the corporate form of business, which precipitates, sustains, and develops management.

Management in Greece

Greek managers in the 1960s and early 1970s were family members. In most cases, the management of the organization was in the hands of the owners or their children. Managers were not willing to undertake any risks for improving, expanding, or developing their organizations, and only 16 percent of them were willing to consider employing consultants and specialists to assist in the development of the ownership and management of the firm itself.[51] Furthermore, it was noted that the lack of understanding and appreciation of the owners and managers of long-term organizational development would have detrimental effects upon the process of industrialization in the country.[52]

In the small number of large Greek enterprises, managers did not have the necessary management education to pursue developmental changes, and their lack of will or ability to use advanced management practices was impeding the introduction and use of innovation and development management.[53] The selection of managers was a simple process, since the persons selected had to be members of the family.[54] In the majority of Greek companies, the founder and proprietor is traditionally involved with all aspects of the company, so most firms have a paternalistic management style, which explains the relative lack of professional personnel management.[55] Also, promotions among managers were based on age, not performance, and the personnel department was unknown because the owners and managers did not understand its importance.[56]

The education of Greek managers in the 1960s and early 1970s was limited. Those who were graduates of a university had degrees in areas unrelated to management. Nineteen percent of mangers working in small enterprises and 35 percent of those working in large enterprises had university degrees, but only 21 percent of them had degrees in business and economics. Over half of them were engineers and chemists.[57] Fifty years after Alec Alexander's groundbreaking study of Greek industrialists and entrepreneurs, the private sector still has problems attracting educated persons for management positions. Although the public sector in Greece offers relatively low-paid jobs, it remains the most popular employer of university graduates because it offers employees the stability and security of a permanent job in which dismissal is almost impossible.[58] Xenophon Zolotas, one of the key personalities in Greek economic affairs, exposed the poor state of management education that existed due to the backward mentality of Greek business owners, a situation that also had detrimental effects upon the work of employees.[59]

A small number of commensurately educated managers were making attempts to break the chains of ownership and managerial retardation and open the way for management development. Lamentably, most of the efforts were abortive. This retardation was very difficult for educated managers and employees who suffocated under the pressure of the obsolete mentality of the ownership of their organizations.[60] Forty years after Ioannis Dialysmas' investigation of management education and the condition of human resources in Greek private enterprises, Greek management education is beginning to take off in Greek universities. Professors are currently introducing and experimenting with new instructional methods such as the portfolio process, which was determined to be valuable because it enables students to connect theory with practice.[61]

Due to the mentality of the ownership and management, delegation of authority and responsibility was absent. Since most Greek organizations had been under the control of one person—usually the owner—it was very difficult for them to delegate authority and responsibility to subordinates.[62]The same situation prevails fifty years later, but today strong forces of change emanating from professors and management consultants suggest that Greek organizations should try to reduce power centralization and decrease the distance between the employees and their supervisors.[63]

In most cases, the employees of private organizations were either family members or close friends who had no definite job descriptions but were asked to perform every task dictated to them by the ownership and management of the firm. Sales personnel were also in charge of legal affairs and lower-level managerial duties, while employees assigned to maintain machinery were also responsible for productivity projects.[64] Owners made decisions by themselves without any input from managers and employees.[65] Furthermore, it was determined in 1971 that a definite line of demarcation existed between workers and employees in Greek organizations. Although they constituted the majority of the non-managerial personnel, workers always occupied a second-class position. In industrial enterprises, only 13.5 percent of employees had a high school or university education,[66] whereas in all enterprises of the country only 35 percent of employees had completed the mandatory nine years of education.[67] In 1967, only seventy Greek enterprises employed persons who were attending either high schools or universities.[68]

Unemployment, especially among young persons, was very high in the twentieth century, and the same lamentable situation exists today. During the period from 1995 to 2001, the Greek economy grew on average by 3.3 percent per year, as opposed to 2.4 percent for the EU. However, over the same period, the average yearly employment growth stood at 0.3

percent and 1.2 percent respectively.[69]

Greece still has problems providing good technical and vocational education for its labor force. There is a wide consensus in Greece that to ensure a high quality of technical and vocational education, priority should be given to recruitment, initial education, training of well-qualified teachers, instructors and administrators, and to the provision of continuous professional education throughout their careers.[70]

Up to the 1970s, Greek employees were controlled through their physiological and safety needs, with monetary compensation and job security being the key issues in employment. Labor unions had started their developmental process and provided the necessary protection for their members. However, labor unions did not provide any assistance for the development of employees due to their orientation, the mentality of the owners and managers, and the large number of small business organizations, whose size did not allow management and employee development.[71] Until 1971, the clear majority of Greek employees in the private sector were male.[72] Due to pressure from the EU to provide equal employment opportunities, today a large percentage of women are employed, but lamentably, women earn approximately 75 percent of what men do.[73] Additional changes in the area of employment are currently taking place. There has been a sharp rise in the number of foreign workers in almost all sectors, especially in jobs shunned by native workers. Large numbers of jobs are being created for native and foreign workers in sectors like construction (especially for men) or the hospitality industry (mainly for women), reflecting joint growth of both native and foreign labor.[74]

It is important to mention that management was well known in ancient Greece. For example, Socrates spoke about the use of management in all areas of social and economic operations, and Plato referred to the importance of specialization more than 2000 years before Adam Smith.[75]

Since the completion of my initial research project on Greek management in 1971, insufficient development has taken place in the management of private Greek organizations due to the stubborn mentality of owners of small business enterprises, who could not see the benefits derived from mergers leading to larger-size organizations and the corporate form of business. Furthermore, the owners of small- and medium-size corporations appear to be reluctant to invest in management development. Formal management education and management development programs are now in their embryonic stages. Briefly speaking, in order to develop management during this critical period of economic and social development of the country, there is need for mergers of small organizations, formal management education, formal and informal management and employee training, emphasis on commensurate organizational designs and structures, advanced organizational policies, good communication channels, and leadership development.

A striking difference between my research in 1971 and that of the present is the adequate presence of qualified and well-educated university professors, writers, and management consultants who have great concerns about the predicament of the management of private enterprises in Greece. This is a powerful force that can create miracles in changing the present situation, because in 1971, only a handful of university professors and consultants were cognizant of the situation. The rest of them viewed management as accounting, banking, or finance; the human factor did not exist in their mind.

During the short but prolific period of industrialization in Greece from 1960 to 1990, labor unions took the opportunity to develop themselves into strong entities. Lamentably, the business sector failed to create medium- and large-size organizations in the corporate form, an entity which is responsible for the development of management. This failure has arrested the development of management in the country.

References

Ai Anthropinai Sheseis eis tas Synhronous Epihirisis. Meletai Epitropis Anthropinon Sheseon. Athinai: Ellinikon Kentron Paragogikotitos, 1966.

Alexander, A. *Greek Industrialists. An Economic and Social Analysis.* Athens: Center of Planning and Economic Research, 1964.

Apographi Viomihanias kai Viotehnias ta eti 1958 kai 1963. Athinai: Ethniki Statistiki Ypiresia Ellados, 1964.

Apospori, E., I. Nikandrou, and L. Panayotopoulou. "Mentoring and Women's Career Advancement in Greece." *Human Resource Development International* 9, 4. (December 2006): 521. doi:10.1080/13678860601032627

Apotelesmata Etisias Biomihanikis Erevnis etous 1959. Athinai: Ethniki Statistiki Ypiresia Ellados, 1962. Ekdosis A 4 Biomihania.

Barbosa, N., and H. Louri. "Corporate Performance: Does Ownership Matter? A Comparison of Foreign- and Domestic-Owned Firms in Greece and Portugal." *Review of Industrial Organization* 27, 91. (2005). doi:10.1007/s11151-005-4920-y

Bernard, B., M. Katsouros, and T. Jones. "Privatisation and the Euro-
pean Union: The Case of the Public Power Corporation of Greece."
International Journal of Public Sector Management 17, 1. (2004): 70,
ProQuest LLC database.

Bruton, J. *The European Union: Political, Social, and Economic Cooperation. Greece.* Philadelphia, PA: Mason Crest Publishers, 2006.

Burnes, Bernard. *Managing Change: A Strategic Approach to Organizational Dynamics.* 4th ed. Harlow: Prentice-Hall, 2004.

Chorianopoulos, I. "Urban Restructuring and Governance: North-South
Differences in Europe and the EU URBAN Initiative." *Urban Studies*
39, 4. (2002): 209. doi:10.1080/0042098022011953 4

Coutsoumaris, G. *The Morphology of Greek Industry.* Athens: Center of
Economic Research, 1963.

Dagkas, A. "Ideological Inclinations and Cultural Changes in a Globalized Europe: Effects on Greece." *Nature, Society, and Thought* 19, 1.
(2006): 95.

Damaskinidis, A. *Oikonomiki ton Epiheiriseon.* Thessaloniki: Ekdotikos
Oikos Adelphoi Zakouli, 1963.

Damaskinides, A. Synkrisis Ellinikos kai Europaikon Epiheiriseon en
opsi tis endehomenis Syndeseos is Ellados me tin Europaikin Koinin Agoran. Meletai Europaikon Thematon. Thessaloniki: Europaiki
Leshi Thessalonikis, 1961.

Damaskinidis, A. *To Provlima tis Ekpaideuseos, kai idia tis Tehnikis,
exetazomenon apo Oikonomikis Apopseos.* Thessaloniki: Aristotelion
Panepistimion Thessalonikis. Epistimoniki Epetiris Scholis Nomikon
kai Oikonomikon Epistimon. Tomos AB, 1968.

Dialysmas, I. *I Poiotiki Stathmi tis Viomihanias.* Athinai: Oikonomikos
Tachydromos, 1969.

Directory of Education Online. http://www.directoryofeducation.net/
colleges/worldwide/greece/

Dioikisis Biomihanikon Epiheiriseon eis Hypoanaptiktous Horas. Athinai: Ellinikon Kentron Paragogikotitos, 1960.

Domingo, A., and F. Gil-Alonso. "Immigration and Changing Labour
Force Structure in the Southern European Union." *Population* 62, 4.
(2007): 719, ProQuest LLC database.

Economic Development Plan for Greece, 1968-1972. Athens: Central
Committee for the Elaboration of the Economic Development Plan,
1968.

Ekpaidefsis Ypallilon Viomihanikon Epiheirison. Athinai: Ethniki

Statistiki Ypiresia Ellados, 1961.

Eleftheriou, A., and I. Robertson. "A Survey of Management Selection Practices in Greece." *Management Selection Practices in Greece* 7, 4. (December 1999): 203, Academic Search Complete database.

Ellis, H., D. Psilos, R. Westebee, and K. Nicolaou. *Industrial Capital in Greek Development*. Athens: Center of Economic Research, 1964.

European Commission. *Growing Regions, Growing Europe: Fourth Report of Economic and Social Cohesion*. Luxembourg: Office for the Official Publications of the European Communities, 2007.

Featherstone, K. "Introduction: 'Modernisation' and the Structural Constraints of Greek Politics." *West European Politics* 28, 2. (March 2005): 223-241. doi:10.1080/01402380500058753

Featherstone, K. and D. Papadimitriou. *The Limits of Europeanization: Reform Capacity and Policy in Greece*. Houndmills, England: Palgrave McMillan, 2008.

Gravani, M. N., and John, P. D. "'Them and Us': Teachers' and Tutors' Experiences of 'New' Professional Development Courses in Greece." *Compare* 35, 3. (2005): 310. doi:10.1080/03057920500212597

Hatzikian, Y., and J. Bouris. "Innovation Management and Economic Perspectives: The Case of Greece." *Journal of Enterprising Culture* 15, 4. (December 2007): 415.

I Elliniki Viomihania kata to etos 1968. Athinai: NA Syndesmos Ellinikon Viomihanon, 1969.

I paragogikotis eis tin Ellada. Ypologismos Drastiriotitos mias eptaetias (1954-1960). Athinai: Ellinikon Kentron Paragogikotitos, 1961.

Kantonidou, M. M., and G. E. Chatzarakis. "Technical Teacher Training in Greece: Trends, Concerns and Innovative Attempts." *European Journal of Teacher Education* 28, 3. (October 2005): 247. doi:10.1080/02619760500268766

Kapopoulos, P., and P. Papadimitriou. "Preliminary Evidence on Wage Setting in Greek Manufacturing." *Labour* 18, 1. (2004): 170.

Karalis, T., and D. Vergidis. "Lifelong Education in Greece: Recent Developments and Current Trends." *International Journal of Lifelong Education* 23, 2. (March-April 2004): 108. doi:10.1080/0260137042000184200

Katzourakis, G. D. *Oi Diefthintai to Epiheiriseon*. Athinai: Ellinikon Kentron Paragotikotitos, 1963.

Kavali, S., N. Tzokas, and M. Saren. "Corporate Ethics: An Exploration of Contemporary Greece." *Journal of Business Ethics* 30, 2001: 87-

104.

Kioukias, D. "Reorganizing Social Policies Through Social Partnerships: Greece in European Perspective." *Social Policy & Administration* 37, 2. (April 2003): 130.

Koulaidis, V., K. Dimopoulos, A. Tsatsaroni, and A. Katsis.
"Young People's Relationship to Education: The Case of Greek
Youth." *Educational Studies* 32, 4. (December 2006): 356.
doi:10.1080/0305569060085099

Kyriazis, D. Dioikisis Epiheiriseon Synoptiki Anaskopisis—Elliniki
Pragmatikotis. Athinai: Ellinikon Kentron Paragogikotitos, 1961.

Louri, H., and I. P. Minoglou. "A Quantitative Exploration on the
Determinants of (De-)Industrialization: The Case of Greece." *International Review of Applied Economics* 15, 4. (2001): 407.
doi:10.1080/02692170110081930

Mastaganis, M. "Union Structures and Pension Outcomes in Greece."
British Journal of Industrial Relations 45, 3. (September 2007): 545.
doi:10.1111/j. 1467-8543.2007.00627.x.

Mihail, D. M. "Working Students at Greek Universities." *Journal of
European Industrial Training* 29, 7. (2005): 563-564, ProQuest LLC
database.

Mitsopoulos, M., and T. Pelagidis. "Economic and Social Turbulence in Greece: The Product Markets are a No-Brainer, the Labour Market is Not." *Intereconomics*, July-August 2009: 246.
doi:10.1007/s/10272-009-0302-2

Nakos, G. E., and Y. A. Hajidimitriou. "Conducting Business in Greece:
A Brief for International Managers." *Global Business and Organizational Excellence* 74. (July-August 2009): doi:10.1002/joe

NationMaster.com. "Trade Union Membership by Country." Accessed
October 1, 2010 from http://www.nationmaster.com/graph/lab_tra_
uni_mem-labor-trade-union-membership

Nomiki Morphi ton Ellinkon Epiheiriseon. Athinai: Ethniki Statistiki
Ypiresia Ellados, 1960.

Pagoulatos, G. *Greece's New Political Economy: State, Finance and
Growth from Postwar to EMU*. Basingstoke, England. Pelgrave Mc-
Millan, 2003.

Papadimitriou, A. "Motivating Freshman Students in a Business Management Course Via Portfolios: Practice from a Greek Public University." *Assessment Update* 21, 1. (January-February 2009): 11.
doi:10.1002/au

Papageorge, A. J. *Transferability of Management: A Case Study of the United States and Greece*. Los Angeles: University of California Press, 1967.

Papapetrou, E. "Evidence on Gender Wage Differentials in Greece." *Economic Change & Restructuring* 41, November 2006: 167. doi:10.1007/s10644-008-9046-4

Petmesidou, M., and P. Polyzoidis. "The 'Social Quality' Perspective in Greece." *European Journal of Social Quality* 5, 1/2. (2005): 119, Academic Search Complete database.

Pitelis, C., and N. Antonakis. "Manufacturing and Competitiveness: The Case of Greece." *Journal of Economic Studies* 30, 5/6. (2003): 544. doi:10.1108/01443580310492826

Problimata prokiptonta ek tis syndeseos tis Ellados meta tis EOK. Athinai: Ellinikon Kentron Paragogikotitos, 1964.

Saiti, A. "Management in Education: Evidence from Greek Secondary Education." *Management in Education* 17, 2. (2003): 37, Academic Search Complete database.

Saiti, A., and G. Prokopiadou. "The Demand for Higher Education in Greece." *Journal of Further and Higher Education* 32, 3. (August 2008): 286. doi:10.1080/03098770802221080

Spanos, L. "Corporate Governance in Greece: Developments and Policy Implication." *The International Journal of Finance* 5, 1. (2005): 19.

Sofroniou, A. *The Philosophical Concepts of Management through the Ages*. Swindon, England: PsySys Limited, 2005.

Stratoudakis, P. *Ta stelehi tis Ellinikis Viomihanias*. Athinai: Ellinikon Kentron Paragogikotitos, 1967.

Theodore, John D. *I Exelixis tou Thesmou tis Dioikiseos ton Epiheiriseon eis Inomenas Politeias tis Amerikis kai i Parousa Katastasis os kai i Provlepomeni Exelixis tou Thesmou toutou eis tin Ellada*. Athinai: Adelphoi Ioannidi, 1971.

Voulgaris, F, D. Asteriou, and G. Agiomirgianakis. "Capital Structure, Asset Utilization, Profitability and Growth in the Greek Manufacturing Sector." *Applied Economics* 34, 2002: 1380. doi:10.1080/0003684011009682 2

Zolotas, X. E. *I Ellas is to stadion Ekviomihaniseos. Seira Eidikon Melenton*. Athinai: Trapeza Ellados, 1964.

Endnotes

1   W. G. Runciman, *Social Science and Political Theory* (Cambridge:

Cambridge University Press, 1963).

2   S. Kavali, N. Tzokas, and M. Saren, "Corporate Ethics: An Exploration of Contemporary Greece," *Journal of Business Ethics* 30, 2001: 95.

3   A. Dagkas, "Ideological Inclinations and Cultural Changes in a Globalized Europe: Effects on Greece," *Nature, Society, and Thought* 19, 1 (2006): 91.

4   M. Mitsopoulos and T. Pelagidis, "Economic and Social Turbulence in Greece: The Product Markets are a No-Brainer, the Labour Market is Not," *Intereconomics*, July-August 2009: 246. doi:10.1007/s/10272-009-0302-2

5   European Commission, *Growing Regions, Growing Europe: Fourth Report of Economic and Social Cohesion* (Luxembourg: Office for the Official Publications of the European Communities, 2007), 191.

6   G. E. Nakos and Y. A. Hajidimitriou, "Conducting Business in Greece: A Brief for International Managers," *Global Business and Organizational Excellence* 74. (July-August 2009): 72. doi:10.1002/joe

7   A. Damaskinidis, *To Provlima tis Ekpaideuseos, kai idia tis Tehnikis, exetazomenon apo Oikonomikis Apopseos* (Thessaloniki: Aristotelion Panepistimion Thessalonikis. Epistimoniki Epetiris Scholis Nomikon kai Oikonomikon Epistimon. Tomos AB, 1968).

8   A. Saiti and G. Prokopiadou, "The Demand for Higher Education in Greece," *Journal of Further and Higher Education* 32, 3 (August 2008): 37. doi:10.1080/03098770802221080

9   V. Koulaidis, K. Dimopoulos, A. Tsatsaroni, and A. Katsis, "Young People's Relationship to Education: The Case of Greek Youth," *Educational Studies* 32, 4 (December 2006): 356. doi:10.1080/0305569060085099

10 Saiti and Prokopiadou, "The Demand for Higher Education in Greece," 286.

11 Directory of Education Online. http://www.directoryofeducation.net/colleges/worldwide/greece/

12 T. Karalis and D. Vergidis, "Lifelong Education in Greece: Recent Developments and Current Trends," *International Journal of Lifelong Education* 23, 2 (March-April 2004): 184. doi:10.1080/0260137042000184200

13 Karalis and Vergidis, "Lifelong Education in Greece: Recent Developments and Current Trends," 188.

14 M. N. Gravani and P. D. John, "'Them and Us': Teachers' and Tutors' Experiences of 'New' Professional Development Courses in Greece," *Compare* 35, 3 (2005): 316. doi:10.1080/03057920500212597

15 I. Chorianopoulos, "Urban Restructuring and Governance: North-South Differences in Europe and the EU URBAN Initiative," *Urban Studies* 39, 4 (2002): 709. doi:10.1080/0042098022011953 4

16 G. Pagoulatos, *Greece's New Political Economy: State, Finance and Growth from Postwar to EMU* (Basingstoke, England. Pelgrave McMillan, 2003).

17 K. Featherstone, "Introduction: 'Modernisation' and the Structural Constraints of Greek Politics," *West European Politics* 28, 2 (March 2005): 244. doi:10.1080/01402380500058753

18 Dagkas, "Ideological Inclinations and Cultural Changes in a Globalized Europe: Effects on Greece," 90.

19 M. Petmesidou and P. Polyzoidis, "The 'Social Quality' Perspective in Greece," *European Journal of Social Quality* 5, 1/2 (2005): 119. Academic Search Complete database.

20 D. M. Mihail, "Working Students at Greek Universities," *Journal of European Industrial Training* 29, 7 (2005): 246. ProQuest LLC database.

21 Ibid., 35.

22 Featherstone, "Introduction: 'Modernisation' and the Structural Constraints of Greek Politics," 230.

23 D. Kioukias, "Reorganizing Social Policies Through Social Partnerships: Greece in European Perspective," *Social Policy & Administration* 37, 2 (April 2003): 130.

24 Petmesidou and Polyzoidis, "The 'Social Quality' Perspective in Greece," 120.

25 H. Ellis, D. Psilos, R. Westebee, and K. Nicolaou, *Industrial Capital in Greek Development* (Athens: Center of Economic Research, 1964), 15.

26 Apographi Viomihanias kai Viotehnias ta eti 1958 kai 1963, (Athinai: Ethniki Statistiki Ypiresia Ellados, 1964)

27 Nakos and Hajidimitriou, "Conducting Business in Greece: A Brief for International Managers," 74.

28 J. Bruton, *The European Union: Political, Social, and Economic Cooperation. Greece* (Philadelphia, PA: Mason Crest Publishers, 2006).

29 C. Pitelis and N. Antonakis, "Manufacturing and Competitiveness: The Case of Greece," *Journal of Economic Studies* 30, 5/6 (2003): 544. doi:10.1108/01443580310492826

30 K. Featherstone and D. Papadimitriou, *The Limits of Europeanization: Reform Capacity and Policy in Greece* (Houndmills, England: Palgrave McMillan, 2008).

31 N. Barbosa and H. Louri, "Corporate Performance: Does Ownership Matter? A Comparison of Foreign- and Domestic-Owned Firms in Greece and Portugal," *Review of Industrial Organization* 27, 91 (2005): 47. doi:10.1007/s11151-005-4920-y

32 NationMaster.com. "Trade union membership by country."

33 M. Mastaganis, ' Union Structures and Pension Outcomes in Greece," *British Journal of Industrial Relations* 45, 3 (September 2007): 541. doi:10.1111/j. 1467-8543.2007.00627.x.

34 P. Kapopoulos and P. Papadimitriou, "Preliminary Evidence on Wage Setting in Greek Manufacturing," *Labour* 18, 1 (2004): 163.

35 Mastaganis, "Union Structures and Pension Outcomes in Greece," 545.

36 E. Papapetrou, "Evidence on Gender Wage Differentials in Greece," *Economic Change & Restructuring* 41, November 2006: 157. doi:10.1007/s10644-008-9046-4

37 Apotelesmata Etisias Biomihanikis Erevnis etous 1959, (Athinai: Ethniki Statistiki Ypiresia Ellados, 1962. Ekdosis A 4 Biomihania).

38 Featherstone and Papadimitriou, *Limits of Europeanization: Reform Capacity and Policy in Greece*.

39 A. Damaskinidis, *Oikonomiki ton Epiheiriseon* (Thessaloniki: Ekdotikos Oikos Adelphoi Zakouli, 1963).

40 F. Voulgaris, D. Asteriou, and G. Agiomirgianakis, "Capital Structure, Asset Utilization, Profitability and Growth in the Greek Manufacturing Sector," *Applied Economics* 34, 2002: 1380. doi:10.1080/0003684011009682 2

41 Bruton, *The European Union: Political, Social, and Economic Cooperation. Greece*.

42 Barbosa and Louri, "Corporate Performance: Does Ownership Matter?"

43 *Economic Development Plan for Greece, 1968-1972* (Athens: Central Committee for the Elaboration of the Economic Development Plan, 1968).

44 A. Damaskinides, Synkrisis Ellinikos kai Europaikon Epiheiriseon

en opsi tis endehomenis Syndeseos is Ellados me tin Europaikin Koinin Agoran. Meletai Europaikon Thematon. (Thessaloniki: Europaiki Leshi Thessalonikis, 1961).

45 I Elliniki Viomihania kata to etos 1968 (Athinai: NA Syndesmos Ellinikon Viomihanon, 1969).

46 Y. Hatzikian and J. Bouris, "Innovation Management and Economic Perspectives: The Case of Greece," *Journal of Enterprising Culture* 15, 4 (December 2007): 415.

47 A. Alexander, *Greek Industrialists: An Economic and Social Analysis*, (Athens: Center of Planning and Economic Research, 1964), 108.

48 Nomiki Morphi ton Ellinkon Epiheiriseon, (Athinai: Ethniki Statistiki Ypiresia Ellados, 1960).

49 Bernard Burnes, *Managing Change: A Strategic Approach to Organizational Dynamics,* 4th ed. (Harlow: Prentice-Hall, 2004), p.4.

50 L. Spanos, "Corporate Governance in Greece: Developments and Policy Implication," *The International Journal of Finance* 5, 1 (2005): 19.

51 Ai Anthropinai Sheseis eis tas Synhronous Epihirisis, Meletai Epitropis Anthropinon Sheseon (Athinai: Ellinikon Kentron Paragogikotitos, 1966).

52 G. D. Katzourakis, *Oi Diefthintai to Epiheiriseon* (Athinai: Ellinikon Kentron Paragotikotitos, 1963).

53 John D. Theodore, *I Exelixis tou Thesmou tis Dioikiseos ton Epiheiriseon eis Inomenas Politeias tis Amerikis kai i Parousa Katastasis os kai i Provlepomeni Exelixis tou Thesmou toutou eis tin Ellada* (Athinai: Adelphoi Ioannidi, 1971).

54 A. J. Papageorge, *Transferability of Management: A Case Study of the United States and Greece* (Los Angeles: University of California Press, 1967).

55 A. Eleftheriou and I. Robertson, "A Survey of Management Selection Practices in Greece," *Management Selection Practices in Greece* 7, 4 (December 1999): 203. Academic Search Complete database.

56 Alexander, *Greek Industrialists: An Economic and Social Analysis*.

57 Ibid.

58 Saiti and Prokopiadou, "The Demand for Higher Education in Greece," 285.

59 X. E. Zolotas, *I Ellas is to stadion Ekviomihaniseos. Seira Eidikon*

Melenton (Athinai: Trapeza Ellados, 1964).

60 I. Dialysmas, *I Poiotiki Stathmi tis Viomihanias* (Athinai: Oikonomikos Tachydromos, 1969), 24.

61 A. Papadimitriou, "Motivating Freshman Students in a Business
Management Course Via Portfolios: Practice from a Greek Public
University," *Assessment Update* 21, 1 (January-February 2009): 10.
doi:10.1002/au

62 D. Kyriazis, Dioikisis Epiheiriseon Synoptiki Anaskopisis—Elliniki
Pragmatikotis (Athinai. Ellinikon Kentron Paragogikotitos, 1961).

63 E. Apospori, I. Nikandrou, and L. Panayotopoulou, "Mentoring
and Women's Career Advancement in Greece," *Human Resource
Development International* 9, 4 (December 2006): 520.
doi:10.1080/13678860601032627

64 Dioikisis Biomihanikon Epiheiriseon eis Hypoanaptiktous Horas
(Athinai: Ellinikon Kentron Paragogikotitos, 1960).

65 P. Stratoudakis, *Ta stelehi tis Ellinikis Viomihanias* (Athinai: Ellinikon Kentron Paragogikotitos, 1967).

66 *Economic Development Plan for Greece 1968-1972.*

67 Ibid.

68 Stratoudakis, *Ta stelehi tis Ellinikis Viomihanias*, 123.

69 Featherstone and Papadimitriou, *The Limits of Europeanization:
Reform Capacity and Policy in Greece.*

70 M. M. Kantonidou and G. E. Chatzarakis, "Technical Teacher
Training in Greece: Trends, Concerns and Innovative Attempts,"
European Journal of Teacher Education 28, 3 (October 2005): 247.
doi:10.1080/02619760500268766

71 G. Coutsoumaris, *The Morphology of Greek Industry* (Athens:
Center of Economic Research, 1963).

72 Theodore, *I Exelixis tou Thesmou tis Dioikiseos ton Epiheiriseon
eis Inomenas Politeias tis Amerikis kai i Parousa Katastasis os kai i
Provlepomeni Exelixis tou Thesmou toutou eis tin Ellada.*

73 Papapetrou, "Evidence on Gender Wage Differentials in Greece,"
155.

74 A. Domingo and F. Gil-Alonso, "Immigration and Changing Labour
Force Structure in the Southern European Union," *Population* 62, 4
(2007): 6. ProQuest LLC database.

75 A. Sofroniou, *The Philosophical Concepts of Management through
the Ages* (Swindon, England: PsySys Limited, 2005).

Chapter 8: Italy

Religion and Economic Development

The Roman Catholic Church in Italy had negative views about economic development in the past because the process emphasized mundane benefits at the expense of religious practices. Such negligence had its roots in ancient Greek and Latin philosophies regarding economic development and prosperity, as discussed in the previous chapter. However, after the end of World War II, Italian religious beliefs toward economic development began to rapidly change. This change was officially supported by the Vatican in the Apostolic Letter of Pope Paul VI, which commemorated the eightieth anniversary of the *Rerum Novarum* Encyclical in 1971. Pope Paul VI stated that in order to avoid misery and parasitism in the human race in the future, the Church must support government policies toward economic investments, the organization of production, and the increase of commerce and industry; it must support every aspect of improving the economy.[1] On May 1, 1990, Pope John Paul II reiterated the same concept by indicating that economic growth and the production of wealth are essential to economic justice.

Today, Italy is characterized by good economic development that is not yet equally distributed in all regions of the country. However, managerial and entrepreneurial abilities of small and medium organizations are able to sustain competitive pressures as a vital agent of economic and social development.[2]

The Roman Catholic Church in Italy initially had negative views about economic development because the process emphasized mundane benefits at the expense of religious practices. However, after World War II, the Church changed its position and started to support economic development.

Religion and Education

The Italian education system, under the influence of the Roman Catholic Church, had traditionally leaned toward classical education, such as religion, art, law, medicine, and music. Artistic education, one of the most important educational cores in the country, continues to be emphasized to the degree that the Italian state provides art education to its citizens from childhood on. After the end of World War II, the influence of the Church upon the education system changed, and it now favors vocational, commercial, economic, technical, and technological curricula in addition to the classical basics. The constitution of Italy specifies the educational principles of the country and guarantees that all Italian children have free and compulsory education. The philosophy of the education system is relatively flexible and the education curricula are strongly standardized, a situation that makes transferring from one school to another fairly easy.

After the end of World War II, Italian education underwent many changes. In the 1950s, the responsibility for education and the provisions of educational services were decentralized; twenty years later, administrative powers were also decentralized. In 1999, a law was passed making the attendance of schools compulsory between the ages of six and sixteen. At the present time, the Ministry of Public Instruction is in charge of all educational activities from pre-school to high school, whereas the Ministry for Universities and Scientific Research is in charge of higher education. The *scuola primaria* or elementary school for children six to ten years old is followed by the *scuola media*, or lower secondary school for children eleven to fourteen years old, and then the *scuola superiore* or *liceo*, or upper secondary school for teenagers from fourteen to eighteen years old. Secondary education consists of six years of studies, and it is divided into three years of lower secondary schools and three years in the classical gymnasium, scientific lyceum, or technical institutes. Virtually all Italian children attend the lower secondary school, for the Italian constitution states that the first eight years of education shall be obligatory and free. Also, Italian attitudes toward increasing vocational-technical education are coming more and more in line with the necessity for economic growth and the demands of modern society.

Italy's higher education system underwent a number of deep changes during the first part of the last decade in order to be more effective, efficient, and dynamic. At the same time, significant changes have also occurred over the past ten years in the Italian university system in order to develop decentralization, autonomy, and evaluation.[3]

As the result of the famous Sorbonne and Bologna Declarations of May 1998, the United Kingdom, France, Italy, and Germany adopted the two-tier university model with the purpose of creating a standard of harmonization among European university structures. In Italy, like the other Southern European states of the European Union, universities were highly centralized. Traditionally, universities held little autonomy and were subject to strong control by the central government.[4] Universities are now receiving a high degree of autonomy pertinent to degrees and teaching activities, and university instruction has become student-centered for the first time in its long history. There are currently eighty-five colleges and universities in the country.[5]

The Italian education system, under the influence of the Roman Catholic Church, favored classical curricula such as religion, art, law, medicine, and music. Due to the dramatic changes that took place in the country after World War II, the Church recognized the need for curricula in economics, business, and related areas. Consequently, the education system was modified to serve the needs of an advanced socioeconomic system without neglecting the need for classical curricula.

Religion and Social Structure

The Roman Catholic Church historically contributed to a traditional Italian social structure, dominated by large land owners that enjoyed great wealth and privileged status. At the other end of the social scale were the tenants of the land owners, the agricultural workers that formed the great bulk of the population. These social conditions impeded the development of the human factor and constrained the individual to his inherited class. Only a small and insufficient portion of the population was capable of pursuing careers demanded by the emergence of industrialization in the country. This semi-feudal social structure persisted until industrialization took hold in the twentieth century.[6]

World War II upset the socioeconomic structure and destroyed the barriers of social mobility. The Catholic Church was no longer able to sustain an obsolete social structure that militated against the interests of the people. The Italians worked hard in order to create a new state out of the ashes of the past. They adopted a new and dynamic constitution, and abolished the dysfunctional monarchy that had created substantial instability in Italian society in the past. In the long run, these changes were undoubtedly for Italy's benefit. Taken together, this meant that the country had finally crossed a decisive social watershed and was close to meeting desired socio-economic development.[7]

Furthermore, the advancement of social mobility was necessary for the economic development of Italy to change despite the fact that the Italian economy had faced more economic cyclical fluctuations than other states that signed the Treaty of Rome in 1957. Italian society has always favored European integration, but it is not in favor of expansion of the European Union, at least at this point and time.[8] Currently, Italy has the fourth largest economy in the European Union. A strong indication of social mobility is that Italian women have been entering into the labor market in large numbers, especially in professional areas. The difference between the education level of men and women has been substantially reduced. Italian women prefer their professional careers over having children, at least during the initial part of their work experience.[9]

The continuous economic development of the country is creating drastic social changes and thus maintaining a high degree of social mobility. When Italian society became exposed to the cultures of the other EU members and the rest of the world, it allowed extrinsic forces to dissolve former barriers. Furthermore, the Italian society is witnessing an increase in the number of civil society organizations, which are powerful instruments for participating in social, economic, and political affairs.[10]

Today, the best indicator of the Italian social structure is based on personal income. Modern Italy has an advanced industrial complex, which is not equally shared throughout the nation but still reflects upon the social structure of the various regions in the country. The northern part of the country is substantially industrialized under the auspices of large private organizations. On the other hand, the central and southern parts of the nation are agricultural, and socioeconomic problems prevail due to high unemployment rates. Italy has made every effort to combat unemployment because high unemployment rates eventually lead to social exclusion, often to the extent that unemployed populations have serious problems finding jobs. Social exclusion in Italy (and other southern states of the European Union) lamentably includes a high percentage of young citizens experience followed by people with limited professional and skills preparation, immigrants, and women.

Beginning in 1990, under the auspices of the European Union Italy enacted laws which precipitated more employment, resulting in a substantially large number of new jobs during the second half of the 1990s. Similar laws have followed, aiming at the creation of additional new jobs. Immigration has created xenophobia, which mainly emanates from pensioners, house people, and those with the least education.[11]

Italian society requires tremendous amounts of healthcare services for its citizens due to the longevity of the population. At this point, the healthcare system has not been able to satisfy the needs of the country's aging population. Currently, there is a strong movement to modernize the healthcare system and make it more effective, efficient, and cheaper to operate.

The Roman Catholic Church favored an antiquated social structure and social immobility until the beginning of the 1900s; after this period, it started to gradually support flexibility in the social structure of the country. After World War II, the Church supported a flexible social structure and social mobility.

Extent of Industrialization

Italy did not begin to develop industries on a significant scale until the early part of the twentieth century as it had not reached the necessary pre-industrialization stage, due to its rigid social structure and inadequate education system oriented toward classical curricula. Handicapped by shortages of industrial raw materials, the Italian economy was beginning to develop when progress was halted by World War I.[12]

Economic advance was further disturbed by the dominance of Fascism during World War II. It took nearly fifteen years for the reconstruction of the Italian economy and industry to take place. This situation obstructed the development of large industries and subsequently the development of an industrial society. Starting in the second half of the twentieth century, industrialization started to receive increasing support from a growing economy, a flexible and dynamic social structure, and a modern education system.

In 1951, Italy joined the European Coal and Steel Complex, which was the first step toward integration with Western Europe and precipitated a period of economic growth during the 1950s and 1960s. Before World War II, the importation of raw materials was difficult and costly due to an elaborate structure of preferential tariff charges and other impediments, whose purpose was to prevent international competition within the steel industry in Europe. Italy's affiliation with the European Coal and Steel Complex erased these impediments, and access to steel and iron sources at competitive prices opened the way for a vigorously expanding Italian industry. A second milestone was Italy's affiliation with the European Economic Community in 1957.

Today, Italy is a major industrialized nation. The industrial sector in the country occupies one quarter of the nation's economic activities. A small number of gigantic industries are responsible for most industrial production, whereas a large number of small and family controlled entities make up the remaining portion of industrial production. Heavy industries have grown more than manufacturing as a whole and the capital per worker has increased. Employment has concentrated in small- and medium-size firms, while both the very small (below ten employees) and very large units (over 500 employees) have decreased.[13] The large industrial organizations are both private and state-controlled. However, recent European Union legislative enactments are pushing for more privatization of state enterprises, as is the case in the remaining southern states of the European Union.

After World War II, the growing economy, the modern education system, and the flexible social structure of the country provided the necessary support for the growth and development of industrialization in Italy.

Labor Unions

Due to the slow and ineffectual process of industrialization, unionism in Italy was weak until the middle of the twentieth century. Worst of all, unions briefly came under the influence of the Fascist regime. However, after the end of World War II, they re-emerged and became a powerful force in the Italian economy. Strong labor unions provide the necessary support for their members and the entire Italian society and economy. Individuals engaged in industrial work and clerical employees belong to labor unions. The clerical middle class is at least partially organized; both civil servants and clerical workers are represented by major labor federations.

Currently, there are eleven labor unions in the country: Italian General Confederation of Labour, Italian Confederation of Workers' Trade Unions, Italian Labour Union, Italian Confederation of Free Workers' Unions, Confederazione Italiana Sindacati Autonomi Lavoratori (CONFSAL), Confederazione del Comitati di Base (COBAS), Confederazione Unitaria di Base (CUB), General Labour Union (Italy) (UGL), Sindacato Padano (SIN.PA.), Sindacato Nazionale dei Dirigenti, dei Direttivi del Corpo Forestale dello Stato (DIRFOR), and Unione Sindacale Italiana.[14]

Italian labor union membership has been dynamic, and the turnover ratio of union membership has dramatically increased, rising up to 30 percent in the last decade and making the length of union membership a top issue for union officials.[15] Unions are strong and have the right to veto the Italian government's social and economic policy initiatives by fostering up a *state of necessity* within Italian policy development.[16]

Like France, unionized organizations in Italy experience a more productive working environment, with the retention of higher skilled workers who voice worker grievances and demand improved communication channels.[17] Salaried employees are represented by commensurate labor unions with high membership numbers.[18]

Labor unions in Italy were influenced by the state of development in the industrialization of the country. Unionization was weak before World War II, but after the war unions gained tremendous power and contributed both to the well-being of its members and the nation in general.

The Corporation

The origins of Italian corporations date back to the Italian trading centers of Genoa and Venice, which operated in the Eastern Mediterranean after the decline of the Byzantine Empire. The relatively weak degree of industrialization in Italy up to the 1960s did not foster development of the corporate form of business. The corporate form of business was not sufficiently developed until the 1980s because, among other things, modern Italy had only a small number of public companies that operated under the Anglo-American modus operandi.[19] Furthermore, family businesses persisted for a long time because of the absence of regulatory intervention and the abundance of government corruption.[20] In addition, the majority of Italian firms were closely held by the founders' families, who shunned the stock market and operated on a relatively small scale in niche markets.[21]

As Italian corporations grew in size and numbers as a result of the industrialization process, the positive relationship between size and profitability became even more convincing, with an increase in performance accompanying the increase in size.[22] In addition to the increasing numbers and power of its domestic corporations, Italy has witnessed the emergence of European Union corporations. Currently, both the government and corporations have seen good results from their attempts to advance the private corporate form of business. This is highly important, for even today Italy stands out in Europe for the small size of its business organizations, which is a long-term feature.[23] Solid corporate governance and greater ability to reinvest profits was understood to be better than family control, which reduces the amount of resources available for long-term growth, the capacity for innovation, and the potential to compete in the international market.[24]

The lack of sufficient industrialization in Italy until the middle the twentieth century had a negative impact upon the development of corporations. However, after the country started its rapid acceleration of industrialization, more private and larger corporations appeared, resulting in the separation of ownership from management and thus precipitating the increase of the managerial development in the country.

Management in Italy

Until the second half of the twentieth century, Italian labor unions were relatively weak and the presence of the corporate form of business in the economy was limited; thus both had a negative impact upon the development of management in the country. The origin of Italian managers goes back to traders, who operated with limited factors of production, and who eventually became a source of power that was subsequently integrated into the other socioeconomic power centers of the country. The owner-managers placed heavy emphasis on their personal power to operate their organizations, but they put limited importance on external input, making decisions without the assistance of their long-term employees. This situation continued until the 1960s and was characterized by obsolete and antiquated principles of management and organization, and with limited knowledge on monitoring and evaluating the external environment of the organization. Furthermore, due to relatively poor management, organizations had not managed internal communications in a systematic way.[25] The development of owner-managers was viewed as an unnecessary expense that did not merit any serious consideration. Professional managers only existed in large private organizations, which constituted a very small percentage of Italian commercial organizations.

In the 1960s, labor unions became stronger and the corporate form of business increased. For this reason, serious attempts were made by both the government and the private sector to take advantage of the potential of owner-managers and create professional managers who did or did not have ownership in the organization. As the country interacted more with advanced members of the European Union and the outside world, especially the United States, the development of professional managers started to rapidly take place. Italian managers today are recruited to be professional managers with skills that can match present and future corporate requirements.[26]

Management education in Italy was neglected until the 1970s, when the inadequacy of management education and the indifference toward management per se was finally understood. In the late 1970s and early 1980s, Italy developed a good network of management education opportunities both in universities and other institutions of higher learning. Programs were developed to provide an international center for advanced training of managers in Turin.[27]

This process continues to this date, having fostered a number of fine business schools in the country that need to become players on the international stage while retaining their position in the country.[28]

The majority of Italian universities and practically all colleges provide management education, from undergraduate curricula to doctoral studies. Concentrations pivot around the behavioral sciences of management (organizational behavior, development, and human resources) in accounting, finance, and marketing and other business management subjects. In addition, specialized institutions in the country and in the European Union offer an abundant number of courses and curricula in management education. The Italian management apprentice program, which it has its roots in the German system of *Berufsakademie*, is becoming more common.[29]

Until the 1970s, managers controlled their employees through negative methods, such as fear of punishment and losing their jobs. Weak labor unions made desperate attempts to change the situation, but management strongly resisted any efforts to share managerial prerogatives or undercut managerial authority. Certain improvements did take place in the 1970s, and Italian management was modified to paternalism. By the beginning of the 1990s, employee control became democratic in many organizations. During the same period, managers came to understand the importance of human resource management and started to form human resource departments. Today, managers and owners believe that human resource management is highly important work, recognizing that its primary task is managing the network of complex contacts and relationships between employees and the organization.[30] Human resource management has moved from an administrative role to a specialized functional and strategic role; it is in a transitional phase, moving from personnel management towards human resource management.[31]

Italian employees are no longer controlled by lower physiological needs such as wages and job security because they have experienced substantial improvement in their wages and salaries as the direct effect of sustained growth in the economy. Due to the increased strength of labor unions and the presence of more corporations in the economy in the 1970s, employers were able to satisfy their employees' physiological needs though equitable wages, a situation that enabled employees to purchase basic products as the domestic production and availability of consumer goods substantially increased. Particularly significant was the availability of packaged food, health care, clothing, and other similar commodities for consumer consumption.[32] Currently, incentives and bonus payments are common in Italian enterprises.

Italian society supports long-term employment, which provides the employer with incentives to support its staff, and motivates employees to make the best of opportunities offered and invest in their work.[33] Although a high degree of unemployment still exists in the country today, Italy has the lowest regional unemployment differentiation in the EU.[34] The European Union has also made available funds for research relevant to industrial fatigue and similar matters pertinent to the well-being of employees. Employee participation in the decision-making process in the functional areas of their operation is highly encouraged. The Italian process-driven enterprise demands high participation, requiring employees to participate in the decision-making process in their organization.[35] The High Authority of the European Union participates in the financing of research institutions dealing with physiopathology and clinical studies of employees. Expenditure on research and development is of particular importance to the advanced technology section of industry throughout the European Union.

Employee education became extensively available through industrial firms and other enterprises. National agencies and the High Authority of the European Union have been providing intensive technical education for employees in the production areas of their organization, exchanging employees among European Union countries and teaching European languages to all employees. Today, a significant number of employees of large industrial enterprises have acquired university education in their respective areas of specialization.

Italian labor unions were relatively weak and corporations played a limited role in the economy of Italy until the last half of the twentieth century; consequently, both had a minimal impact upon the development of management. However, during the second half of the century, labor unions acquired substantial strength and corporate enterprises increased in numbers and size. These events had a positive impact accelerated the development of management in Italy.

References

Agasisti, T. "Performance Based Funding of Universities: The Italian Experience." *International Educator* 18, 20. (March-April 2009): 13. http://proquest.umi.com/pqdweb?did=1667435091&sid=1&Fmt=2&clientId=11123&RQT=309&VName=PQD

Angot, J., H. Malloch, and B. Klyemann. "The Formation of Professional Identity in French Apprenti Managers." *Education & Training*

50, 5. (2008): 408. doi:10.11080/00400910810889084

Ashlund, A. and M. Dabrowski. *Europe after Enlargement*. Cambridge, MA: Cambridge University Press, 2007.

Biggeri, L., and M. Bini. "Evaluation at University and State Level in Italy: Need for a System of Evaluation and Indicators." *Tertiary Education and Management* 7, 2. (2001): 150. http://proquest.umi.com/pqdweb?did=355911151&sid=1&Fmt=2&clientId=11123&RQT=309&VName=PQD

Bradshaw, Della. "Italian Roots, Global Ambitions: The Milan-Based Bocconi School is Pursuing a Twin-Track Approach, says Della Bradshaw." *Financial Times* (Surveys Edition), May 15, 2006: 8. http://proquest.umi.com/pqdweb?did=1036835341&sid=2&Fmt=3&clientId=11123&RQT=309&VName=PQD

Camuffo, A., and G. Costa. "Strategic Human Resource Managements–Italian Style." *Sloan Management Review* 34, 2. (Winter 1993): 61.

Cesaria, R. "Organizational Communication Issues in Italian Multinational Corporations." *Management Communication Quarterly* 14, 1. (August 2000): 165-171. http://proquest.umi.com/pqdweb?did=57311193&sid=3&Fmt=2&clientId=11123&RQT=309&VName=PQD

Cohen, J. F. *The Development of Italian Economy, 1820-1960*. Cambridge, MA: Cambridge University Press, 2001.

Colli, A., and E. Merlo. "Family Business and Luxury Business in Italy." *Enterprises et Historie* 46, 114. (April 2007).

Departimento per L'informazione e L'editorial. *Conoscere L'Italia*. Roma, Italy: Departimento per L'informazione e L'editorial, 1988.

Directory of Education Online. http://www.directoryofeducation.net/colleges/worldwide/italy/

Doucouliagos, H., and P. Laroche. "Unions and Tangible Investments: A Review and New Evidence in France." *Relations Industrielles* 58, 2. (Spring 2003): 315. http://proquest.umi.com/pqdweb?did=378109041&sid=27&Fmt=4&clientId=11123&RQT=309&VName=PQD

Dufour, C., and A. Hege. *L'Europe Syndicale au Quotidian. La Representations des Salaries en France, Allemagne, Grand Bretagne, et Italie*. Bruxelles, Germany: Institut de Recherches Economiques et Social (IRES), 2002.

European Commission. *Community Charter of Fundamental Social Rights of Workers*. Luxembourg: Office for the Official Publications of the European Communities, 1990.

Giannetti, R., and M. Vasta. *Evolution of Italian Enterprises in the 20th*

Century. New York, NY: Physica-Verlag, Heidelberg, 2006.

Hughes, S. *The United States and Italy*. Cambridge, MA: Harvard University Press, 1965.

Kalff, D. *An Unamerican Business: The Rise of the New European Enterprise*. London, England: Kogan Page, 2006.

Kalwij, A. S. "The Effects of Female Employment Status on the Presence and Number of Children." *Journal of Population Economics* 13, 2000: 225.

Morck, R. K., ed. *A History of Corporate Governance around the World*. Chicago, IL: University of Chicago Press, 2007.

NationMaster.com. "Trade Union Membership by Country." Accessed October 1, 2010 from http://www.nationmaster.com/graph/lab_tra_uni_mem-labor-trade-union-membership

Paul VI. "Octogesima Adveniens (A Call to Action)." Apostolic Letter, May 14, 1971.

Plato. *The Republic*. Athens, Greece: Organismos Edkoseos Scholikon Biblion, 1955.

Pulignano, V. "Unions Struggling and the Crisis of Industrial Relations in Italy." *Capital & Class* 79, Spring 2005: 5. http://proquest.umi.com/pqdweb?did=301701121&sid=3&Fmt=2&clientld=11123&RQT=309&VName=PQD

Rodriguez-Pose, A. *The European Union: Economy, Society, and Polity*. Oxford, England: Oxford University Press, 2003.

Silipo, D. B., ed. *The Banks and the Italian Economy*. Berlin, Germany: Physical-Verlag, 2009.

Sirianni, A. C. "Human Resource Management in Italy." *Employee Relations* 14, 5. (1992): 23. http://proquest.umi.com/pqdweb?did=1073029&sid=33&Fmt=3&clientd=11123&RQT=309&VName=PQD

Smismans, S., ed. *Civil Society and Legitimate European Governance*. Shelenham, England: Edward Elgar Publishing, 2006.

Vamvakidis, A. "Regional Wage Differentiation and Wage B Bargaining Systems in the European Union." *Financial Theory and Practice* 33, 1. (January 14, 2009): 74.

Vaona, A. "The Duration of Union Membership in Italy: A Research Note." *Industrial Relations* 47, 2. (April 2008): 261.

Endnotes

1   Paul VI., "Octogesima Adveniens (A Call to Action)," Apostolic Letter, May 14, 1971, p.5.

2 D. B. Silipo, ed., *The Banks and the Italian Economy* (Berlin, Germany: Physical-Verlag, 2009).

3 L. Biggeri and M. Bini, "Evaluation at University and State Level in Italy: Need for a System of Evaluation and Indicators," *Tertiary Education and Management* 7, 2 (2001): 150. http://proquest.umi.com/pqdweb?did=355911151&sid=1&Fmt=2&clientId=11123&RQT=309&VName=PQD

4 T. Agasisti, "Performance Based Funding of Universities: The Italian Experience," *International Educator* 18, 20 (March-April 2009): 13. http://proquest.umi.com/pqdweb?did=1667435091&sid=1&Fmt=2&clientId=11123&RQT=309&VName=PQD

5 Directory of Education Online. http://www.directoryofeducation.net/colleges/worldwide/italy/

6 Ibid.

7 Ibid.

8 A. Ashlund and M. Dabrowski, *Europe after Enlargement* (Cambridge, MA: Cambridge University Press, 2007).

9 A. S. Kalwij, "The Effects of Female Employment Status on the Presence and Number of Children," *Journal of Population Economics* 13, 2000: 225.

10 S. Smismans, ed., *Civil Society and Legitimate European Governance*, (Shelenham, England: Edward Elgar Publishing, 2006).

11 A. Rodriguez-Pose, *The European Union: Economy, Society, and Polity* (Oxford, England: Oxford University Press, 2003).

12 J. F. Cohen, *The Development of Italian Economy, 1820-1960* (Cambridge, MA: Cambridge University Press, 2001).

13 R. Giannetti and M. Vasta, *Evolution of Italian Enterprises in the 20th Century* (New York, NY: Physica-Verlag, Heidelberg, 2006).

14 NationMaster.com. "Trade union membership by country."

15 A. Vaona, "The Duration of Union Membership in Italy: A Research Note" *Industrial Relations* 47, 2 (April 2008): 261.

16 V. Pulignano, "Unions Struggling and the Crisis of Industrial Relations in Italy," *Capital & Class* 79, Spring 2005: 5. http://proquest.umi.com/pqdweb?did=301701121&sid=3&Fmt=2&clientId=11123&RQT=309&VName=PQD

17 H. Doucouliagos and P. Laroche, "Unions and Tangible Investments: A Review and New Evidence in France," *Relations Industrielles* 58, 2 (Spring 2003): 315. http://proquest.umi.com/pqdweb?did=378109041&sid=27&Fmt=4&clientId=11123&RQT=309&VNam

e=PQD

18 C. Dufour and A. Hege, *L'Europe Syndicale au Quotidian: La Representations des Salaries en France, Allemagne, Grand Bretagne, et Italie* (Bruxelles, Germany: Institut de Recherches Economiques et Social (IRES), 2002).

19 Giannetti and Vasta, *Evolution of Italian Enterprises in the 20th Century*.

20 Morck, *A History of Corporate Governance around the World*.

21 Ibid.

22 Giannetti and Vasta, *Evolution of Italian Enterprises in the 20th Century*.

23 Ibid.

24 Ibid.

25 R. Cesaria, "Organizational Communication Issues in Italian Multinational Corporations," *Management Communication Quarterly* 14, 1 (August 2000): 165-171. http://proquest.umi.com/pqdweb?did=57 311193&sid=3&Fmt=2&clientId=11123&RQT=309&VName=PQD

26 D. Kalff, *An Unamerican Business: The Rise of the New European Enterprise* (London, England: Kogan Page, 2006).

27 Departimento per L'informazione e L'editorial, *Conoscere L'Italia* (Roma, Italy: Departimento per L'informazione e L'editorial, 1988).

28 Della Bradshaw, "Italian Roots, Global Ambitions: The Milan-Based Bocconi School is Pursuing a Twin-Track Approach, says Della Bradshaw," *Financial Times* (Surveys Edition), May 15, 2006: p.8. http://proquest.umi.com/pqdweb?did=1036835341&sid=2&Fmt =3&clientId=11123&RQT=309&VName=PQD

29 J. Angot, H. Malloch, and B. Klyemann, "The Formation of Professional Identity in French Apprenti Managers," *Education & Training* 50, 5 (2008): 408. doi:10.11080/00400910810889084

30 A. Camuffo and G. Costa, "Strategic Human Resource Managements–Italian Style," *Sloan Management Review* 34, 2 (Winter 1993): 61.

31 A. C. Sirianni, "Human Resource Management in Italy," *Employee Relations* 14, 5 (1992): 23. http://proquest.umi.com/pqdweb?did=10 73029&sid=33&Fmt=3&clientd=11123

32 A. Colli and E. Merlo, "Family Business and Luxury Business in Italy," *Enterprises et Historie* 46, 114 (April 2007).

33 Kalff, *An Unamerican Business: The Rise of the New European Enterprise*.

34 A. Vamvakidis, "Regional Wage Differentiation and Wage B Bargaining Systems in the European Union," *Financial Theory and Practice* 33, 1 (January 14, 2009): 74.

35 Cesaria, "Organizational Communication Issues in Italian Multinational Corporations."

Chapter 9: France

Religion and Economic Development

The situation in France relevant to religion and economic development is quite similar to that of Italy, since both countries are mostly Roman Catholic. However, France underwent drastic changes in the eighteenth and nineteenth centuries that altered the socio-religious beliefs of the people. Religion was profoundly attacked, weakening its impact upon French society and culture in general.[1]

The French Revolution was also a catalyst for the change of the people's attitudes, customs, and beliefs, and it gave birth to French secularism. The French acquired a more positive attitude toward economic development after the downfall of the French nobility because the aristocracy had demeaned those who performed labor. On the other hand, important personalities in the country like the philosopher Jean Jacques Rousseau emphasized the value of the working man. French society managed to enact the Law of 1905, which separated the Catholic Church from the French State. This separation between the two entities is better known as *laicite*, derived from the Greek *laicos*, denoting pertaining to the common people. French society is now characterized by the large number of active civil society organizations that are powerful instruments participating in social, economic, and political affairs.[2]

Today, France is one of the most economically developed nations, characterized by substantial diversity that incorporates both civilian and military products, including large numbers of facilities that produce and utilize nuclear power. The economy of France highly depends on the production and sale of advanced military aircraft, vessels, submarines, land vehicles, and advance offensive weapons. France may well be the first advanced nation in the world that uses nuclear energy instead of petroleum for a large extent of consumer, commercial, industrial, and governmental consumption.

Although the Catholic Church opposed economic development in the past, its power and control in France were attacked and limited by both the government and the people. The French Revolution and the governments that followed supported economic development. Subsequently, the impact of religion upon economic development was steadily altered and eventually became positive.

Religion and Education

The French education system was also influenced by the Roman Catholic Church for centuries, but the influence of the Church diminished substantially after the French Revolution and the Industrial Revolution, which was imported from England. French education had traditionally been inclined toward classical studies. Both the French government and the French people made drastic changes in their education system to cope with the changing demands of a modern society now incorporated into the broader society of the European Union. In the 1950s and 1960s, the increase in the population with higher average income and standards of living, the shift from general to skilled labor, and the educational demands of technological civilization placed enormous pressures on the French school system.[3]

French elementary education is compulsory and secondary education has been divided into two sectors or cycles. The first sector includes students from ages eleven to fifteen. This is called the *college* and students attend either private high schools or public schools. The basic curricula are divided into technical-vocational training and classical studies with a strong emphasis on Greek, Latin, Humanities, and Modern Languages.

The second sector includes the *lycee*, which includes students from fifteen to eighteen years of age and is divided into four types. The first type, the *enseignement general long*, has been traditionally devoted to classical types of curricula. The second type, the *enseignement technique*, leans toward technical education. The third type, the *enseignement technique agricole long*, relates to agricultural education, and fourth type, the *enseignement court*, is pertinent to a basic technical education concerned merely with fundamental concepts.

The upper part of secondary education is separated into academic and vocational sectors, as mentioned previously. The graduates from the academic sector *lycees* continue their studies in institutions of higher learning, leading to a degree in classical subjects, such as law or medicine. Graduates from the vocational sector may seek employment, or they may aspire to technical institutions of higher learning, which make up a large proportion of the French secondary education. The *baccalaureat* degree is awarded after the completion of secondary education.

The French government provides higher education in universities and in special schools, and through private individuals in free faculties and schools. The Law of 1968 created guidelines for improving higher education and brought several disciplines together. Another highly successful reform took place in 2003.[4] The first modern business school established in France and the European Union is the now famous *Institute European d'Administration des Affairs*. This organization, better known as INSEAD, was established in 1966 in Fontainebleau, France. Its impact upon managerial education in the EU countries and the rest of Western Europe has been tremendous.[5]

Currently, higher education in France is under a dual system. In the first system, education is provided by universities, which include national polytechnic schools. Universities are easily accessible by all students because these are public institutions, and enrollment is open to students who have graduated from French or from foreign high schools with equivalent accreditation. The curricula taught in these universities are technical, academic, and professional. In the second system, there are the *grandes ecoles*, prestigious institutions limited to a small number of students able to pass strict admission examinations. The matriculation cost is substantially high, and entrance to such institutions is highly selective.

French institutes that have university affiliation offer short degree programs that range between two to three years of studies pivoting around manufacturing, services, and commerce. As a result of the Sorbonne and Bologna Declarations of the European Union Commission on Education, France has been continuously modernizing its higher education system to comply with the international harmonization of the structure of Europe's higher education system. There are currently 252 colleges and universities in the country.[6]

Another important milestone in France's higher education system is the Equal Opportunity Act of 2006. Specifically, the government created a charter to provide work placement for graduates of higher education. French industry also participated in signing the charter, thus officially becoming an integral part of higher education in the country.

The French education system was strongly influenced by the Roman Catholic Church for centuries, which favored classical curricula such as religion, art, law, medicine, and music. Due to the dramatic changes brought about by the French Revolution and the Industrial Revolution, the influence of the Church substantially diminished. Today, France has one of the finest education systems in the world.

Religion and Social Structure

French society has been diverse since its formation. The Law of 1905 separated the Catholic Church from the French State, opening society to

people of all religions. In addition to incorporating various European eth-
nic groups, the country has attracted non-European elements, especially
from former colonies. The country has a large number of Muslims, most
of who emigrate from North Africa.

France was occupied by the Germans during World War II; upon its
liberation, the Fourth Republic was formed and a new constitution was
created. The country continued to face social and political unrest due to
its involvement in wars in Algeria and Vietnam, a situation that caused
the collapse of the government in the 1950s. When General Charles De
Gaulle entered into the political arena, he became a pivotal force for the
creation of the Fifth Republic. Since De Gaulle's time, France has attained social and political stability.

French society is currently confronting social problems due to its Mus-
lim population demanding equal rights and equal treatment. French society is considering an addendum to its basic elements, that of *French
Islam*. There is, however, great dispute among social sectors about how
French Islam is going to be financed by domestic sources. French society
is also confronting racial issues. Racism is illegal in the country, but it is
still practiced.

Social mobility has its roots in the French Revolution and early industrialization. Conflicts between the poor and the rich, the new and the old,
and the rural and the urban were responsible for the social mobility and
change that took place in nineteenth century France.[7] Under the influence
of the reformers and modernists, with their eyes on foreign models, a
more open and egalitarian spirit appeared to be emerging.[8]

Social mobility and change were highly visible and widely practiced
in the second half of the twentieth century. Furthermore, French society
is now characterized by the large and active number of civil society organizations, which are powerful instruments for participating in social,
economic, and political affairs.[9] French women have been entering into
the labor market in large numbers, especially in professional areas, thus
postponing childbirth and choosing their professional careers over having children, at least during the initial part of their work experience.[10]

French society requires tremendous amounts of healthcare services
for its citizens due to the longevity of the population. At this point, the
current healthcare system has not been able to satisfy the needs of el-
derly citizens. At the present time, the healthcare system is undergoing
developmental changes in order to be more effective, more efficient, and
cheaper to operate.

The middle class in France produces most of the wealth and participates in most of the socioeconomic and political activities. It is basically an urban culture, but recently the middle class is moving out of urban areas to close suburbs. This is due to the increase of wealth in the middle class.

French society is well-established and integrated into the European Union, but the country is not inclined to accept any new members.[11] The country is now changing from a socioeconomic structure that had been profoundly controlled by the government—which supported the high standard of living and the wealth of the French people—to a market-oriented economy. It is now facing the privatization of many formerly government-owned and operated business organizations, which is creating additional changes in the fabric of the society and economy.

French society was influenced by the Roman Catholic Church for centuries. The incoming industrialization era that started at the beginning of the twentieth century and its revival the end of World War II substantially diminished the influence of the Church, and allowed the creation of a dynamic society characterized by social mobility.

Extent of Industrialization

Industrialization in France was regarded as a compromise necessary to compete with the heavily industrialized nations of Great Britain and Germany. In the first part of the twentieth century, the country had a growing economy, a flexible social structure, and a good education system which favored the gradual development of modern industrialization. At first, the positive attitude toward industrial prosperity was limited to important personalities like French economist Jean Monnet, but this attitude eventually permeated most of French society. Gradually, over the past thirty years, this new spirit has gained social acceptance. Ordinary people have started to believe in progress and accept the need for industrial change; however, whenever change actually presents itself, many Frenchmen were loathe giving up some of their vested interest.[12]

The French government recognized the benefits to be derived from industrialization and did an excellent job in implementing its achievement. President De Gaulle's philosophy of advocating national economic independence called for a greater advancement of the French industrial complex, and the same program continued under successive leaders. The government began to modify French industry in the 1960s, and as a result of this, each sector of the economy started to have locally-owned enterprises that were able to compete viably in international markets. The recent strength of French enterprises means more power to compete in world markets, and their diversity protects the economy from a slump in a single product line. Mergers, joint ventures, and broad specialization between large industrial complexes and minor sectors became necessary. Furthermore, strong industrial restructuring has been taking place during the last ten years due to the increase in international competition, especially for traditional heavy industries.[13] The industrial sector in the country accounts for close to 20 percent of the nation's economic activities, and large industrial organizations are both private and state controlled. However, as is the case with most states in the European Union, the French government is under pressure to privatize its state-controlled organizations.

The post-World War II industrialization process in France received the necessary support from a relatively good economy, a flexible social structure, and a modern and developing education system. Today, France is a highly industrialized nation.

Labor Unions

Labor unions in France were relatively weak until the end of World War II, but stronger than their counterparts in Italy because of the greater extent of industrialization. In 1966, Parliament passed a law requiring enterprises to grant official recognition to union delegates, to notify the workers committees in due time of planned reductions in the workforce, and to inform and consult the committee on the enterprise's operations in general and on labor matters in particular.[14]

French unions bargain not only with private employers and employers associations (such as the Conseil National de Patronat Francais and the Confederation Generale des Petites et Moyennes Enterprises), but also with the management of the nationalized industries (railroads, coal mines, electricity and gas producers, and the Renault automobile enterprise in particular), and in this respect they apply pressure to the government in the normal conduct of their economic bargaining activities. French unions also act as interest groups in a more generalized fashion, being especially concerned with social welfare legislation. Enterprises that employ fifty or more workers must have a *Comite d'Enterprise*, a person who has the right to sit in on board meetings as an observer and to be informed of the financial situation of the enterprise. Recently, it has been noted that French unionized organizations experience a more productive working environment and the retention of higher skilled workers due to mechanisms for voicing worker grievances and improved communication channels.[15]

There are currently five large labor confederations: the Confédération Générale du Travail (CGT), the Force Ouvrière (FO), the Confédération Française Démocratique du Travail (CFDT), the Confédération Française des Travailleurs Chrétiens (CFTC), and the Confédération Française de l'Encadrement-Confédération Générale des Cadres (CFE-CGC). There are also five important unions: the Solidaires Unitaires Démocratiques (SUD), the Fédération Syndicale Unitaire (FSU), the Union Nationale des Syndicats Autonomes (UNSA), the Confédération Nationale du Travail (anarcho-syndicalists), and the Confédération Autonome du Travail.[16]

In the context of pluralism and union division, the SUD unions have seen strong development in the country. Leaders of SUD labor unions are involved in political activities and are strong political entities that cannot be removed without serious consequences.[17] It is important to note that trade unions have emerged much weaker from the changes of the past three decades. The decline has led to sociological changes that accompanied the attendant shift in employment patterns, which have been a major factor for the additional declining trade union strength.[18]

Labor unions in France were relatively weak until the end of World War II. The rapid advancement of industrialization within the country created stronger labor unions with tremendous power and influence over the well-being of their members and the entire country.

The Corporation

The corporate form of business has played a very important role in the social and economic life of France. Corporations first appeared during the late sixteenth and early seventeenth centuries. However, as was the case in Great Britain and Germany, the most important forms of business organization until the middle of the nineteenth century were the partnership and the joint stock company. The Industrial Revolution inherited from England demonstrated that the development of large-scale enterprises in France demanded large-scale capital. The corporate form of business offered the advantages of broadly distributed ownership, limited liability, and the ability to attract many French and European investors by offering common stock at reasonable prices. France imitated Germany's strong effort to create industrial and governmental corporations, and in 1982, corporations spread across the country.[19] This form of business managed to raise capital much more easily than the partnership and the joint stock company. Furthermore, with the presence of the corporate form of business came the expansion of investment banks to serve as intermediaries for corporations and investors.

Many French corporations remained family-owned and operated until the late 1990s. In 2004, about a third of the firms were widely held, another third were founder-controlled, and the remaining third were heir-controlled family firms.[20] In the 1990s, corporations began to open up to the public, thus creating the separation of ownership from management which led to the acceleration of the appearance of professional managers, and, subsequently, the development of management. However, the most important developments may be expected to take place not at the national level but at the transnational level, as both national business and politics become increasingly dependent on transnational business and politics.[21]

The expansion of private European corporations in France that appeared at the end of last decade was hampered by a legal framework that included European law requirements.[22] French and European Union corporations are now resolving governmental restrictions on these corporations in order to allow them to operate more effectively and efficiently.

France inherited industrialization from England, and as a result of France's well-balanced industrialization process, it became necessary for enterprises to follow the corporate form of business in order to create the necessary factors of production demanded by an industrialized socioeconomic system.

Management in France

Industrialization came to France at the same time it reached Germany, but it was not initially strong because France depended more on agriculture. In small enterprises in the past, the owners of organizations were also the managers. They were viewed as the owners, rather than as the managers of the enterprise. Professional managers first appeared in the country at the beginning of the 1900s. However, as industrial enterprises started to develop, the appearance of industrial managers who were separate from the owners of organizations gained ground. The French word for manager, *cadre*, has its origin in the military. In the mind of the French people, the cadre is a professional manager working in the private sector. Today, most managers are not related to the owners of the organizations. In addition, the French *grandes ecoles* have been used intensively by family-owned corporations to ensure that their successors are capable of handling the *patrimoine* in an appropriate manner.[23] Managers now acquire their positions on the basis of educational and professional qualification. Furthermore, the profession of manager started to develop a distinct identity based on respect and admiration.

Consequently, the French manager of today has a professional identity. France has come closer than any other nation in turning management into a separate profession with its own entry requirements and regulations.[24] Professional identity is constructed at a very early stage of initial management education.[25] The French believe that managers played a very important role in saving the country from the socioeconomic collapse after World War II and bringing it to the level of prosperity the country enjoys today. Today's French managers are now recruited to be professional managers with skills that can match present and future corporate requirements.[26] Furthermore, because of reforms and the reorganization of enterprises, young managers are rapidly reaching top executive positions.[27] Good communication is considered to be an important tool for the development of managers, especially the younger managers, with feedback being an important mechanism for adjusting and improving performance.[28] There are still some difficulties that negatively affect French managers, such as regulation by bureaucratic authority and peer pressure, both amplified by greater reliance on internal labor markets.[29]

Until the 1970s, managerial education was neglected in France. People believed that managerial qualities were innate and could not be developed in a formal way through education.[30] The inadequacy of management education and the indifference toward management per se was finally understood in the 1970s. A letter I received from the Chamber of Commerce and Industry of Paris revealed that management education was neglected in France, and that it was finally being considered as a basic factor in enterprise immobility.[31]

Historically, most managers in France had a degree either in engineering or economics from a local institution.[32] During the 1970s, France started a number of universities that offered management education, an effort that has continued to this day. Additionally, management education began to be offered by their prestigious institutions such as the *Ecole de Hautes Etudes Commerciales*, the *Ecole Superieure de Commerce*, the *Ecole Centrale*, the *Ecole des Mines*, and the *Ecole Politechnique*, among others.[33]

At the present time, universities and other institutions of higher learning offer managerial education. The number of business schools offering

MBA programs in France has increased substantially over the last decade.[34] Furthermore, the French management apprentice program is now increasingly common in France.[35]

In France, where socioeconomic conditions were better than those in Italy and where industrialization was more advanced, employees were less autocratically controlled by management than their Italian counterparts. Nevertheless, paternalism was the key to employee control. The decrease in European unemployment in the late 1990s coincided with the passing of flexible labor laws in many European countries. Economies noted for their incapacity to create jobs during the 1980s and early 1990s are now creating jobs at much faster rate than before the reforms.

French society supports long-term employment, providing the employer with incentives to encourage its staff and employees to make the best of opportunities offered and to invest in their work.[36] French employees have experienced substantial improvement in their wages and salaries as the direct effect of sustained growth in the economy. Four out of five business organizations in France use forms of incentive pay. Managers and employees get bonuses and profits through company-sponsored programs or government-sponsored programs applicable to French companies with more than fifty employees.[37]

French employees are encouraged to participate in the decision-making process in their areas of functional jurisdiction, and they have always been prone to question a supervisor's orders if they do not agree with its relevance to the task at hand.[38] Other state measures have been used to encourage employee share ownership and financial participation.[39] Equal opportunities for men and women still must be assured and deployed.[40]

Employee education is being extensively provided by industrial firms and other enterprises. In France, national agencies and the High Authority of the European Union have been providing intensive technical education of production employees, promoting the exchange of employees among European Union countries, and teaching European languages to all employees. This policy has been established for both young and old employees. Consequently, a significant number of employees of large industrial enterprises have acquired university education in their respective areas of specialization.

The European Union has also made funds available for research relevant to industrial fatigue and similar matters pertinent to the well-being of employees. The High Authority of the European Union participates in the financing of a number of research institutions dealing with physiopathology and clinical studies of the employees. Expenditure on research and development is of particular importance to the advanced technology sector of industry throughout the European Union.

Industrialization came relatively late in France, and did not begin to accelerate until the first part of the twentieth century. This acceleration precipitated the formation of strong labor unions and the rise of the corporate form of business. Both entities have contributed to the continuous development of management in the country.

References

Angot, J., H. Malloch, and B. Klyemann. "The Formation of Professional Identity in French Apprenti Managers." *Education & Training* 50, 5. (2008): 408. doi:10.11080/00400910810889084

Ardagh, J. *The New French Revolution*. New York, NY: Harper & Row, 1968.

Ashlund, A., and M. Dabrowski. *Europe after Enlargement*. Cambridge, MA: Cambridge University Press, 2007.

Barsoux, J. L., and P. Lawrence. "The Making of a French Manager." *Harvard Business Review*, 58, July-August 1991.

Béréziat, G. "Radical Reform of the French University System." *Higher Education in Europe* 33, 1. (April 2008): 164. doi:10.1080/03797720802228316

Boland, L. G. A. *Théorie Du Pouvoir Politique & Religieux Dans Le Société Civile, Démontrée Par Le Raisonnement Et Par l'Histoire: Suivie De La Théorie De l'Éducation Sociale ... L'administration Politique*. Breinigsville, PA: Nabu Public Domain Reprints, 2010.

Bonneuil, N., and P. A. Rosental. "Changing Social Mobility in Nineteenth-Century France." Historical Methods 32, 2. (Spring 1999): 19-21.

Burt, R. S., R. M. Hogarth, and C. Michaud. "The Social Capital of French and American Managers." *Organization Science* 11, 2. (March-April 2000): 123-147. doi:1047-7039/00/1102/0123/$05.00

Business International Corporation. "Investing, Licensing, and Trading Conditions Abroad: France." August 1969.

Comission de Communautes Europeenes. *La Politique Industrielle* (Industrial Policy). Brussels, Germany: Comission de Communautes Europeenes, 1970.

Damesin, R., and J. Denis. "SUD Trade Unions: The New Organizations Trying to Conquer the French Trade Union Scene." *Capital &*

Class 86, Summer 2005: 22-23. http://proquest.umi.com/pqdweb?did =857820081&sid=27&Fmt=3&clientld=11123&RQT=309&VName =PQD

Directory of Education Online. http://www.directoryofeducation.net/ colleges/worldwide/france/

Doucouliagos, H., and P. Laroche. "Unions and Tangible Investments: A Review and New Evidence in France." *Relations Industrielles* 58, 2. (Spring 2003): 315. http://proquest.umi.com/pqdweb?did=378109041 &sid=27&Fmt=4&clientld=11123&RQT=309&VName=PQD

Dufour, C., and Hege. *L'Europe Syndicale au Quotidian. La Represen-tations des Salaries in France, Allemagne, Grand-Bretagne et Italie.* Bruxelles, Germany: Institut de Recherches Economiques et Social (IRES), 2002.

European Commission. *Community Charter of Fundamental Social Rights of Workers.* Luxembourg: Office for the Official Publications of the European Communities, 1990.

Essounga, Y. N. "A Review of the Effect of National Culture on Cor-porate Culture: An Example of the United States & France." *Review of Business Research* 9, 5. (2009): 71. http://search.ebscohost.com/ login.aspx?direct=true&db=bth&AN=45463177&site=ehost-live

Guterl, F. V. "Europe's Secret Weapon." *Business Monthly*, 134, Octo-ber 1989: 63.

Hoffman, S., and C. P. Kindleberger, et al. *In Search of France.* New York, NY: Harper & Row, 1965.

Kalff, D. *An Un-American Business: The Rise of the New European En-terprise.* London, England: Kogan Page, 2006.

Kalwij, A. S. "The Effects of Female Employment Status on the Pres-ence and Number of Children." *Journal of Population Economics* 13, 2000: 225.

Kumar, R., and J. Usunier. "Management Education in a Globalizing World: Lessons from the French Experience." *Management Learning* 32, 3. (September 2001) 367. http://proquest.umi.com/pqdweb?did= 83520290&sid=13&Fmt=3&clientd=11123&RQT=309&VName=P QD

Chevalier, Antoine. Letter from the director of the French Chamber of Commerce and Industry. (1969, October 9). Paris, France.

Mala, G. A. "Education in France." *U.S. Department of Health, Educa-tion, and Welfare Bulletin* 33, 1. 1968.

Marsden, D., R. Belfield, and S. Benhamou. *Incentive Pay Systems and*

the Management of Human Resources in France and Great Britain.
London, England: Centre for Economic Performance, 2007.

McCahery, J., T. Raaijmakers, and E. Verneulen. *The Governance of Close Corporations and Partnerships: US and European Perspectives*. Oxford, England: Oxford University Press, 2004.

Morck, R. K., ed. *A History of Corporate Governance around the World*. Chicago, IL: University of Chicago Press, 2007.

Myers, A., A. Kakabadse, and C. Gordon. "Effectiveness of French Management: Analysis of the Behavior, Attitudes, and Business Impact of Top Managers." *Journal of Management Development* 14, 6. (1995): para. 73-79.

NationMaster.com. "Trade Union Membership by Country." Accessed October 1, 2010 from http://www.nationmaster.com/graph/lab_tra_uni_mem-labor-trade-union-membership

Ongaro, E. *Public Management Reform and Modernization: Trajectories of Administrative Change in Italy, France, Greece, Portugal and Spain*. Cheltenham, England: Edward Elgar Publishing, 2010.

Parsons, N. *French Industrial Relations in the New World Economy*. London, England: Routledge Taylor & Francis, 2005.

Paucar-Caceres, A. "Mapping the Structure of MBA (AMBA-Accredited) Programs in the UK and France." *International Journal of Educational Management* 22, 2. (2008): 187. doi:10.1108/09513540810853576

Smismans, S., ed. *Civil Society and Legitimate European Governance*. Shelenham, England: Edward Elgar Publishing, 2006.

van Schendelen, Rinus. *More Machiavelli in Brussels: The Art of Lobbying the EU*. Aldershot, Netherlands: Darmouth, 2010.

Endnotes

1 L. G. A. Boland, *Théorie Du Pouvoir Politique & Religieux Dans Le Société Civile, Démontrée Par Le Raisonnement Et Par l'Histoire: Suivie De La Théorie De l'Éducation Sociale ... L'administration Politique* (Breinigsville, PA: Nabu Public Domain Reprints, 2010).

2 S. Smismans, ed., *Civil Society and Legitimate European Governance*. (Shelenham, England: Edward Elgar Publishing, 2006).

3 G. A. Mala, "Education in France," *U.S. Department of Health, Education, and Welfare Bulletin* 33, 1 (1968): 1.

4 G. Béréziat, "Radical Reform of the French University System," *Higher Education in Europe* 33, 1 (April 2008): 164.

doi:10.1080/03797720802228316

5   F. V. Guterl, "Europe's Secret Weapon," *Business Monthly*, 134, October 1989: 63.

6   Directory of Education Online. http://www.directoryofeducation.net/colleges/worldwide/france/

7   N. Bonneuil and P. A. Rosental, "Changing Social Mobility in Nineteenth-Century France," *Historical Methods* 32, 2 (Spring 1999): 18.

8   S. Hoffman and C. P. Kindleberger, et al., *In Search of France* (New York, NY: Harper & Row, 1965).

9   Smismans, *Civil Society and Legitimate European Governance*.

10 A. S. Kalwij, "The Effects of Female Employment Status on the Presence and Number of Children," *Journal of Population Economics* 13, 2000: 225.

11 A. Ashlund and M. Dabrowski, *Europe after Enlargement* (Cambridge, MA: Cambridge University Press, 2007).

12 J. Ardagh, *The New French Revolution* (New York, NY: Harper & Row, 1968).

13 N. Parsons, *French Industrial Relations in the New World Economy* (London, England: Routledge Taylor & Francis, 2005).

14 *Business International Corporation*, "Investing, Licensing, and Trading Conditions Abroad: France," August 1969, p.49.

15 H. Doucouliagos and P. Laroche, "Unions and Tangible Investments: A Review and New Evidence in France," *Relations Industrielles* 58, 2 (Spring 2003): 315. http://proquest.umi.com/pqdweb?did=378109041&sid=27&Fmt=4&clientId=11123&RQT=309&VName=PQD

16 NationMaster.com. "Trade union membership by country."

17 R. Damesin and J. Denis, "SUD Trade Unions: The New Organizations Trying to Conquer the French Trade Union Scene," *Capital & Class* 86, Summer 2005: 22-23. http://proquest.umi.com/pqdweb?did=857820081&sid=27&Fmt=3&clientId=11123&RQT=309&VName=PQD

18 Parsons, *French Industrial Relations in the New World Economy*.

19 J. McCahery, T. Raaijmakers, and E. Verneulen, *The Governance of Close Corporations and Partnerships: US and European Perspectives* (Oxford, England: Oxford University Press, 2004).

20 Morck, *A History of Corporate Governance around the World*.

21 Rinus van Schendelen, *More Machiavelli in Brussels: The Art of*

Lobbying the EU (Aldershot, Netherlands: Darmouth, 2010).

22 McCahery, Raaijmakers, and Verneulen, *The Governance of Close Corporations and Partnerships: US and European Perspectives.*

23 Morck, *A History of Corporate Governance around the World.*

24 Barsoux, J.L., and P. Lawrence, "The Making of a French Manager," *Harvard Business Review*, 58, July-August 1991.

25 J. Angot, H. Malloch, and B. Klyemann, "The Formation of Professional Identity in French Apprenti Managers," *Education & Training* 50, 5 (2008): 408. doi:10.11080/00400910810889084

26 Kalff, *An Unamerican Business: The Rise of the New European Enterprise.*

27 E. Ongaro, *Public Management Reform and Modernization: Trajectories of Administrative Change in Italy, France, Greece, Portugal and Spain* (Cheltenham, England: Edward Elgar Publishing, 2010).

28 A. Myers, A. Kakabadse, and C. Gordon, "Effectiveness of French Management: Analysis of the Behavior, Attitudes, and Business Impact of Top Managers," *Journal of Management Development* 14, 6 (1995): para. 73-79.

29 R. S. Burt, R. M. Hogarth, and C. Michaud, "The Social Capital of French and American Managers," *Organization Science* 11, 2 (March-April 2000): 123-147. doi:1047-7039/00/1102/0123/$05.00

30 Barsoux and Lawrence, "The Making of a French Manager."

31 Antoine Chevalier, Letter from the director of the French Chamber of Commerce and Industry (1969, October 9). Paris, France.

32 R. Kumar and J. Usunier, "Management Education in a Globalizing World: Lessons from the French Experience," *Management Learning* 32, 3 (September 2001) 367. http://proquest.umi.com/pqdweb?did=83520290&sid=13&Fmt=3&clientd=11123&RQT=309&VName=PQD

33 Comission de Communautes Europeenes, *La Politique Industrielle* (Brussels, Germany: Comission de Communautes Europeenes, 1970).

34 A. Paucar-Caceres, "Mapping the Structure of MBA (AMBA-Accredited) Programs in the UK and France," *International Journal of Educational Management* 22, 2 (2008): 187. doi:10.1108/09513540810853576

35 Angot, Malloch, and Klyemann, "The Formation of Professional Identity in French Apprenti Managers," 408.

36 Kalff, *An Unamerican Business: The Rise of the New European*

Enterprise.

37 Dufour and Hege, *L'Europe Syndicale au Quotidian la Representation des Salaries en France, Allemagne, Grande-Bretange et Italie.*

38 Y. N. Essounga, "A Review of the Effect of National Culture on Corporate Culture: An Example of the United States & France," *Review of Business Research* 9, 5 (2009): 71. http://search.ebsco-host.com/login.aspx?direct=true&db=bth&AN=45463177&site=ehost-live

39 D. Marsden, R. Belfield, and S. Benhamou, *Incentive Pay Systems and the Management of Human Resources in France and Great Britain* (London, England: Centre for Economic Performance, 2007).

40 European Commission, *Community Charter of Fundamental Social Rights of Workers* (Luxembourg: Office for the Official Publications of the European Communities, 1990).

Chapter 10: Germany

Religion and Economic Development

The impact of religion upon economic development in Germany has been very positive since the Protestant Reformation. Max Weber believed that his fellow Germans favored economic development because of the impact of Calvinism upon the German people. In his *Gessamelte Aufsatze zur Reigionssoziologie (Collected Essays on Sociology of Religion)*, Weber stated that the influence of Protestantism upon the idea of hard work and industrial prosperity was a definite factor.[1] Specifically, Weber indicated that Protestant Dogma deviated from the Catholic theological philosophies and promulgated mundane prosperity, culturally defined as earthly rather than posthumous. Encouragement of this type of personal orientation had selective effects in different spheres, the most important of which were in economy and science. The Lutheran Reformation, and thus the emancipation from the Catholic Church, was central to the rise of internal responsibility. Protestantism assigns much higher accountability to the individual.[2]

Economic development came rapidly in the country, and in the early 1900s, the nation started to utilize the factory system. German industrialists created a strong alliance with the German military, establishing new industrial organizations based on private ownership for the main purpose of producing goods for the armed forces. The military made attempts to take over these industrial organizations, but it lacked the capability of managing them. For this reason, an agreement was made that allowed both sides to coexist and meet their respective goals, making products for the army, navy, and eventually the air force.

The impact of religion upon economic development in Germany has been positive since the Protestant Reformation. Economic, industrial, and commercial prosperity have been traditionally emphasized, thus making it one of the most economically developed nations in the world.

Religion and Education

The German education system has been positively influenced by the Protestant Reformation. The system was designed to satisfy the needs of an industrialized socioeconomic system after the arrival of the Industrial Revolution in the country. After World War II, the Germans realized that education should not only be used as a medium for social prestige, but also as a preparation for life as a citizen in a democratic society. For this reason, the adoption of civics has been strongly supported by the government. After the unification of country in the early 1990s, the Germans confronted the problem of unifying two education systems, and they also looked at the various dysfunctions that continued to exist between educational opportunities and labor market needs.[3]

Elementary education starts with the basic school known as *grundschule* for children aged six to ten. Children then enter into different high schools based on a holistic evaluation of their performance. Secondary schools have been traditionally divided into three subcategories: *Humanities Gymnasium* (classical languages), *Modern Gymnasium* (modern languages), and *Mathematics and Science Gymnasium*. The *gymnasium*—now a part of a combined education entity—is important because it leads to higher schooling. This school imparts to the students a scholarly approach to all aspects of social and cultural life. It provides a nine-year course following the fourth primary school year. Methods of teaching the *gymnasium* are based on the assumption that students are intellectually capable and are concerned with academic learning.

Currently, secondary education is divided between various schools. Junior secondary education consists of grades five and six, during which students explore various academic choices. There is another type of school, the *hauptsdhule*, whose duration is between five to six years and includes grades five to nine. The *realschule* is an intermediate primary school for grades five to ten that prepares students for medium-level private and governmental jobs. Students can also enter into a high technical school known as *fachberschule* or a *fachgymnasium*, which is a profoundly specialized high school. Although one segment of the German society continued to emphasize the value of a classical education, vocational education gained considerable ground in the first part of the 1900s. There have been three types of vocational and technical schools: the *berufsschulen*, a part-time vocational school; the *berufsfachschulen*, a full-time vocational school; and the *fachschulen*, an advanced full-time vocational school that trains students to become specialized workers, masters of their trades, technicians, and practical engineers.

Students who enroll in the part-time school or *berufsschulen* do not continue into an intermediate school after they finish their compulsory education. Consequently, this school trains them for a career by providing on-the-job experience and general education subjects. The full-time vocational school provides for one, two, or three years of study with thirty to thirty-six hours of practical and theoretical instruction per week. These schools are primarily administered by districts and municipalities, and sometimes by business organizations, private bodies, or other organizations. The advanced full-time vocational schools also provide education for other fields, such as art, nursing, and social welfare work. As a general rule, all students must be eighteen years old and have two years of practical experience.

German universities are excellent, and they provide education in every necessary academic area in the German and European Union socioeconomic structures. Reforms of higher education have been under way in Germany, introducing many structural elements that resemble parts of the American education system.[4] A new super-university, the *Universistestsseminar der Winterschaft*, was built at the end of the 1980s. It was supported by many other universities and business leaders and offers both short and extensive managerial courses for all three managerial levels. There are currently 272 colleges and universities in the country.[5]

The German education system was positively influenced by the Protestant Reformation, and was created to serve the needs of the people in a highly industrialized socioeconomic environment. The education system since World War II and the unification of the country in 1990 has been continuously developing in order to effectively and efficiently serve the needs of German citizens.

Religion and Social Structure

The Protestant Reformation had a positive impact upon German society, but German social structure has gone through a large number of disruptions and tragedies. To begin with, there had not been a single German society in the history of the various German states (as was the case with the Greek states in the past) that inhabited North-Central Europe. Most of those German states were small entities at the mercy of the larger powers of the time. French troops occupied most of those states until the final defeat of Napoleon in 1813. The French withdrew from the occupied territories and left behind them approximately forty small German states. German politicians looked at the unification of other European nations that took place centuries in the past, such as in Spain and France, and created a strong impetus for a united German state. The elite of the German social stratifications were instrumental in promoting unification, which finally came in 1871 under Wilhelm von Bismarck, who declined to incorporate Austria in the unification process. The top echelon of the newly established united German society consisted of the military and the own-ers of large- and medium-size industries associated with the military.

The newly formed united German state suffered a humiliating defeat in World War I that brought an end to the former socioeconomic structure. The Weimar Republic's social and economic reorganization which fol-lowed World War I and the Nazi regime that appeared shortly thereafter contributed to further changes in the social structure and social mobility. Germany's defeat in World War I resulted in continuous turmoil in the country that had detrimental social and economic effects. This turmoil also had detrimental effects upon the psyche of the German people, driv-ing them to seek salvation in the hands of Hitler, who led the country to a second humiliating defeat of unprecedented dimensions in 1945. At-titudes, behavior, and social interaction in Germany were influenced by an undemocratic, hierarchical society, in which the ideas of liberty and equality of a non-hierarchal society had not unfolded.[6]

After World War II, the country was divided into West Germany (the German Federal Republic under the control of the United States, Unit-ed Kingdom, and France), and East Germany (the German Democratic Republic under the control of the Soviet Union). The territory covered by the German Democratic Republic is actually Middle Germany; East Germany was generously given to another nation. The two new societies that emerged were diagonally opposed in their socioeconomic stratifica-tion. West Germany underwent drastic social changes after World War II. A great achievement was the absorption of approximately 8.5 million refugees from the eastern regions of the former German Reich, and some 3.5 million refugees from the communist German Democratic Republic and East Berlin, who occupied the lowest social stratification of German society. In many respects, this successful social fusion serves as a model for the integration of other minority groups.[7]

In the 1960s and 1970s, Germany came to an ideal type of a Fordist social structure. However, in 2003, the German social and occupational structure declined due to the crisis of Fordism.[8] In 1990, the two German states were unified to form a single Germany. The unification was con-fronted with serious problems concerning the fusion of the two societies and two economies. The former East German socioeconomic element initially occupied the lower stratification level of the new German society and economy. However, the fusion and forces of change started to shape a socioeconomic stratification that is now based on factors other than the geographic origin of the German people.

German women have been entering into the labor market, especially in professional areas, and the educational gap between men and women in the country has been substantially reduced. German women prefer their professional careers over having children, at least during the initial part of their work experience.[9] Germany has been instrumental in European integration, but it is not in favor of accepting other states into the European Union at this time.[10]

German society requires tremendous amounts of healthcare services for its citizens due to the longevity of the population. At the present time, the healthcare system is undergoing developmental changes in order to be more effective, efficient, and cheaper to operate.

Germany today has several million Muslims who are immigrant workers or their descendants, and the government is paying significant sums of money for their repatriation.

The Protestant Reformation had a positive impact upon German social structure. German history was characterized by the turmoil of wars, military occupations, and the socioeconomic destruction and dislocation of the population. After the final unification of the German state in 1990, the country created a dynamic new social structure.

Extent of Industrialization

Industrialization in Germany came much later than in England. The country witnessed a large population growth in the late 1800s and early 1900s that was accompanied by changes in the infrastructure of the economy. The gap closed between 1850 and 1875, when modern technology replaced traditional methods on the Continent and German industry could compete on an equal footing with the British.[11]

In the early 1900s, new industrial organizations based on private ownership were established for the main purpose of producing goods for the German military, and periodic abortive attempts were made by the military to take over these organizations. After World War II, Germany rapidly developed a good economy, formed a flexible social structure, and created a modern education system. These three elements provided the infrastructure needed for a strong industrial complex. With the help of the state, the Germans acquired the most advanced technologies available at the time, and because they were latecomers in the industrial arena, they were able to create firms that started out at the most efficient scale of production.[12]

Germany today is the most industrialized nation in the European

Union. The industrial sector makes up 27.9 percent of all economic activities. Service is the number one sector, accounting for 71.3 percent of economic activity, whereas agriculture only accounts for less than 1 percent. Germany has the heaviest industries in Europe, which are continuously restructuring to replace inferior industrial complexes inherited from the former East Germany and to compete effectively and efficiently against other European Union industries and international industries.

After World War II, Germany rapidly developed a good economy, formed a flexible social structure, and created a modern education system. These three elements provided the infrastructure needed for a strong industrial complex.

Labor Unions

Due to the early and powerful industrialization of the nation, labor unions quickly developed, and although victimized during various political periods, German labor unions have endured and are now a potent force in the country. Currently, there are three major German trade union confederations: Deutscher Gewerkschaftsbund (DGB) (German Confederation of Trade Unions), Deutscher Beamtenbund (DBB) (German Civil Service Federation), and the Christlicher Gewerkschaftsbund (CGB) (German Christian Workers' Federation).[13]

Most German workers belong to commensurate trade unions affiliated with the German trade union federation DGB, whose task is to coalesce all trade unions into an effective unit to protect their common interests, particularly in economic, social, and cultural policy. German labor legislation prescribes free collective bargaining and negotiation of labor-employer agreements on pay, working hours, vacations entitlements, and general working conditions.[14] German trade unions are highly involved in the political arena of the country. Today, collective bargaining is based on trade unions and employer confederations. Employees often stay for several decades in the same organization and the same trade union. Labor unions are obliged to fight all antidemocratic influence; to support the expansion and maintenance of the social and democratic constitutional state; to encourage international understanding; and to advocate for the preservation of peace and freedom.

There are also Workers Councils that examine production issues, handle individual grievances, and implement collective agreements; they have extensive codetermination rights that convey power that can be exercised sotto voce.[15] Corporatism in Germany refers to the often tight network of representatives from industry, unions, and politics, and to the habit of making important decisions on economic policy on the basis of a consensus between government politicians, employer associations, and unions.[16] Salaried employees in Germany are represented by a unique organization known as *Betriebstrat*.[17]

Labor unions in Germany developed under the powerful influence of the early industrialization of the country. Although they went through many painful experiences before the unification of the country, modern labor unions are strong and provide sufficient support for their members. German labor unions are contributing to the well-being of their members and the entire country.

The Corporation

After the Industrial Revolution reached the country from England, German corporations appeared and turned to the exploration of minerals and other raw materials.[18] One of the earliest German corporations is Friedrich Bayer, which began to emerge in 1865 by expanding to the United States, France, Belgium, and Russia. By 1990, this corporation was operating in seventy nations around the world. Currently, there is a rapid spread of private corporations across Germany, an event that started at the end of the twentieth century.[19]

Today, German corporations play a vital role in the modern German economy, which consists of family-controlled pyramidal groups and nominally widely held firms that are actually controlled by the top few banks via proxies.[20] The German corporation functions as an infrastructure between itself and its internal and external stakeholders. The closely knit network of personal relations between representatives of different institutions is a classical feature of German corporatism.[21]

The early industrialization of Germany precipitated the creation of private corporations of all sizes, which were characterized by having all the factors of production required for a modern industrial socioeconomic system. The impact of industrialization upon the German corporate form of business is of paramount importance.

Management in Germany

Due to the strong industrialization of the country, labor unions and the corporate form of business rapidly developed, which precipitated the formation of management development. The roots of German management go back to the history of the numerous German states that existed until the unification of the country by Bismarck in 1871. As in Italy and France, owner-managers existed in guilds and merchant entities that eventually gained prestige and power, and they managed their enterprises based on their personal power. Industrialization from England reached Germany quickly and started to develop with the assistance of private funds, the government, and the military. As industrial enterprises started to develop, the appearance of industrial managers who were different than the owners of the organization gained ground and became abundant in Germany at the turn of the 1900s.

One of the principal issues that confronted German management after World War II was the complete democratization of the organizational structure. This involved expunging paternalism to provide uninhibited access to all managerial positions, increasing the social responsibility of management, liberalizing employee control to increase participation, and implementing managerial and organizational decentralization. What was needed was a revolution in management attitudes and a vigorous attack on the status quo in four areas: strategy, organizations, operations, and people.[22]

Until the second half of the twentieth century, professional managers in Germany had academic degrees that were not related to management, such as engineering. However, this situation changed rapidly due to the availability of commensurate education and related training. Management in Germany was not initially regarded as a distinct profession that merited recognition and respect because of the unfounded beliefs of employers, who regarded the profession as bureaucratic and the center of conspiracies against the organization. These inaccurate ideas have disappeared due to the development of the cultural factors in the country, a situation depicted in the studies in organizational culture that have exposed many misconceptions about management. Modern managers, who may or may not be related to the ownership, are being treated as independent, responsible persons who are accountable for their performance.[23]

Currently, German managers are recruited to be professional managers with skills that can match present and future corporate requirements.[24] It is important to note that middle-level managers have gained their due recognition as professionals, and are now viewed as colleagues who supervise their subordinates and execute their prescribed tasks in synergy with top management.[25]

In the early 1900s, German professors who taught business and economics placed elements pertinent to management under different classifications and curricula, making the emerging field of management in private organizations a distinct discipline that could be better understood by students, managers, and employers. The first academic business school in Germany, the *Handelshochschule*, was founded in 1898; these type of institutions were separate from universities, but were categorized as academic institutions.[26]

Management education in Germany was relatively limited until the 1960s; in the decades that followed, the country started to establish and develop many universities and other institutions of higher learning which offer management education. Curricula in business economics grew as an integrated body of knowledge for the management of a firm.[27]

The Marshal Plan, in reference to management education in Germany, aimed at creating managers and business people who think like American managers.[28] One of the major concerns in German management education was the movement to create a democratic style of management, in which the new managers are more entrepreneurial.[29] Today, the country has many universities and other institutions of higher learning, that offer management education and training, as there are about 400 organized occupations which require such training.[30] The Universistestsseminar der Winterschaft is offering both short and extensive managerial courses for all three managerial levels.

Entrepreneurship education appeared at the beginning of the 1970s in universities and colleges, and is employed as a promising method that arouses entrepreneurial interest in students.[31] In addition, during the last two decades of the twentieth century, entrepreneurship and management training institutions were established with the explicit goal of making German managers familiar with American management approaches.[32]

Germany is a pioneer in the apprenticeship training system, where the state runs and pays for the vocational schools, and the firms pay the costs of training the apprentices in the firm.[33] A new institution specializing in management is the *corporate university*, a company-owned and operated institution ensuring an education that is directly related to the business; most of them are strategically oriented.[34]

After the war destroyed much of the country, it was subsequently divided into several sectors of occupation. For this reason, the autocratic control of the German employee was overshadowed by other significant concerns such as politics and military occupation, as well as the reconstruction of industry, commerce, and the economy. Being ardent patriots, the German people did not oppose managerial control, which was primarily directed toward an individual's basic physiological and safety needs, with paternalism as a secondary consideration.

The late 1950s and the 1960s witnessed a tremendous improvement in the socioeconomic sectors of the country, and German employees experienced substantial improvement in their wages and salaries as the direct effect of sustained growth in the economy. Furthermore, equal treatment and equal opportunities for men and women have been assured.[35] Working conditions profoundly improved due to private and government efforts, and employees enjoy satisfactory health and safety conditions in their working environment.[36]

Employee participation became possible through the efforts of labor unions and the cooperation of the country's new professional managers, because one of the major concerns of German firms has been the movement to create a democratic style of management.[37] German employees are protected by strong labor unions and by Workers Councils that focus on production issues, handle individual grievances, and implement collective agreements. Their extensive codetermination rights convey a power which can be exercised sotto voce.[38] German employees fully understand that German management is based on consistent patterns of business-related practices built around a "competence first" principle that has to be followed all the time.[39]

Human resource departments and human resource management exist in the majority of German enterprises for the benefit of employees, managers, and the organization itself, and they are rooted in its historically grown and legally shaped institutional environment.[40] A recent development in German management is the appearance of temporary workers under the auspices of commensurate work agencies, a situation characterized as a triangular employment relationship involving a temporary work agency, a client company, and temporary agency workers.[41]

One of the top priorities in Germany has been Strategic Management, which includes capability, open-mindedness, assertiveness, truth, minimum game playing, and desire to overcome functional and hierarchical barriers. Strategic Management also promotes positive and creative thinking, good relationships, and a healthy balance between concern for work and people,[42] thus ensuring corporate survival.[43]

Labor unions and corporations appeared early in Germany during the industrialization process of the country. Both precipitated the development of management with several interruptions until the end of World War II. Since the unification of Germany, the development of management is taking place in a continuous and evolutionary manner with great success.

References

Addison, J. T., C. Schnabel, and J. Wagner. "The (Parlous) State of German Unions." *Journal of Labor Research* 28, 1. (Winter 2007): 4. http://search.ebscohost.com/login.aspx?direct=true&db=bth&AN=23815050&site=ehost-live

Allen, R. *The British Industrial Revolution in Global Perspective*. Cambridge, MA: Cambridge University Press, 2009.

Andresen, M., and B. Lichtenberger. "The Corporate University Landscape in Germany." *Journal of Workplace Learning* 19, 2. (2007): 110. doi:10.1108/13665620710728484

Armbruster, T. *Management and Organization in Germany*. Bodmin, Cornwall, England: MPG Books, 2005.

Ashlund, A., and M. Dabrowski. *Europe after Enlargement*. Cambridge, MA: Cambridge University Press, 2007.

Business Week. "Taking Over the Helm of Germany, Inc." December 1989: 66.

Directory of Education Online. http://www.directoryofeducation.net/colleges/worldwide/germany/

Dufour, C., and A. Hege. *L'Europe Syndicale au Quotidian la Representation des Salaries en France, Allemagne, Grande-Bretange et Italie*. Bruxelles, Germany: Presses Interuniversitaries Européennes, 2002.

El-Khawas, E. "Uniting German Higher Education." *Change* 22, 6. (1990): 39. http://proquest.umi.com/pqweb?did=1566022&sid=5&Fmt=2&clientld=2186&RQT=309&VName=PQD

European Commission. *Community Charter of Fundamental Social Rights of Workers*. Luxembourg: Office for the Official Publications of the European Communities, 1990.

European Commission. *Health and Safety at Work in the European Community*. Luxembourg: Office for the Official Publications of the European Communities, 1990.

Federal Republic of Germany. *Facts about Germany*. Bonn, Germany: Lexikon-Institut Bertelsman, 1989.

Federal Republic of Germany. *The Educational System*. Bonn, Germany: Press and Information Office of the Federal Republic of Germany, 1988.

Giardini, A., R. Kabst, and M. Müller-Camen. "HRM in the German

Business System: A Review." *Management Revue* 16, 1. (2005): 70. http://proquest.umi.com/pqdweb?did=820630351&sid=1&Fmt=3&cl ientId=2186&RQT=309&VName=PQD

Geppert, M., D. Matten, and K. Williams. *Challenges for European Management in a Global Context.* Basinsgtoke, England: Palgrave McMillan, 2003.

Glunk, U., C. Wilderom, and R. Ogilvie. "Finding the Key to German-Style Management." *International Studies of Management & Organization* 26, 3. (1997): 102.

Herrigel, H. *Constructions: The Source of German Industrial Power.* Cambridge, MA: Cambridge University Press, 2000.

Hunsicker, Q. J. "Innovation and Renewal: A European Perspective." *McKinsey Quarterly*, Spring 1984.

Kalff, D. *An Un-American Business: The Rise of the New European Enterprise.* London, England: Kogan Page, 2006.

Kalwij, A. S. "The Effects of Female Employment Status on the Presence and Number of Children." *Journal of Population Economics* 13, 225. (2000).

Kieser, A. "The Americanization of Academic Management Education in Germany." *Journal of Management Inquiry* 13, 2. (June 2004): 93. http://proquest.umi.com/pqdweb?did=647513621&sid=3&Fmt=3clie ntId=11123&RQT=309&VName=PQD

Klandt, H. and C. Volkmann. "Development and Prospects of Academic Entrepreneurship Education in Germany." *Higher Education in Europe* 31, 2. (July 2006): 201. doi:10.1080/03797720600940880

Koch, M. *Roads to Post-Fordism: Labor Markets and Social Structures in Europe.* Hampshire, England: Ashgate Publishing, 2006.

Locke, R., and K. Schone. *The Entrepreneurial Shift: Americanization in European High-Technology Management Education.* Cambridge, MA: Cambridge University Press, 2004.

Locke, R. "Comparing the German and American Systems." *Business History Review* 82, 2. (Summer 2008): 336-342. http://proquest.umi.com/pqdweb?did=1543534881&sid=30&Fmt=3&clientId=11123&RQT=309&VName=PQD

Management Today. "What Management Needs in the 1990s." October 1987: 102.

McCahery, J., T. Raaijmakers, and E. Verneulen. *The Governance of Close Corporations and Partnerships: US and European Perspectives.* Oxford, England: Oxford University Press, 2004.

Mitlacher, L. W. "Job Quality and Temporary Agency Work: Challenges for Human Resource Management in Triangular Employment Relations in Germany." *International Journal of Human Resource Management* 19, 3. (March 2008): 447.

Morck, R. K., ed. *A History of Corporate Governance around the World*. Chicago, IL: University of Chicago Press, 2007.

NationMaster.com. "Trade Union Membership by Country." Accessed October 1, 2010 from http://www.nationmaster.com/graph/lab_tra_ uni_mem-labor-trade-union-membership

Termporal, R. P. "Strategic Management for the 80s." *Industrial Management and Data Systems* 8, November-December 1982.

Weber, M. *The Protestant Ethic and the Spirit of Capitalism*. New York, NY: Charles Scribner's Sons, 1948.

Endnotes

1 M. Weber, *The Protestant Ethic and the Spirit of Capitalism* (New York, NY: Charles Scribner's Sons, 1948).

2 Armbruster, *Management and Organization in Germany*.

3 E. El-Khawas, "Uniting German Higher Education," *Change* 22, 6 (1990): 39. http://proquest.umi.com/pqweb?did=1566022&sid=5&F mt=2&clientld=2186&RQT=309&VName=PQD

4 A. Kieser, "The Americanization of Academic Management Education in Germany," *Journal of Management Inquiry* 13, 2 (June 2004): 93. http://proquest.umi.com/pqdweb?did=647513621&sid=3 &Fmt=3clientld=11123&RQT=309&VName=PQD

5 Directory of Education Online. http://www.directoryofeducation.net/ colleges/worldwide/germany/

6 Armbruster, *Management and Organization in Germany*.

7 Federal Republic of Germany, *Facts about Germany* (Bonn, Germany: Lexikon-Institut Bertelsman, 1989).

8 M. Koch, *Roads to Post-Fordism: Labor Markets and Social Structures in Europe* (Hampshire, England: Ashgate Publishing, 2006).

9 A. S. Kalwij, "The Effects of Female Employment Status on the Presence and Number of Children," *Journal of Population Economics* 13, 225 (2000).

10 A. Ashlund and M. Dabrowski, *Europe after Enlargement* (Cambridge, MA: Cambridge University Press, 2007).

11 R. Allen, *The British Industrial Revolution in Global Perspective* (Cambridge, MA: Cambridge University Press, 2009).

12 H. Herrigel, *Constructions: The Source of German Industrial Power* (Cambridge, MA: Cambridge University Press, 2000).

13 NationMaster.com. "Trade union membership by country."

14 Federal Republic of Germany, *Facts about Germany*.

15 J. T. Addison, C. Schnabel, and J. Wagner, "The (Parlous) State of German Unions," *Journal of Labor Research* 28, 1 (Winter 2007): 4. http://search.ebscohost.com/login.aspx?direct=true&db=bth&AN=23815050&site=ehost-live

16 Armbruster, *Management and Organization in Germany*.

17 C. Dufour and A. Hege, *L'Europe Syndicale au Quotidian la Representation des Salaries en France, Allemagne, Grande-Bretange et Italie* (Bruxelles, Germany: Presses Interuniversitaries Européennes, 2002).

18 McCahery, Raaijmakers, and Verneulen, *The Governance of Close Corporations and Partnerships: US and European Perspectives*.

19 Ibid.

20 Morck, *A History of Corporate Governance around the World*.

21 Armbruster, *Management and Organization in Germany*.

22 Q. J. Hunsicker, "Innovation and Renewal: A European Perspective," *McKinsey Quarterly*, Spring 1984, p.62.

23 Armbruster, *Management and Organization in Germany*.

24 Kalff, *An Unamerican Business: The Rise of the New European Enterprise*.

25 M. Geppert, D. Matten, and K. Williams, *Challenges for European Management in a Global Context* (Basingstoke, England: Palgrave McMillan, 2003).

26 Kieser, "Americanization of Academic Management Education in Germany," 93.

27 R. Locke, "Comparing the German and American Systems" *Business History Review* 82, 2 (Summer 2008): 336-342. http://proquest.umi.com/pqdweb?did=1543534881&sid=30&Fmt=3&clientId=11123&RQT=309&VName=PQD

28 Kieser, "Americanization of Academic Management Education in Germany."

29 *Business Week*, "Taking Over the Helm of Germany, Inc," December 1989: 66.

30 R. Locke and K. Schone, *The Entrepreneurial Shift: Americanization in European High-Technology Management Education* (Cambridge, MA: Cambridge University Press, 2004).

31 H. Klandt and C. Volkmann, "Development and Prospects of Academic Entrepreneurship Education in Germany," *Higher Education in Europe* 31, 2 (July 2006): 201. doi:10.1080/03797720600940880

32 Kieser, "Americanization of Academic Management Education in Germany," 93.

33 Armbruster, *Management and Organization in Germany*.

34 M. Andresen and B. Lichtenberger, "The Corporate University Landscape in Germany," *Journal of Workplace Learning* 19, 2 (2007): 110. doi:10.1108/13665620710728484

35 European Commission, *Community Charter of Fundamental Social Rights of Workers* (Luxembourg: Office for the Official Publications of the European Communities, 1990).

36 European Commission, *Health and Safety at Work in the European Community* (Luxembourg: Office for the Official Publications of the European Communities, 1990).

37 Kieser, "Americanization of Academic Management Education in Germany," 93.

38 Addison, Schnabel, and Wagner, "The (Parlous) State of German Unions," 4.

39 U. Glunk, C. Wilderom, and R. Ogilvie, "Finding the Key to German-Style Management," *International Studies of Management & Organization* 26, 3 (1997): 102.

40 A. Giardini, R. Kabst, and M. Müller-Camen, "HRM in the German Business System: A Review," *Management Revue* 16, 1 (2005): 70. http://proquest.umi.com/pqdweb?did=820630351&sid=1&Fmt=3& clientId=2186&RQT=309&VName=PQD

41 L. W. Mitlacher, "Job Quality and Temporary Agency Work: Challenges for Human Resource Management in Triangular Employment Relations in Germany," *International Journal of Human Resource Management* 19, 3 (March 2008): 447.

42 R. P. Termporal, "Strategic Management for the 80s," *Industrial Management and Data Systems* 8, November-December 1982: 8.

43 *Management Today*, "What Management Needs in the 1990s," October 1987: 102.

Chapter 11: The United Kingdom

Religion and Economic Development

The Protestant Ethic had a significant impact upon economic development in Great Britain. The country created a large commercial and industrial complex that dominated the entire world for centuries. The best proof of the British people's esteem for economic, commercial and industrial prosperity is the unprecedented English Industrial Revolution. Without the inspiration of English Industrial Revolution, the creation of the Industrial Revolutions in Continental Europe and America in would not have occurred.

In the latter half of the eighteenth century, the factory system appeared in England transforming the production of cotton, a vital industry in the country. The Industrial Revolution started between 1830 and 1850, when new industries appeared on the scene, starting with the railroad and steamship industries and then novel manufacturers like Bessemer steel.[1] Subsequently, other industries were transformed and developed, using machines to replace human labor. This process was accelerated because of the importation of agricultural products from Britian's colonies and the ensuing advances in domestic agriculture, transportation, and technology.

During the nineteenth century, the country secured a leading position in the world as a manufacturer, merchant, carrier, banker, and investor. Consequently, it was able to support a rapidly increasing population with a rising standard of living.

The impact of religion on economic development in Great Britain has always been positive under the auspices of the Protestant Reformation.

Religion and Education

The education system of Great Britain was positively influenced by the Protestant Reformation; consequently, it is one of the best education systems in Europe and the entire world. Curricula in classical studies, economics, and business have been present during the last two centuries, especially in higher education. In the 1960s, increased attention was focused on technological, commercial, and managerial education.

Primary education at the present covers six years of instruction, whereas secondary education is mandatory for children between the ages of eleven to sixteen. Traditionally, there have been three types of secondary schools: the *grammar school*, which provides a classical education to prepare students for a university with a classical curriculum; the *modern secondary school*, designed to provide general education; and the *technical school*, which provides an education for students who want to enter industry, commerce, or agriculture. The secondary school today is called the *comprehensive school* and includes students between the ages of eleven to eighteen. In tenth grade, students begin a long preparation for the *General Certificate of Secondary Education*, in which the students can select four of nine subjects. After completing the *General Certificate of Secondary Education*, students are free to leave school in order to pursue professional and career endeavors, or they can continue studying for an additional two years to prepare for university entrance examinations.

The Further and Higher Education Act passed in 1992 ended the separation between universities and polytechnic schools, allowing polytechnic schools to receive university status. British universities offer courses on every subject, and they are the oldest institutions of higher learning in the world to offer curricula in business administration and management. The courses offered in management are classified under many categories. They offer undergraduate courses leading to three-year and four-year undergraduate degrees on many subjects, including economics, behavioral sciences, human relations, engineering management, and hotel and catering management. Graduate work is also offered by many institutions of higher learning.

Universities and other institutions of higher learning have traditionally offered programs in every subject including professional studies, which can lead to qualifications in specialist fields of management such as personnel, office, sales, marketing, and work study. Looking back at the *Franks Report* published in 1963, we realize that no country had such widespread determination to improve the provision of management education, training, and development as the United Kingdom.[2] Currently, there are 168 colleges and universities in the country.[3]

The education system of the United Kingdom has developed under the positive influence of the Protestant Reformation. Curricula in classical studies, economics, and business have been present during the last two centuries, especially in higher education.

Religion and Social Structure

The Protestant Reformation has had a positive impact on the social structure of the United Kingdom. It has created a society with sufficient flexibility and freedom for developmental change, a situation that enabled the country to create the Industrial Revolution, which in turn had a tremendous influence upon its social structure. Prior to the advent of the Industrial Revolution, the socioeconomic fabric of the country pivoted around agriculture, fishing, and trade. Although London had become a relatively large city, most of the people of England lived in rural areas. The focal point of the socioeconomic element was that of the family, better known as the domestic system.[4]

The Industrial Revolution started with improving food production by developing the agricultural system. At that time, the country had already increased the variety of foodstuffs by importing them from its various colonies in the New World. The construction of machines that made human labor less necessary in producing food for domestic consumption became of paramount importance. Subsequently, machines constructed for industrial production led to the creation of mass production, mass consumption, and the inevitable appearance of a mass society that totally revolutionized and changed the former socioeconomic structure. The impact of industrialization changed the traditional social structure of Great Britain during the third part of the 1800s, and this change continued on a steady and gradual basis, making social mobility and social changes easy to attain. Skilled labor gradually infiltrated the lower middle class, increasing its size.[5]

Since beginning of the Industrial Revolution, Great Britain has not witnessed any abrupt or destructive socioeconomic changes similar to those that took place on the European Continent. The country went through two major victorious conflicts in War World I and World War II that did not eradicate the existing socioeconomic structure, but still affected it in some ways, such as increasing social mobility and creating new industries. This led to a Fordist social structure in the 1960s and 1970s.[6] Modern British society still has a traditional class system much like any other European state, with an upper class, a middle class, and a lower class (better known as the working class). Education, profession, income, and origin of birth are the forces that shape the nation's social and economic stratification today. However, there is social mobility not only for those who are of British origin but for the descendants of those who emigrated from other areas, especially from former British colonies in Asia and Africa. This is important because migration in the 1950s and 1960s was often employer-initiated and state-managed, as employers in expanding job markets looked into other areas for cheap and amenable labor.[7]

British society has faced a number of problems. One serious problem is the tragic violence between Catholics and Protestants pivoting around the status of Northern Ireland; at this time, violence has subsided, but no solution has been attained. Another problem is the sporadic confrontations between labor unions and the British government. Some of those confrontations have been related to privatization policies initiated by Prime Minister Margaret Thatcher, an issue which continues to explode from time to time. Britain has also confronted less painful problems, such as integration into the European Union. The United Kingdom for centuries has remained mentally, emotionally and strategically insular, resisting integration into the Western European fabric of nations. The United Kingdom never had a strong inclination for European integration, and it is not in favor of accepting other states into the European Union at this time.[8]

British women have been postponing childbirth and entering into the labor market in large numbers, and the educational gap between men and women has been substantially reduced.

Modern British society requires tremendous amounts of health care services for its citizens due to the increasing longevity of its population. At this point, the health care system has not been able to satisfy the needs of the country's aged population. At the present time, the health care system is undergoing developmental changes in order to be more effective, more efficient, and cheaper to operate.

The social structure in the United Kingdom has gone through a long evolutionary process during the last three centuries. Although it still adheres to tradition, it allows social mobility through its customary evolutionary movement and development.

Extent of Industrialization

Great Britain had a good pre-industrial economy, an advanced education system, and a relatively flexible and cosmopolitan society. These three elements created a strong infrastructure on which the Industrial Revolution was built. In the last half of the eighteenth century, the factory system appeared as the result of the transformation of cotton production, which proved to be a vital industry in the country. Subsequently, other industries transformed and developed by using machines to replace human labor. In the early 1890s, it became necessary to separate management from ownership, a seminal event that created the birth of professional management. The Second Industrialization involved the beginning of the separation of ownership and control, and moved Britain toward managerial capitalism.[9] Today, the industrial sector accounts for close to 25 percent of total economic activity in the country. British industries are strong and well diversified, and possess plenty of international experience based on traditional international activities during the last three hundred years. For example, the British steel industry is one of the best in the world, and the energy industry in the country is exemplary.

The United Kingdom had a strong economy, a relatively flexible social structure, and an advanced education system prior to the first phases of industrialization. These three elements created a strong infrastructure on which the oncoming industrialization phases were built. Today, the United Kingdom is one of the most industrialized nations in the world.

Labor Unions

Early industrialization contributed to the early formation and continuous development of labor unions in the nineteenth century. Currently, there are three trade union confederations in the country: General Federation of Trade Unions (UK), Trades Union Congress (TUC), and Scottish Trades Union Congress (STUC).[10] The Trade Union Congress, founded in 1886 is the national center of the trade movement.[11]

Employees join labor unions in order to attain optimum working conditions in terms of wages, safety, health, and welfare provisions. Labor unions also provide facilitation and representation in negotiations between employees and employers. Additionally, labor unions offer advisory and training services for their members, thus indirectly aiding employers.

Labor unions are no longer open exclusively to those employees who do manual work, but also include clerical, supervisory, technical, and administrative manpower. The basic component of British labor unions is the local branch, as is the case in the United States. Each local branch preoccupies itself with matters of direct concern. If further assistance is needed, help is sought from regional or national offices. Shop stewards and other appropriate officers are present in order to insure the effective and efficient performance of union members, and because most industry is based on locality and not factory, the steward has had a chance to become a powerful negotiator.[12]

Labor Unions help provide better compensation through unified strength in dealing with management. One of the central features of state and trade union policy in terms of the labor market has been the development of lifelong learning and training strategies.[13] Furthermore, the legal regulations that govern the relationship between employers and their employees require collective consultation with recognized labor unions, or with elected employee representatives in a number of specific situations. Employers also benefit from the presence of labor unions in their organizations because employees are mainly concerned with job security, better wages, and better working conditions in which the economic well-being of employers is crucial.[14] In the *Companies Act of 2006*, employees' interests have been retained as one of the factors to be considered by directors in relation to the performance of their duties.[15] Salaried employees in Britain are also represented by various organizations.[16]

Labor unions in the United Kingdom have been influenced by early and continuous industrialization and have followed the same developmental path. They have always been strong and democratic, and have provided all the required support for the well-being of their members and for the entire nation.

The Corporation

The corporate form of business has played a very important role in the social and economic life of the British people. Corporations first appeared in Continental Europe during the late sixteenth and early seventeenth centuries. However, the most important forms of business organization until the middle of the nineteenth century were the partnership and the joint stock company. As the direct result of the Industrial Revolution, the development of large-scale enterprises in Great Britain demanded large-scale capital. The corporate form of business offered the advantages of broadly distributed ownership, limited liability, and the ability to attract many British investors by offering common stock at reasonable prices.[17] The corporate form of business managed to raise capital much easier than proprietorships and partnerships. The dispersed ownership that characterizes the corporate system today emerged early in the twentieth century, and with the corporate form of business came the expansion of investment banks to serve as intermediaries for corporations and investors.[18]

The development of the corporate form of business also contributed to the industrial concentration that began in the latter part of the nineteenth century. During that period, many industries came to be dominated by large corporations. As corporations became more complex, concentration of industries became a necessity. The corporation operated on a large-scale basis through its ability to raise capital from the sale of stocks and bonds. Gradually, the ownership of organizations changed to professional investors. It was this transformation in ownership structure that led to change in the nexus of power, which greatly affected the governance of organizations and the way that managers behaved. Consequently, management as a process became professional.[19]

The corporate form of business developed rapidly as the result of the industrialization of Great Britain because corporations provided all the factors of production necessary to sustain an industrial society.

Management in the United Kingdom

The appearance of labor unions and the corporate form of business took place immediately after the Industrial Revolution. Both entities continued to develop on an uninterrupted evolutionary basis, and they precipitated the development of management under the same auspices. The roots of British management in history appear prior to the Industrial Revolution, but its presence in the economy evolved as the result of the Industrial Revolution. A cadre of managers emerged from the late eighteenth century and the early nineteenth century from which the true figure of the manager appeared.[20] Being a leader in international commerce, the country developed small commercial enterprises that were initially managed by their respective owner-managers. The first part of the Industrial Revolution improved the agricultural system of the country by developing machinery for food production. Subsequently, machines were constructed for industrial production leading to the creation of mass production, mass consumption, and the inevitable appearance of a mass society that totally revolutionized and changed the former socioeconomic structure. Industrial firms needed a new type of managers: industrial managers who, as salaried employees, had no financial interests in the organization.[21] It must be noted that while families relinquished ownership, they retained control through their positions on the board of directors and still exerted power without responsibility.[22] Such families placed persons in selected managerial positions with tremendous accountability for their performance.

Initially, management was not regarded as a distinct profession, and there was no legal definition of a manager, especially middle and lower managers, for all three levels were classified as employees. However, in the 1970s, government policies affecting privatization, the support for small business entities and more effective and efficient operation of business and government organization elevated the prestige of British managers. Employers today recognize their managers' individual responsibility, especially their interactions with their subordinates.[23] British managers are involved in many innovations and developments; they are recruited to be professional managers with skills that can match present and future corporate requirements.[24]

Managers have access to both academic and practical management courses offered at universities, whose purpose is to develop the greatest scope for management development in the immediate future. These courses include operational resources, work study, critical path analysis, linear programming, and statistical methods. Higher education programs training managers in small- and medium-size firms have been in existence for a long time in Britain.[25] Furthermore, providers of management education benefit from feedback from recent graduates about their experiences in the workplace, and use that feedback to identify the relevant skills that should be developed in their graduate and undergraduate programs.[26] There is ample cooperation between business organizations and educational institutions. The main impetus for the spread of management education in the post-war period came not from industry or universities, but from the creation of the Foundation for Management Education (FME) in 1960.[27]

At the present time, every university and institution of higher learning offers managerial education. In addition, specialized institutions in the country offer an abundant number of courses in management education, and the number of business schools offering MBA programs in Britain has increased substantially over the last decade.[28] During the 1960s, behavioral sciences emphasized the study of management education. When the universities became involved in management issues in the late 1960s, the rise of structural analysis in social science was mostly led by Britain.[29] Furthermore, the country has a wide range of professional institutes that contribute to the development of management.[30]

There is also great emphasis on research and development in management and management studies. One of the agencies responsible for such activities is the *British Association for Commerce and Industrial Education* (BACIE). It has been extremely active in doing consultant and research work to improve the management and organizational structure in British enterprises. Furthermore, research assessment exercises were established to rate universities in the United Kingdom, which were used as a basis for allocating much of the research funding from the central government.

British business schools are now well-established and mature, having

stabilized after a major growth phase in the last quarter of the twentieth century, and now focus on degree-level qualifications.[32] Management
education is currently concerned with the major challenges of management training and the appropriateness of curricula for preparation and
learning in the outside world.[33] Furthermore, business schools need to
become more enterprising, more protective of reputation, more flexible,
more competitive, and less averse to risk.[34] Finally, the development of
management education and its provision in England over the past two
decades has been dominated by the need for postgraduate education.[35]

Employee control has traditionally been more democratic than that in
the European Continent due to the Britain's strong democratic tradition
and its economic and social evolutionary development. Employees have
experienced substantial improvement in their wages and salaries as the
direct effect of sustained growth in the economy. The United Kingdom
was of the first countries to introduce flexible work schedules, and thus
has enjoyed lower unemployment levels than the rest of the EU since the
late 1990s, with United Kingdom rates remaining several points below
the EU average.[36] Furthermore, equal opportunities for women have been
effectively implemented, and equal treatment for men and women is assured.[37] The British government has also provided a number of measures
to encourage employee share ownership and financial participation.[38]

The increased presence of human resources management and human
resource departments has provided the basis for a new win-win relationship between employees and managers. Such practices offer management
the prospect of improved performance while improving the employees'
job satisfaction, security, pay, and benefits.[39] However, in some employment sectors, the traditional routes to professional development are well
established and somewhat slow to change.[40]

Many types of enterprises have provided extensive employee education. A significant number of employees of large industrial enterprises
have acquired university education in their areas of specialization. The
European Union has also made funds available for research relevant to
industrial fatigue and similar matters that are pertinent to the well-being
of employees.

In 1963, Mason Haire indicated that British and American management were parallel and that Britain and the United States seem to move
in sync.[41] Other studies on the same subject provide additional support to
this thesis and add that British managers are very close to their American
counterparts.[42]

Labor unions and the corporate form of enterprise appeared early during the industrialization period in Great Britain, and thus precipitated the continuous and uninterrupted development of management.

References

Allen, R. *The British Industrial Revolution in Global Perspective*. Cambridge, MA: Cambridge University Press, 2009.

Ashlund, A., and M. Dabrowski. *Europe after Enlargement*. Cambridge, MA: Cambridge University Press, 2007.

Ball, D. F., and J. Butler. "The Implicit Use of Business Concepts in the UK Research Assessment Exercise." *R&D Management* 34, 1. (2004): 88.

Bieler, A. "Labour and the Struggle over the Future European Model of Capitalism: British and Swedish Trade Unions and their Positions on EMU and European Co-Operation." *British Journal of Politics & International Relations* 10, 2008: 89. doi:10.1111/j.1467-856x.2007.00319.x

Brech, E. *The Evolution of Modern Management: A History of the Development of Managerial Practice, Education, Training and other Aspects in Britain from 1852-1979*. Bristol, England: Thoemmes Press, 2002.

Brech, E., A. Thompson, and J. Wilson. *Lyndall Urwick, Management Pioneer: A Biography*. Oxford, England: Oxford University Press, 2010.

Central Office of Information. *Employment in Britain*. London, England: Central Office of Information, 1990.

Cox, S. "Global Management Education: A Perspective from the Dean of Lancaster University Management School." *Malaysian Journal of Economic Studies* 41, 1/2. (June-December 2005): 6.

Crouzet, F. *The First Industrialists*. Cambridge, MA: Cambridge University Press, 1985.

Directory of Education Online. http://www.directoryofeducation.net/colleges/worldwide/united-kingdom/

Dufour, C., and A. Hege. *L'Europe Syndicale au Quotidian la Representation des Salaries en France, Allemagne, Grande-Bretange et Italie*. Bruxelles, Germany: Presses Interuniversitaries Européennes, 2002.

European Commission. *Community Charter of Fundamental Social Rights of Workers*. Luxembourg: Office for the Official Publications of the European Communities, 1990.

Haire, M., E. E. Chiselli, and L. W. Porter. "Cultural Patterns in the Role of the Manager." *Industrial Relations*, February 1963: 108.

Heaton, N., and C. Ackah. "Changing HR Careers: Implications for Management Education." *Journal of Management Development* 26, 10. (2007): 959. doi:10.1108/02621710710833405

Granick, David. *The European Executive*. Garden City, NY: Doubleday, 1962.

Granick, David. *Management of the Industrial Firm in the U.S.S.R.* New York, NY: Columbia University Press, 1954.

Kalff, D. *An Un-American Business: The Rise of the New European Enterprise*. London, England: Kogan Page, 2006.

Kalwij, A. S. "The Effects of Female Employment Status on the Presence and Number of Children." *Journal of Population Economics* 13, 2005: 225.

Koch, M. *Roads to Post-Fordism: Labor Markets and Social Structures in Europe*. Hampshire, England: Ashgate Publishing, 2006.

Little, B. "Graduate Development in European Employment: Issues and Contradictions." *Education & Training* 50, 5. (2008): 10. doi:10.1108/00400910810889066

Machin, S., and S. Wood. "Human Resource Management as a Substitute for Trade Unions in British Workplaces." *Industrial and Labor Relations Review* 58, 2. (January 2005): 202.

Marsden, D., R. Belfield, and S. Benhamou. *Incentive Pay Systems and the Management of Human Resources in France and Great Britain*. London, England: Centre for Economic Performance, 2007.

Montague, J. *Class and Nationality*. Pullman, WA: New College and University Press, 1963.

Morck, R. K., ed. *A History of Corporate Governance around the World*. Chicago, IL: University of Chicago Press, 2007.

NationMaster.com. "Trade Union Membership by Country." Accessed October 1, 2010 from http://www.nationmaster.com/graph/lab_tra_uni_mem-labor-trade-union-membership

Paucar-Caceres, A. "Mapping the Structure of MBA (AMBA-Accredited) Programs in the UK and France." *International Journal of Educational Management* 22, 2. (2008): 187. doi:10.1108/09513540810853576

Perrett, R., and M. Martinez-Lucio. "The Challenge of Connecting and Coordinating the Learning Agenda: A Case Study of Trade Union Learning Centres in the UK." *Employee Relations* 20, 6. (2008): 623-

624. doi:10.1108/01425450810910028

Personnel Management. "From Franks to the Future: 25 Years of Management Training and Prescriptions." May 1988: 48.

Rodriguez-Pose, A. *The European Union: Economy, Society, and Polity.* Oxford, England: Oxford University Press, 2003.

Storey, D. J. "Exploring the Link, among Small Firms, between Management Training and Firm Performance: A Comparison Between the UK and other OECD Countries." *International Journal of Human Resource Management* 15, 1. (February 2004): 119. doi:10.1080/0958519032000157375

Venkatesh, A., and D. Wilemon. "American and European Product Managers: A Comparison." *Columbia Journal of World Business*, Fall 1980: 68.

Wilson, J. F., and A. Thomson. "Management in Historical Perspective: Stages and Paradigms." *Competition & Change* 10, 4. (December 2006): 356. doi:10.1179/102452906X160996

Wilson, J. F., and A. Thomson. *The Making of Modern Management.* Oxford, England: Oxford University Press, 2009.

Wilton, N. "Business Graduates and Management Jobs: An Employability Match Made in Heaven?" *Journal of Education and Work* 21, 2. (April 2008): 148. doi:10.1080/13639080802080949

Wynn-Evans, C. "The Companies Act of 2006 and the Interests of Employees." *Industrial Law Journal* 36, 2. (June 2007): 189. doi:10.1093/indlaw/dwm004

Endnotes

1   R. Allen, *The British Industrial Revolution in Global Perspective* (Cambridge, MA: Cambridge University Press, 2009).

2   *Personnel Management,* "From Franks to the Future: 25 Years of Management Training and Prescriptions," May 1988: 48.

3   Directory of Education Online. http://www.directoryofeducation.net/colleges/worldwide/united-kingdom/

4   A. Rodriguez-Pose, *The European Union: Economy, Society, and Polity* (Oxford, England: Oxford University Press, 2003).

5   J. Montague, *Class and Nationality* (Pullman, WA: New College and University Press, 1963).

6   M. Koch, *Roads to Post-Fordism: Labor Markets and Social Structures in Europe* (Hampshire, England: Ashgate Publishing, 2006).

7   Rodriguez-Pose, *The European Union: Economy, Society, and*

Polity.

8   A. Ashlund and M. Dabrowski, *Europe after Enlargement* (Cambridge, MA: Cambridge University Press, 2007).

9   J. F. Wilson and A. Thomson, *The Making of Modern Management* (Oxford, England: Oxford University Press, 2009).

10 NationMaster.com. "Trade union membership by country."

11 Central Office of Information, *Employment in Britain* (London, England: Central Office of Information, 1990), 364.

12 David Granick, *The European Executive* (Garden City, NY: Doubleday, 1962).

13 R. Perrett, and M. Martinez-Lucio. "The Challenge of Connecting and Coordinating the Learning Agenda: A Case Study of Trade Union Learning Centres in the UK." *Employee Relations* 20, 6 (2008): 623-624. doi:10.1108/01425450810910028

14 A. Bieler, "Labour and the Struggle over the Future European Model of Capitalism: British and Swedish Trade Unions and their Positions on EMU and European Co-Operation," *British Journal of Politics & International Relations* 10, 2008: 89. doi:10.1111/j.1467-856x.2007.00319.x

15 C. Wynn-Evans, "The Companies Act of 2006 and the Interests of Employees," *Industrial Law Journal* 36, 2 (June 2007): 189. doi:10.1093/indlaw/dwm004

16 C. Dufour and A. Hege, *L'Europe Syndicale au Quotidian la Representation des Salaries en France, Allemagne, Grande-Bretange et Italie* (Bruxelles, Germany: Presses Interuniversitaries Européennes, 2002).

17 E. Brech, *The Evolution of Modern Management: A History of the Development of Managerial Practice, Education, Training and other Aspects in Britain from 1852-1979* (Bristol, England: Thoemmes Press, 2002).

18 Morck, *A History of Corporate Governance around the World.*

19 Brech, *The Evolution of Modern Management.*

20 F. Crouzet, *The First Industrialists* (Cambridge, MA: Cambridge University Press, 1985).

21 E. Brech, A. Thompson, and J. Wilson, *Lyndall Urwick, Management Pioneer: A Biography* (Oxford, England: Oxford University Press, 2010).

22 Morck, *A History of Corporate Governance around the World.*

23 J. F. Wilson and A. Thomson, "Management in Historical Perspec-

tive: Stages and Paradigms," *Competition & Change* 10, 4 (December 2006): 356. doi:10.1179/102452906X160996

24 Kalff, *An Unamerican Business: The Rise of the New European Enterprise*.

25 D. J. Storey, "Exploring the Link, among Small Firms, between Management Training and Firm Performance: A Comparison Between the UK and other OECD Countries," *International Journal of Human Resource Management* 15, 1 (February 2004): 119. doi:10.1080/0958519032000157375

26 N. Wilton, "Business Graduates and Management Jobs: An Employability Match Made in Heaven?" *Journal of Education and Work* 21, 2 (April 2008): 148. doi:10.1080/13639080802080949

27 Wilson and Thomson, "Management in Historical Perspective: Stages and Paradigms," 356.

28 A. Paucar-Caceres, "Mapping the Structure of MBA (AMBA-Accredited) Programs in the UK and France," *International Journal of Educational Management* 22, 2 (2008): 187. doi:10.1108/09513540810853576

29 Wilson and Thomson, "Management in Historical Perspective: Stages and Paradigms," 356.

30 Ibid., 356.

31 D. F. Ball and J. Butler, "The Implicit Use of Business Concepts in the UK Research Assessment Exercise," *R&D Management* 34, 1 (2004): 88.

32 Wilson and Thomson, "Management in Historical Perspective: Stages and Paradigms," 356.

33 N. Heaton and C. Ackah, "Changing HR Careers: Implications for Management Education," *Journal of Management Development* 26, 10 (2007): 959. doi:10.1108/02621710710833405

34 S. Cox, "Global Management Education: A Perspective from the Dean of Lancaster University Management School," *Malaysian Journal of Economic Studies* 41, 1/2 (June-December 2005): 6.

35 Paucar-Caceres, "Mapping the Structure of MBA Programs in the UK and France."

36 Kalff, *An Unamerican Business: The Rise of the New European Enterprise*.

37 European Commission, *Community Charter of Fundamental Social Rights of Workers* (Luxembourg: Office for the Official Publications of the European Communities, 1990).

38 D. Marsden, R. Belfield, and S. Benhamou, *Incentive Pay Systems and the Management of Human Resources in France and Great Britain* (London, England: Centre for Economic Performance, 2007).

39 S. Machin and S. Wood, "Human Resource Management as a Substitute for Trade Unions in British Workplaces," *Industrial and Labor Relations Review* 58, 2 (January 2005): 202.

40 B. Little, "Graduate Development in European Employment: Issues and Contradictions," *Education & Training* 50, 5 (2008): 10. doi:10.1108/00400910810889066

41 M. Haire, E. E. Chiselli, and L. W. Porter, "Cultural Patterns in the Role of the Manager," *Industrial Relations*, February 1963: 108.

42 A. Venkatesh and D. Wilemon, "American and European Product Managers: A Comparison," *Columbia Journal of World Business*, Fall 1980: 68.

Chapter 12: The United States

Religion and Economic Development

Although the United States is a nation that includes all Christian and some non-Christian religions, Calvinism is credited for the dedicated American belief in economic development.

The Protestant work ethic exerted its influence in the Netherlands in the seventeenth century, the Golden Century of Holland. The first groups of immigrants to the United States were Puritans, who brought these beliefs with them. Because Calvinists were harshly persecuted in Europe, many early immigrants in America were Calvinists, who lived according to their beliefs and thereby established reverence for Calvinism. They favored economic development and worked assiduously to be successful, and since they had to live modestly, they reinvested their profits in their various commercial and industrial enterprises. Consequently, they amassed large fortunes and promulgated the Protestant work ethic in the United States. Thus, the doctrine of Calvinism, which included the belief that power, prestige, and wealth are gained through success in commerce and industry and are analogous to living a good life, made the United States economy dynamic from its very beginning. Protestantism, a central figure in the formation of early industrial discipline, also made workers more aware of the distinction between work and leisure, and of the value of time itself.[1]

The impact of the Protestant work ethic upon economic development is reinforced in the United States. A good example is the work of Dr. Norman Vincent Peale, who knows quite a bit about business ethics because he directs much of his ministry towards the business audience.[2] Generally speaking, both the government and the American people have traditionally encouraged commerce and industrial prosperity. Social institutions will always support industry, for as one prospers so does the other. Industry must prosper to support society.[3]

The impact of religion upon economic development in the history of the United States has been very positive. Strong impact, accompanied by the entrepreneurial motive, resulted in a decentralized and independently owned and operated industrial complex, a democratic education system, and a flexible social structure.

Religion and Education

The Protestant Reformation and the Second Industrial Revolution has a positive influence on the education system in the United States. America's education system is complex and always changing. The United States is comparatively young in its development, but its education system is based on many ideas of various European civilizations. Although there are several problems in American education today, the nation's education system remains advanced. Schools are organized to provide opportunity, primarily for those who would be unable to transcend their environment without the opportunity for social mobility.[4]

The United States has flexible education institutions in order to adapt to changes within society. Because of the increasing emphasis on progress and change, the American school focuses on creativity and preparing students for further humanistic and technological evolution. The average American school developed as a separate institution to achieve the goals of society, or at least the goals of the dominant portion of society, through the education of the young.[5] American education is based on social evolution. The educational structure is concrete evidence of the deep concern among Americans for a fluid, casteless society in which it is possible for everyone to move as far as their perseverance and abilities will take them.[6]

The way a society educates its people determines the character and objectives of that society. As an agent for social change and as a factor directed toward implementing the ideas of society, the education system must somewhat disturb the status quo, as one of the basic values of this society is equal opportunity for all.[7] Free and compulsory schooling has been the cornerstone of the American educational philosophy, offering educational opportunity that is open to everyone. The illiteracy rate is low in America because practically all children in the country attend elementary schools.

Vocational and technical education is a continually expanding force that elevates national standards of living. As the number of recognized occupations increases, the growth of vocational education is accelerating in the United States. The country has excellent vocational schools and many more well-equipped educational departments. Formal vocational education has been in existence for many decades, giving many opportunities to numerous young Americans who would ordinarily be unable to acquire an education, either due to personal finances or a lack of desire to attend a university.

College and university enrollment in the country has been growing due to population growth and the many opportunities to freely enter into higher education. However, the percentage of high school graduates that enter into higher education is not excessively high. The hallmark of the American education system is its access, but the United States is not among the top countries in terms of the percentage of high school graduates who matriculate in higher education;[8] nevertheless, access to higher education is relatively easy. The American education system provides adequate general and specialized education to all who seek it. There are currently 3,360 colleges and universities in the country.[9]

One of the impressive characteristics of the American education system is that higher education is available to all. Consequently, American employees have one of the highest average incomes in the world and a very strong position when interacting with management. The role of education in assisting the American people to reach higher socioeconomic levels has always been of paramount importance. Education has long been regarded as the principal vehicle for ameliorating socioeconomic problems.[10]

The education system of the United States has developed under the positive influence of the Protestant Reformation. It is continually developing to serve the increasing needs of the American people in a complex post-industrial socioeconomic environment.

Religion and Social Structure

Since the formation of the country, Protestant churches in the United States have played a very positive role in creating a flexible society and allowing social developmental changes. Despite the fact that Americans legally and traditionally subscribe to the credo that all men are created equal, sociologists have recognized that American society is structured into classes. The demarcations between the various classes are not incisive, for lineage, land, or affluence is not the sole determining factor of class, as is the case elsewhere. The United States, which prides itself on being the land of opportunity, has always emphasized the work of the individual. It has been a quintessential belief in the United States that the promotion of the individual's self-interest is tantamount to the promotion of the general interest. Despite all the changes in the economy, the majority of Americans are working-class people.[11] The great degree of social mobility, the facility with which a person can attain a higher class than that into which he was born, serves to emphasize the plasticity of class structure in the United States.

The criteria which delineate the classes of American society are historical status, class attributes, income, education, and the job the individual is performing. Affluence and the inherent prestige which usually accompanies it are not the sole determinants of social class.

Loosely, there is a basic five-class structure, with people distributed in approximately the same proportion for each class in the various size cities. The actual percentage distribution in any particular community is determined by the age and the economic character of the community. For the purposes of this work, the five divisions of society into classes offered by the eminent sociologist Robert Havighurst have been employed. These divisions are defined as upper class, upper middle class, lower middle class, upper lower class and lower lower class.[12]

The American democratic society is characterized by the ideal of equal opportunity and the emphasis on social mobility. The two types of social mobility are horizontal, movement within the same class; and vertical, which is the change from one social class to another. It should be noted that in the social structure of the United States there is both upward and downward social mobility. There are many ways to attain advancement by class mobility; the most frequent are through prestige gained through marriage, socially valued talent, intellectual ability, or the most influential factor, education.

Within the United States, the expanding economy and increasing industrialization influence or promote vertical mobility, as does differential birthrates among the various social classes. When upper and upper middle class families do not produce enough children, children from the lower classes grow up and move into the vacant economic positions within society. Although most people are keenly aware of differences in social standing, and judge status levels primarily in terms of income, occupation, and education, they also emphasize the openness of the system.[13] This belief in upward mobility is itself a salient factor when one considers the social structure. The American Dream probably operates as an added and somewhat independent factor in promoting overall mobility. The great advantage of American society is that it created a state of democracy without having to endure a democratic revolution, and that all citizens are born free without having to fight for that right.[14]

The social attitude toward change in America is far more receptive than in most countries throughout the world. With freedom being a matter of birthright and not of conquest, the American assumes liberalism as one of the presuppositions of life. With no social revolution in his past, the American has no sense of the role of catastrophe in social life.[15] This is primarily true because the United States is a highly industrialized nation, and because the feudalism that was rampant in European countries never existed in the United States. Consequently, anachronistic traditions were never established, traditions that were the remnants of the feudal system and so often the cause of social stagnation humorously known as seniorities. On the contrary, the Calvinistic Ethic that asserted every person's success to be equal to their own endeavors, served to obliterate deference for inherited seniority

Social structure in the United States has been flexible since its formation and has allowed social mobility. American society has gone through a number of evolutionary stages, allowing the American people to enjoy the fruits of a dynamic, ever-changing society.

Extent of Industrialization

The United States had a strong pre-industrial economy, a flexible and democratic social structure, and a good and liberal education system. These three elements served as a strong foundation on which the Second Industrial Revolution (also known as the American Industrial Revolution) was built. A combination of the Protestant work ethic and the ideals of the Enlightenment shaped American culture and institutions. They pushed Americans toward industrialization and development of their infrastructure instead of expanding the agricultural sector with more and more land.[16] Consequently, industry plays a very important role in the economy of the United States. Since 1945, the American public has become increasingly more dependent on the advancements and conveniences manufactured by industry.

Despite the fact that the American economy has suffered in recent years, it has been one of the leaders in both industrial scale and efficiency of operations. A decisive factor in the growth of American industry and commerce has been its successful maintenance of a unified economy on a tremendous scale. This has allowed maximum resource utilization to standardize production for mass market consumption, thus creating strong economies of scale. For this reason, managers need to have good knowledge about the economics of the mass market. Because of this, the development of management lies on strong economic foundations.

The intensive geographical and occupational specialization that has been the foundation of cost reduction would not have been possible on any other basis. Of the many directions that specialization has taken, the most fundamental has been the development of agricultural industry. The United States farmer forsook more domestic crafts in order to concentrate on the production of cash crops, which he exchanged for manufactured goods. This economic relationship was contingent upon the economy's ability to afford the costs of the necessary transportation. To meet these costs, two conditions had to be fulfilled. First, an agricultural surplus had to be amassed that was sufficient to support a large number of people in the transportation, manufacturing, and marketing trades. Second, the country had to develop efficient overland transportation. Concurrently, advances in physical mobility were augmented by increasing social mobility, an important aid to occupational differentiation. The United States economy has been predicated on such mobility from the outset, and it is difficult to suppose that it could cease to be except with most serious consequences.

Due to high rates of production, the American people have been free to develop novel ways of disposing of the national output for consumption purposes. Above all, the aspirations of the general public have concentrated more and more intensively on the preeminently American goal: achieving higher standards of living. Advanced standards of consumption are not only a precondition of mass production, but they have also helped to shape the organization of industry and the structure of modern technology.[17]

Prior to the Second Industrial Revolution, the United States had a strong pre-industrial economy, a flexible and democratic social structure, and a good and liberal education system. These three elements served as a strong foundation on which the industrialization process was built.

Labor Unions

American labor unions are the strongest in the world, having been influenced by the Second Industrial Revolution and the continuous industrialization of the country. The labor movement in the United States gained strength and power with the overall economic development of the country. The growth of labor unions was slow and sporadic until the 1930s. The repression of unions by the courts and by management were major factors retarding growth. Currently, The American Federation of Labor and the Congress of Industrial Organizations are the two great labor federations that include a large number of unions under their umbrella. There are also independent labor unions.[18]

The American Federation of Labor (AFL) dominated the American labor movement from 1889 until 1936, when the Congress of Industrial Organization (CIO) was formed. The AFL's philosophy was basically that of its leader, Samuel Gompers, who favored business unionism, political neutrality, and craft unionism. In the early 1950s, the American Federation of Labor and Congress of Industrial Organization merged and formed the powerful AFL-CIO.

American labor unions have been losing memberships during the last thirty years, mainly due to leadership apathy and mismanagement; however, efforts are being made to correct this situation. Economics can provide guidance in determining which unions or union movements have been successful and which have not. These indicators of union well-being rest on the conventional characterization of unions as being concerned with their members' wages and employment outcomes.[19]

There are two basic types of unions in the United States: craft unions and industrial unions. Craft unions are organized by skilled workers engaged in various crafts or trades. Industrial unions are not restricted to skilled workers; they also include semi-skilled and unskilled workers. The nature of the industry, rather than the special skill of the individual worker, determines the basic union membership.

Many classifications of white-collar employees, such as actors and pilots, have been unionized for decades. Other groups, such as professors and nurses, are currently beginning to organize. There is a strong movement to increase union membership in the immediate future. This is based on two factors: the revitalization of manufacturing, and the prediction that many low-paid service workers will look toward unionization to improve their plight.[20] It is also necessary for labor unions to employ well-qualified and educated leaders and to provide their leadership with more time for strategic planning, implementation of operations, and low-level functions. An extraordinary high level of ideological and personal commitment is necessary to endure the constant travel, the long hours, the social isolation, and the arduous work that is the life of a labor organizer.[21]

In addition to the support received by labor unions the American employee is also supported in many cases by government legislative enactments that are part of the Civil Rights Laws. Although labor unions can significantly affect an organization's human resource management practices, no environmental constraint can match the influence of governmental laws and regulations.[22] However, the establishment of labor unions influenced the American employee long before the enactment of the majority of commensurate government laws.

American labor unions have been influenced by the continuous industrialization of the country. They acquired power early and have been able to support the well-being of their members as well as the socioeconomic fabric of the entire nation.

The Corporation

The Second Industrial Revolution immediately required the presence of the corporate form of business, which provided all the necessary factors of production for the new socioeconomic system of the country. The corporation is one of the pervasive realities in the United States today. Each age is characterized by its dominant social institution. There have been ages in which the church was dominant and ages in which political entities were dominant, but the institution that set the style and pace for the last part of the twentieth century is the corporation.[23] The various needs of the American people are largely supplied by corporations. In many ways, the modern corporation is an institutionalized expression of American life.

The history of the corporation in America may be roughly divided into five periods. Although there were not many organizations in colonial times, the character of those that did exist was to some extent indicative of what was to come. After the Revolutionary War, the number of corporations greatly increased, but the majority continued to perform quasi-public functions. The general business corporation in approximately modern form came into being only at the end of the second period, from 1829 through 1837, during the administration of President Andrew Jackson. The third period, from about 1840 to 1890, saw business corporations performing essential services for the growing country; but at the same time, some of the dangers inherent in increasing corporation power became apparent. The fourth period, the era from 1890 to 1920, is that of the trust and the trustbusters, when corporations seemed to be in fundamental opposition to the interests of the public. The fifth period, from 1920 to the present, covers one world war, a great depression and subsequently, an unparalleled expansion of the great corporations, to the point that some of them have amassed greater assets and higher budgets than many nations. The United States threw off early structures and systems and moved towards a corporate management economy at high speed.[25]

Corporate organizations are extremely concerned with cognitive management, which signifies the role that the enterprise plays within the organization and the entire society. A realistic way of looking at corporations is to consider them as an energy exchange; they are an open system engaged in constant transactions with their environment, which can be visualized as a system of systems.[25] The modern corporation considers itself to be a fundamental component factor of society. When an enterprise reaches maturity, it is concerned less with profit and the creation of goods and services and more with the personal satisfaction of its employees. This is known as institutionalization, which includes the concept that the personal goals of the employees are integrated with those of the enterprise, thus resulting in a perfect harmony within the organization. This complete identification between the personal goals of the participant and the goals of the organization is what most corporations constantly seek.[26]

As the result of the Second Industrial Revolution, the American corporation appeared early and grew quickly, playing an important role in the economic and social spectra of the nation by providing the necessary factors of production within the nation's dynamic socioeconomic system. In turn, the American corporation became a powerful force that precipitated the development of management in the country.

Management in the United States

Labor unions and the corporate form of enterprise started to play a very important role in the socioeconomic structure of the United States during the Second Industrial Revolution, and continued to have a tremendous effect upon the early development of management. The role of the American professional manager is distinguished within society and the economy of the nation. The historical development of the profession is very interesting. After the Industrial Revolution took place, cottage industries expanded to factory production, and the managerial function passed from one to many persons. After this stage, a more advanced development appeared on the managerial horizon. Many former owner-managers prematurely retired due to social pressures demanding more liberal attitudes toward their workers, which in turn resulted in better treatment of employees, higher wages, more humane working conditions, and similar improvements. As professional management departed from the individual-centered viewpoint and became more concerned with external groups, the economic role of managers changed because they operated large enterprises, many of which were corporations. Corporations in the United States are, for the most part, managed by career professionals.[27] A central problem that economists have faced when attempting to account for the effect of management is determining precisely how management practices affect a company's economic performance.[28]

The management of corporate enterprises was passed on to managers who eventually became a semi-professional and later, a professional body. Management increased in size and power and required a new breed of individuals to manage, control, coordinate, and direct the firm's complex activities. This clearly marked the beginning of semi-professional management, since it required the technical, specialized knowledge that owners demanded of their executives.

In the beginning, semi-professional managers were selected from internal sources, and managerial promotions and replacements took place without external impact. This resulted in the escalation of a new management power that invariably challenged owners, who were weak and highly dispersed. Management was engaged in activities unrelated to pure business matters, such as the rearrangement of organizational positions and structures. Striving for success is a moral imperative in American society. In organizations, it means moving up and getting ahead. For managers, it means financial rewards and the freedom and latitude to define their work.[29] Social demands for better educational opportunities and better managers oriented toward human relations through the study of behavioral science resulted in the fact that the average manager in the United States no longer comes from long-established commercial families. They emerge from heterogeneous family backgrounds and from all walks of life.[30]

Managers who are chosen on the basis of ability and qualifications are better able to confront the challenge posed by changes, and they are also more eager to introduce necessary innovations. The majority of professional managers are university graduates with education relevant to their profession. Today, practically all colleges and universities offer degrees in business and business management. Because of the customs and beliefs about commerce and industrial prosperity, American managers are accorded a great deal of respect. They have many civic, social, and club connections, and are concerned about public relations.

Managers in American society usually realize that all authority and power does not stop with them, and that they themselves are managed in some manner. Employee participation in the workplace could only be successful if managers were respected by their employees and their community. American managers enjoy great respect today because they are well educated. Because of the impact of the corporation, American professional managers play an important role in their profession, society, and economy. They come from all social echelons, they have adequate general and commensurate education, and they enjoy a very high degree of prestige.[31]

The United States was one the first nations to offer curricula in the area of business administration and management. Around 1880, the Universities of Chicago, Pennsylvania, and California established their first departments in business administration. There were 12 universities with departments in business administration in 1900, 100 in 1939, and about 120 in 1949. By 1959, there were 160 separately organized schools of business administration and more than 400 departments of business administration in the nation's colleges and universities.[32] Today, the majority of colleges and universities offer curricula in business administration and management.

In the last twenty years, several new elements have been introduced in American business schools in order to make them more global. New qualitative methods, such as business ethnography and business anthropology, are increasingly used in business research and practice. The role of anthropology in business is growing much faster than anticipated only a few years ago.[33] The incorporation of undergraduate and graduate courses and curricula in ethics has increased astronomically in American business schools, with the epicenter in management education. Business schools may attract more students if they offer more courses on corporate responsibility and environmentally friendly business practices, for more than 80 percent of undergraduate students surveyed said that they want more sustainability and corporate responsibility materials in their curricula.[34]

American employees will usually not accept authority when there is no specified reason for them to do so. This attitude is quite normal when one reflects that the United States is built on the ideal of freedom and the rights of the individual. Anyone who wants to interfere with these rights is usually not very well-regarded in society. Nevertheless, Americans accept the fact that there is a hierarchy, and the higher you are in the hierarchy, the more authority you have.[35] For instance, it is acceptable for managers to command employees to do something on the job, but managers will face great opposition if they try to tell employees how to organize their private lives. Rigid and dictatorial managerial control of information and policy will not make an organization successful, since top management may miss important risks that may be identified through a more rational approach to management, where each employee plays an important role.[36] In the United States, authority can really be defined only as a type of communication between managers and subordinates. It does not matter how much authority managers have if their subordinates do not respect it.[37]

Generally speaking, American employees accept managerial control because most of the time they agree with the philosophy of people with more experience and training. Employee control is usually approached under Theory Y beliefs because it is preferred in the United States. American employees have satisfied their basic needs, and are now striving to satisfy their higher needs within Maslow's Hierarchy of Needs.

Employee control in American enterprises is applied to groups as well as individuals, for group behavior highly influences management. The discovery of the importance of groups was made by psychologist and sociologist Elton Mayo. His most important research became the basis of the human relations movement. Above all, Mayo believed that industrial harmony was the key to the achievement and continuation of a stable society, and that understanding the needs of both management and workers was the route to social equilibrium.

Mayo discovered that employees do not react on an individual basis; instead, they form social groups which determine their reactions. He also discovered the importance of such groups within the society and in relation to their managers. The goals of the social group can make the difference in success and failure of organizational goals. If the goals of the group are in agreement with the organization, productivity will improve.[38]

Furthermore, the current use of work groups has resulted in much higher productivity and reductions in waste and employee absenteeism. Groups perform two functions for individuals: a production function and a social function.[39] From the mid-twentieth century to the present, employee control has moved from the mechanistic approach to the organic approach. Mechanistic control involves the extensive use of rules and procedures, and involves top-down authority. Organic control involves the use of flexible authority, flexible job descriptions, individual self-controls, and other informal methods for preventing and correcting deviations from desired behaviors and results.[40] Employee control in American enterprise mainly takes place by preventing mistakes which lead to friction and arguments creating a friendly atmosphere between management and employees. Preventative controls act to ensure that performance objectives are clear and that the correct resources are in place to accomplish them.[41]

During the last twenty years, the role of employees has been recognized and observed from a much more dynamic perspective than in the past. The recognition of the role of employees as key participants in the managerial process signified a move toward an enlightened view of employees in general, which promotes a cooperative relationship among shareholders, top management, and employees in the organizational environment.[42]

American enterprises are aware of their moral obligation to eliminate undesirable working conditions and create pleasant work environments, which is strengthened by legal requirements and the fact that good working conditions increase employee performance. Safety precautions are related to sustaining high employee morale, particularly as they symbolize managerial concern for the well-being of their human resources. Modern buildings are designed and constructed to provide an efficient workflow. Modern organizations provide employees with excellent lavatory facilities, a well-equipped infirmary with first aid facilities, and break rooms, cafeterias, or even small restaurants. In addition, plants are physically designed to contribute to employee morale by means of attractive color dynamics and light, the elimination of noise, comfortable air conditioning and heat, and clean air.

The primary success of dynamic motivation is derived from the top executives, who apply motivational psychology to themselves and their subordinates, and demonstrate how their personal objectives and goals are integrated with those of the organization. Individual members of the organization usually know whether they receive rewards for performance, attendance, innovation, or effort.[43] Another factor that has contributed greatly to employee motivation is good interaction among employees, since it provides them with support and recognition of their importance in the organization. American managers present motivational methods and techniques in the way most desirable and acceptable to their subordinates. From the standpoint of human resources, management development efforts frequently take the form of training programs for managerial and non-managerial personnel.[44]

Generally speaking, organizational purposes in most American enterprises are clearly defined and explained to employees; they are fully aware of the organization's destiny, as well as its present and future objectives. In addition, most organizations present their objectives in an explicit and concrete manner that identifies the employee's goals with those of the firm, to the point that the employees are intrinsically motivated rather than extrinsically motivated.[45] One of the most important aspects in intrinsic motivation is the presence of supervision by results. Results are measured and carefully examined; if they are not sufficient, corrective measures take place. This creates an atmosphere in which employees know whether or not they meet their goals, and what they must do to improve themselves.

Because American employees are specialized, management provides them with job analysis, job description, job classification, job dilution, and job enrichment in order to facilitate their work. Job analysis is a systematic procedure for the acquisition of information about a specific job. Based on relevant data, the human resource department selects the right employee for the right job. The job description deals with the short-term and long-term specifications of the job. Job classification permits jobs to be classified and grouped on the basis of enumeration and importance, and this system is now used instead of job ranking. Job dilution is a very recent innovation that enables the employee to learn his job faster than before. This is accomplished by dividing the job into a number of distinct tasks, so individuals can be trained to perform these distinct tasks in a fraction of the time otherwise required to learn the entire job.[46] In addition, management aids the employee by creating job enrichment, which increases the complexity of the employee's work in order to engender job satisfaction. It attempts to make a job more varied by removing the dullness associated with performing repetitive operations.[47]

Employee participation is of paramount importance in American enterprise, for when different employees with diverse backgrounds contribute their heterogeneous thoughts, it eliminates managerial monopolistic ideas and creates and preserves a democratic atmosphere within the firm. Managers of today are generally intelligent and well educated, although the possibility of error exists. However, when employees participate in manners relevant to their work, managerial errors can usually be forestalled. Participation also entails very strong psychological aspects. Employee participation increases understanding of the reasons underlying the need for change, and employees tend to support changes they help to create.[48]

In the United States, promotions often take place in order for an organization to more effectively utilize the skills and abilities its employees have developed during their employment within and without the firm, and employees are promoted mostly on the basis of merit. Merit applies to an individual's record of performance as well as to his abilities. Employees achieve both monetary and rank promotions upon the completion of a number of objectives that the firm has created and established. If an employee cannot fulfill the requirements and achieve the specified goals, they will have to start looking for another job elsewhere, since management believes that their presence in the firm may demoralize other employees. When a good employee resigns, management attempts to detect the reasons behind this action, using a variety of methods (such as exit interviews) to find the issues, and correct any existing deficiency or malfunction in the organization so that the same mistake will not occur twice.[49]

Most American employees obtain their positions through the human resource departments, which are an integral part of almost every medium- and large-size enterprise, as well as in numerous small enterprises. Since the early 1900s, top and middle management have focused their attention on personnel management, recognizing its important contributions to the successful operation and survival of an organization. This recognition given to personnel management was a result of many factors: the growing enlightenment of management; the compelling pressures exerted by economic competition, organized labor, and labor legislation; the effects of modern scientific and technological advancements on the composition and the necessary qualifications of the labor force; and the methods derived from the experience and research of the growing body of knowledge relating to personnel management principles.[50] Today, the three functions of the human resource department are to improve productivity, improve quality of work life, and ensure legal compliance.[51] Modern human resource departments manage the acquisition, maintenance, and development of the human factor in an organization. Organizations that embrace enhanced training as a critical component to their success average $1,665 in training expenditure per eligible employee.[52]

In the United States, there is an intimate relationship between the business world and educational institutions. The American business world supports cooperation between business and educational institutions in various ways, including scholarships and training programs. Both the business community and the academic community are great forces for change in society.[53]

Although American businessmen are relatively conservative because business culture is based on individualism and competition, they do not hesitate to adjust their behavior to meet environmental demands. They look favorably upon innovation and social reform. Management and organizational changes are the results of stimuli from the external environment; intrinsic changes originate within the organization and are the results of careful planning. Often changes take place in the organization in order to teach employees that innovation is part of their daily work and that organizations cannot remain rigid or stagnant.[54] Changes entail reshaping the culture of an organization to make it more competitive, more efficient, and better able to adapt to a constantly changing environment.[55]

The American manager is accustomed to using research and study to find techniques that can be developed for greater efficiency. Technology and studies in operational research naturally create an internal and external environment where organizational boundaries stimulate the desire of man for knowledge and personal satisfaction. The role of the manager is increasingly of utmost importance to the American society. In order to succeed in the introduction of innovation, management utilizes techniques such as information, participation, consultation, and simulation methods. The resistance to change that springs from fear of the unknown can be reduced by providing appropriate information. This information should explain not only what is to happen, but also why. Changes are generally accepted by employees because they feel pride and pleasure when they identify with increases in efficiency.[56]

The philosophy used by American managers to introduce changes is twofold. First, managers introduce new methods and techniques to deal with oncoming changes. Second, they weaken the resistance to change in their subordinates. A large number of modern American managers consult with employees to a considerable degree before and during the change.

Information serves to change the attitude of the employees and, more importantly, to assure them that such change is legitimate. However, information is not a force by itself; it is based on other factors such as power, authority, and confidence. Modern managers know that secrecy builds distrust, creates rumors, and causes resentment; therefore, they avoid secrecy unless it involves a confidential matter relevant to the operation of the firm.

During the last ten years, many managers have supported the concept of *learning organizations*. Learning organizations are organic entities which learn quickly, effectively, and efficiently. Therefore, they increase their knowledge on an evolutionary incremental basis similar to the total developmental process specified in Kurt Lewin's Action Orientation Theory, and to the organizational development models promulgated by

Ed Schein, Wendell French, Chris Argyris, and other specialists. Building learning organizations requires basic shifts in how one thinks and interacts. The changes go beyond individual corporate cultures, and even the culture of Western management; they penetrate to the bedrock of the assumption and habits of our culture as a whole.[57]

American organizations need to stay ahead of their domestic and international competitors. To do so, they must become learning organizations. The new organization that emerges must possess greater knowledge, flexibility, speed, power, and learning ability to better confront the shifting needs of a new environment, more demanding customers, and more knowledgeable employees.[58]

American employees are legally supported with equal employment opportunities, affirmative action, and diversity. The latter is done voluntarily in most cases. Diversity refers to the qualities of a person that are different from those of others, either on an individual or group basis. Managers need to plan strategically for diversity. As for strategic planning, diversity is defined with attributes relevant to the mission of diversity, with race, ethnicity, and gender prioritized. This management approach should emphasize the creation of an inclusive environment that carefully preserves diversity's unique values and norms.[59] When conflict arises, managers try to get to the roots of it to determine its cause. Internal disagreements among managers or employees need to be avoided because they block change.[60]

The development of management in the United States has continued uninterrupted because of the formation and rapid growth of labor unions, and the increasing importance of the corporate form of business.

References

Albanese, R. *Management*. Cincinnati, OH: South-Western Publishing, 1989.

Arnesen, E., J. Green, and B. Laurie, eds. *Labor Histories: Class, Politics, and the Working Class Experience*. Urbana, IL: University of Illinois Press, 1998.

Bert, A., and M. Van der Linden, eds. *De-Industrialization: Social, Cultural, and Political Aspects*. Cambridge, MA: Press Syndicate of the University of Cambridge, 2003.

Brewer, P. C., A. Gall, and R. M. Smith. "Getting Fit with Corporate Wellness Programs." *Strategic Finance* 91, 11. (May 2010): 27. http://proquest.umi.com/pqdweb?did=2033232691&sid=6&Fmt=3&

clientId=11123&RQT=309&VName=PQD

Chandler, Alfred, D., and B. Mazlish, eds. *Leviathans: Multinational Corporations and the New Global History*. Cambridge, MA: Cambridge University Press, 2005.

Chawla, S., and J. Renesch. *Learning Organizations: Developing Cultures for Tomorrow's Workplace*. Portland, OR: Productivity Press, 2006.

Cohen, A., and C. Kisker. *The Shaping of American Higher Education: Emergence and Growth of the Contemporary System*. San Francisco, CA: Jossey-Bass, 2009.

Directory of Education Online. http://www.directoryofeducation.net/colleges/worldwide/united-states/

Docksai, Rick. "World Trends & Forecasts." *The Futurist*, July-August 2010.

Domhoff, W. G. *Who Rules America: Power and Politics*, 4th ed. Boston, MA: McGraw-Hill, 2002.

DuBrin, A. J. *Essentials of Management*. Cincinnati, OH: South-Western Publishing, 1990.

Evans, R. "Remote Working and its Effects on Business Relationships." *British Journal of Administrative Management*, Winter 2010: 28. http://proquest.umi.com/pqdweb?did=1976129411&sid=1&Fmt=4&clientId=11123&RQT=309&VName=PQD

Fabun, D. *The Corporation as a Creative Environment*. Beverly Hills, CA: Glencoe Press, 1973.

Gibson, J. L., J. M. Ivancevich, and J. H. Donnely, Jr. *Organization*. Homewood, IL: BPI/Irwin, 1988.

Glueck, William F. *Personnel: A Diagnostic Approach*. Dallas, TX: Business Publications, 1974.

Havinghurst, R., and B. Neugarten. *Society and Education*. Boston, MA: Allyn and Bacon, 1962.

Hellriegel, D., S. E. Jackson, and J. W. Slocum, Jr. *Management: A Contemporary-Based Approach*. Mason, OH: South-Western Publishing, 2005.

Hollingshead, A. B. *Social Class and Mental Illness*. New York, NY: John Wiley and Sons, 1958.

Howe, D. W. *What Hath God Brought: The Transformation of America 1815-1848*. Oxford, England: Oxford University Press, 2007.

Jackall, R. *Moral Mazes: The World of Corporate Managers*. Oxford, England: Oxford University Press, 2009.

Keller, G. F. "The Impact of Management Practices on the Economic Performance of Family and Privately Owned Firms Entering the Recession." Speech given at 2010 Academic Business World International Conference, Nashville, TN. http://abwic.org/Proceedings/2010/Proceedings-2010.pdf, p. 449.

Kline, P., and B. Sauders. *Ten Steps to a Learning Organization.* Salt Lake City, UT: Great River Books, 1998.

Kolb, W. R., and D. Schwartz, eds. *Corporate Board: Managers of Risk, Sources of Risk.* West Sussex, England: John Wiley & Sons, 2010.

Koontz, H., and H. Weihrich. *Essentials of Management.* New York, NY: McGraw-Hill, 1990.

Lichtenstein, N. "Why American Unions Need Intellectuals." *Dissent,* Spring 2010: 73.

Lim, N., M. Cho, and K. Curry. *Planning for Diversity: Option and Recommendations for DoD Leaders.* Santa Monica, CA: Rand Corporation, 2008.

Marquartdt, M. *Building the Learning Organization: Mastering the 5 Elements for Corporate Learning,* 2nd ed. Palo Alto, CA: Davies-Black, 2002.

Martindale, D. *American Society.* Princeton, NJ: Van Nostrand Reinhold, 1965.

Massie, J. L., and J. Douglas. *Managing: A Contemporary Introduction.* Englewood Cliffs, NJ: Prentice-Hall, 1983.

Miner, J. B. *Organizational Behavior.* New York, NY: Random House, 1988.

Mondy, W. R., A. Sharplin, and S. R. Premeaux. *Management and Organizational Behavior.* Boston, MA: Allyn and Bacon, 1990.

Morck, R. K., ed. *A History of Corporate Governance around the World.* Chicago, IL: University of Chicago Press, 2007

Morgens, Howard J. *Business and the Universities - A Call for Mutual Understanding.* Founders' Day Keynote Speaker speech at Washington University in St. Louis, February 10, 1973.

Nafukho, F. M., C. M. Graham, and M. H. Muyia. "Determining the Relationship among Organizational Learning Dimensions of a Small-Size Business Enterprise." *Journal of European Industrial Training* 33, 1. (2009): 45. doi:10.1108/03090590910924360

NationMaster.com. "Trade Union Membership by Country." Accessed October 1, 2010 from http://www.nationmaster.com/graph/lab_tra_uni_mem-labor-trade-union-membership

Orwig, S. F. "Business Ethics and the Protestant Spirit: How Norman Vincent Peale Shaped the Religious Values of American Business Leaders." *Journal of Business Ethics* 38, 2002: 82.

Paradise, A., and L. Patel. *2009 State of the Industry Report*. Alexandria, VA: American Society for Training & Development, 2009.

Pencavel, J. "How Successful Have Trade Unions Been? A Utility-Based Indicator of Union Well-Being." *Industrial and Labor Relations Review* 62, 2. (January 2009): 154.

Pounds, R., and J. Bryner. *The School in American Society*. New York, NY: MacMillan, 1959.

Prieto, L. "Some Necessary Conditions and Constraints for Successful Learning Organizations." *Competition Forum* 7, 2. (2009): 519.

Reece, B. L., and R. Brandt. *Effective Human Relations in Organizations*. Boston, MA: Houghton Mifflin, 1990.

Rego, A., N. Ribeiro, and M. P. Cunha. "Perceptions of Organizational Virtuousness and Happiness as Predictors of Organizational Citizenship Behaviors." *Journal of Business Ethics* 93, 2010: 231. doi:10.1007/s10551-009-0197-7

Robbins, S. P., and M. Couiter. *Management*. 8th ed. Upper Saddle River, NJ: Person/Prentice Hall, 2005

Robbins, S. P., and D. A. DeCenzo. *Fundamentals of Management: Essential Concepts and Applications*. 5th ed. Upper Saddle River, NJ: Prentice Hall, 2005.

Ross, W. *Business in a Free Society*. Cleveland, OH: Charles E. Merrill, 1966.

Schemerhorn, J. R., Jr. *Management for Productivity*. New York, NY: John Wiley and Sons, 1986.

Schnake, M. E. *Human Relations*. Columbus, OH: Merrill Publishing, 1990.

Schneider, K. *Destiny of Change*. New York, NY: Alfred Rinehart and Winston, 1960.

Schuler, R. S., N. J. Beutell, and S. A. Youngblood. *Effective Personnel Management*. St. Paul, MN: West Publishing, 1989.

Senge, P. M. *The Fifth Discipline: The Art and Practice of the Learning Organization*. New York, NY: Currency Doubleday, 1990.

Squire, G. D., and C. E. Kurbin. "Privileged Places: Race, Uneven Development and the Geography of Opportunity in Urban America." *Urban Studies* 42, 1. (January 2005): 53. doi:10.1080/0042098042000309694

Tian, Robert G., and Alf H. Walle. "Anthropology and Business Education: Practitioner Applications for a Qualitative Method." *International Journal of Management Education* 64, 2008.

Tipgos, Manuel A., and Thomas J. Keef. "A Comprehensive Structure of Corporate Governance in Post-Enron Corporate America." *CPA Journal* 48, December 2004.

Tocqueville, A. *Democracy in America*. New York, NY: Vintage Books, 1960.

Walczak, S. "Knowledge Management and Organizational Learning: An International Research Perspective." *Learning Organization* 15, 6. (2008): 487.

Wilson, J. F., and A. Thomson. "Management in Historical Perspective: Stages and Paradigms. *Competition & Change* 10, 4. (December 2006): 356. doi:10.1179/102452906X160996

Zweig, M. *The Working Class Majority: America's Best Kept Secret*. Ithaca, NY: Cornell University Press, 2000.

Endnotes

1   E. Arnesen, J. Green, and B. Laurie, eds., *Labor Histories: Class, Politics, and the Working Class Experience* (Urbana, IL: University of Illinois Press, 1998).

2   S. F. Orwig, "Business Ethics and the Protestant Spirit: How Norman Vincent Peale Shaped the Religious Values of American Business Leaders," *Journal of Business Ethics* 38, 2002: 82.

3   D. Martindale, *American Society* (Princeton, NJ: Van Nostrand Reinhold, 1965).

4   R. Havinghurst and B. Neugarten, *Society and Education* (Boston, MA: Allyn and Bacon, 1962).

5   R. Pounds and J. Bryner, *The School in American Society* (New York, NY: MacMillan, 1959).

6   A. B. Hollingshead, *Social Class and Mental Illness* (New York, NY: John Wiley and Sons, 1958).

7   A. Cohen and C. Kisker, *The Shaping of American Higher Education: Emergence and Growth of the Contemporary System* (San Francisco, CA: Jossey-Bass, 2009).

8   Ibid.

9   Directory of Education Online. http://www.directoryofeducation.net/colleges/worldwide/united-states/

10 G. D. Squire and C. E. Kurbin, "Privileged Places: Race,

Uneven Development and the Geography of Opportunity in Urban America," *Urban Studies* 42, 1 (January 2005): 53. doi:10.1080/0042098042000309694

11 M. Zweig, *The Working Class Majority: America's Best Kept Secret* (Ithaca, NY: Cornell University Press, 2000).

12 William F. Glueck, *Personnel: A Diagnostic Approach* (Dallas, TX: Business Publications, 1974).

13 W. G. Domhoff, *Who Rules America: Power and Politics*, 4th ed. (Boston, MA: McGraw-Hill, 2002).

14 K. Schneider, *Destiny of Change* (New York, NY: Alfred Rinehart and Winston, 1960).

15 A. Tocqueville, *Democracy in America* (New York, NY: Vintage Books, 1960).

16 D. W. Howe, *What Hath God Brought: The Transformation of America 1815-1848* (Oxford, England: Oxford University Press, 2007).

17 S. P. Robbins and D. A. DeCenzo, *Fundamentals of Management: Essential Concepts and Applications*, 5th ed. (Upper Saddle River, NJ: Prentice Hall, 2005).

18 NationMaster.com. "Trade union membership by country."

19 J. Pencavel, "How Successful Have Trade Unions Been? A Utility-Based Indicator of Union Well-Being," *Industrial and Labor Relations Review* 62, 2 (January 2009): 154.

20 A. J. DuBrin, *Essentials of Management* (Cincinnati, OH: South-Western Publishing, 1990).

21 N. Lichtenstein, "Why American Unions Need Intellectuals," *Dissent*, Spring 2010: 73.

22 S. P. Robbins and M. Couiter, *Management*, 8th ed. (Upper Saddle River, NJ: Person/Prentice Hall, 2005).

23 D. Fabun, *The Corporation as a Creative Environment* (Beverly Hills, CA: Glencoe Press, 1973).

24 J. F. Wilson and A. Thomson, "Management in Historical Perspective: Stages and Paradigms, *Competition & Change* 10, 4 (December 2006): 356. doi:10.1179/102452906X160996

25 Fabun, *The Corporation as a Creative Environment*.

26 Morck, *A History of Corporate Governance around the World*.

27 Ibid.

28 G. F. Keller, "The Impact of Management Practices on the Economic Performance of Family and Privately Owned Firms

Entering the Recession," Speech given at 2010 Academic Business World International Conference, Nashville, TN. http://abwic.org/Proceedings/2010/Proceedings-2010.pdf, p. 449.

29 R. Jackall, *Moral Mazes: The World of Corporate Managers* (Oxford, England: Oxford University Press, 2009).

30 Arnesen, Green, and Laurie, *Labor Histories: Class, Politics, and the Working Class Experience*.

31 Cohen and Kisker, *The Shaping of American Higher Education: Emergence and Growth of the Contemporary System*.

32 W. Ross, *Business in a Free Society* (Cleveland, OH: Charles E. Merrill, 1966).

33 R.G. Tian and A.H. Walle, "Anthropology and Business Education: Practitioner Applications for a Qualitative Method," *International Journal of Management Education* 64, 2008.

34 Rick Docksai, "World Trends & Forecasts," *The Futurist*, July-August 2010.

35 A.D. Chandler and B. Mazlish, eds., *Leviathans: Multinational Corporations and the New Global History* (Cambridge, MA: Cambridge University Press, 2005).

36 W. R. Kolb and D. Schwartz, eds., *Corporate Board: Managers of Risk, Sources of Risk* (West Sussex, England: John Wiley & Sons, 2010).

37 R. Albanese, *Management* (Cincinnati, OH: South-Western Publishing, 1989).

38 W. R. Mondy, A. Sharplin, and S. R. Premeaux, *Management and Organizational Behavior* (Boston, MA: Allyn and Bacon, 1990).

39 J. L. Massie and J. Douglas, *Managing: A Contemporary Introduction*, (Englewood Cliffs, NJ: Prentice-Hall, 1983).

40 D. Hellriegel, S. E. Jackson, and J. W. Slocum, Jr., *Management: A Contemporary-Based Approach* (Mason, OH: South-Western Publishing, 2005).

41 J. R. Schemerhorn, Jr., *Management for Productivity* (New York, NY: John Wiley and Sons, 1986).

42 Manuel A. Tipgos and Thomas J. Keef, "A Comprehensive Structure of Corporate Governance in Post-Enron Corporate America," *CPA Journal* 48, December 2004.

43 Mondy, Sharplin, and Premeaux, *Management and Organizational Behavior*.

44 J. L. Gibson, J. M. Ivancevich, and J. H. Donnely, Jr., *Organization*

(Homewood, IL: BPI/Irwin, 1988).

45 Chandler and Mazlish, *Leviathans: Multinational Corporations and the New Global History*.

46 Domhoff, *Who Rules America: Power and Politics*.

47 H. Koontz and H. Weihrich, *Essentials of Management* (New York, NY: McGraw-Hill, 1990).

48 M. E. Schnake, *Human Relations* (Columbus, OH: Merrill Publishing, 1990).

49 N. Lim, M. Cho, and K. Curry, *Planning for Diversity: Option and Recommendations for DoD Leaders* (Santa Monica, CA: Rand Corporation, 2008).

50 Ibid.

51 R. S. Schuler, N. J. Beutell, and S. A. Youngblood, *Effective Personnel Management* (St. Paul, MN: West Publishing, 1989).

52 A. Paradise and L. Patel, *2009 State of the Industry Report* (Alexandria, VA: American Society for Training & Development, 2009).

53 Howard J. Morgens, *Business and the Universities - A Call for Mutual Understanding*. Founders' Day Keynote Speaker speech at Washington University in St. Louis, February 10, 1973.

54 Paradise and Patel, *2009 State of the Industry Report*.

55 B. L. Reece and R. Brandt, *Effective Human Relations in Organizations* (Boston, MA: Houghton Mifflin, 1990).

56 M. Marquartdt, *Building the Learning Organization: Mastering the 5 Elements for Corporate Learning*, 2nd ed. (Palo Alto, CA: Davies-Black, 2002).

57 S. Chawla and J. Renesch, *Learning Organizations: Developing Cultures for Tomorrow's Workplace* (Portland, OR: Productivity Press, 2006).

58 Marquartdt, *Building the Learning Organization: Mastering the 5 Elements for Corporate Learning*.

59 Lim, Cho, and Curry, *Planning for Diversity: Option and Recommendations for DoD Leaders*.

60 Chandler and Mazlish, *Leviathans: Multinational Corporations and the New Global History*.

Chapter 13: Conclusion

In this book, we have traced the impact of cultural factors upon the development of management in selected nations of the world. This work demonstrated that cultural factors exert a major influence on the development of management by examining and assessing these factors in eleven nations. It has also shown that a change in one or more cultural factors causes changes in the development of management.

Nation Summary and Analysis

The nations discussed were representative of divergent cultures as well as different levels of management development. They were chosen because of their model character, and were studied in sufficient depth to validate conclusions.

INDIA

The impact of religion upon economic development had been negative because it had been viewed as inimical to India's religious tenets. Although the government and some private sectors were making great efforts to create economic development in the country, the process moved slowly due to the religious beliefs that prevailed in the nation. Also, the education system was heavily influenced by the nation's religious tenets. General curricula have been mainly dedicated to religious and classical studies and are not available to all. The government has made great efforts to provide sufficient education for all, but these endeavors did not materialize. The type of education offered was general in nature, and specialized curricula were also limited and difficult to attain. The majority of the Indian people did not have access to higher education.

Formed under the influence of Hinduism, India's social structure still remains mainly unchanged. The absence of social mobility allows only the occupants of the very small top social echelon to occupy important positions, while the clear majority of the population still remained trapped in social positions due to the caste system, immobility, rigidity, and antiquated environments. India's underdeveloped economy, rigid social structure, and inadequate education system retarded the development of industrialization in the country.

Slow and irregular industrialization retarded the development of strong and functional labor unions. Labor unions were very weak and were developed with a technology that emphasized semi-skilled and unskilled labor. Although industrialization continues to take place under the same slow and irregular basis, trade unions are not serving the interests of their members or that of Indian people because their weakness allows them to be easily manipulated by the interests of internal and external political elements.

Because of the limited extent of industrialization, the corporate form of business in private organizations also remains limited. The majority of corporations in the country are owned and controlled by the government. Therefore, the corporate form of business does not have a positive impact upon the development of management in India.

Due to the negative impact of labor unions and the corporate form of business as well as the indirect negative impact of cultural factors, management authority and employee control are very autocratic. Management philosophy is very conservative, and management's views toward change and development are either nonexistent or excessively limited and impossible to implement. Attempts are currently being made to improve employee control.

ECUADOR

The impact of religion upon economic development was negative from the beginning of the colonial period to the late 1960s. Although the Church changed its position and now favors economic development, the process is slowly taking place and has yet not produced sufficient results. Tremendous efforts are currently taking place to accelerate economic development, which still remains slow and anemic.

From the beginning of the colonial period until the early part of the 1960s, the Roman Catholic Church had full control over the education system, which was based on religious and classical studies. In the 1960s, the Church officially changed its position and started to support curricula in economics, business, technology and related areas commensurate to a modern economy. Ecuadorian education then slowly began to offer such curricula in existing and newly established universities. However, deficiencies in higher education still exist, such as the insufficient preparation of professors, especially in economics, business, management, and related areas. Efforts are being made by the government and the academia to eliminate deficiencies in the education system.

The social structure in Ecuador was rigid and hierarchal from the beginning of the colonial period up to the 1960s. Numerous efforts were made to change the class rigidity and increase mobility in the social structure with some success; this resulted in a less rigid society and change slowly took place. Industrialization was not supported by a sufficient economic development, a modern education system. or a dynamic social structure. All three cultural factors were insufficient to support the needed changes; consequently, industrialization remained slow. However, the industrialization of the country remains one of the most important goals in the Ecuadorian economy.

Due to the limited presence of industrialization, labor unions are weak and disorganized. Employers and the government view unions negatively, and there is ongoing antagonism among the labor unions in the country.

Since industrialization played a minor role in the economy, the corporate form of business was not developed with the exception of a few large corporations. Approximately 97 percent of business organizations are proprietorships and partnerships of limited size, a situation that does not allow organizational growth or the development of the corporate form of business. Economists and consultants suggested that mergers of small organizations would result in larger organizations, thus creating the necessary factors of production for the effective, efficient, and profitable production of their products.

Due to the culture of the country, managers used paternalistic approaches to control their employees, who were not protected by weak labor unions. Furthermore, managers did not have the necessary management education. Worst of all, both the owners and managers of small Ecuadorian organizations were opposed to changes that would lead to the development of management. Management experts and consultants proposed that in order to start management development in small enterprises, it was necessary to change the mentality of the owners and managers, conduct mergers among small enterprises in order to create larger ones, and provide sufficient and commensurate management education to both owners and managers.

Due to the negative impact of labor unions and the corporation, Ecuadorian management has not been developed. Business organizations are small and managed by individuals who are related to the owners. Employees are controlled through their physiological, safety, and security needs. Finally, managers do not have the necessary management education.

BRAZIL

The impact of religion upon economic development was neutral, but in several periods it showed a rather positive influence, as economic development became viewed as a way of supporting the clergy. In turn, the clergy protected Portuguese (and eventually Brazilian) territories while converting African slaves and indigenous people to Christianity and teaching them Portuguese language and culture. The economy of Brazil started with agricultural products during the colonial period and then entered its industrial era in the 1930s. The economy of Brazil personifies a strong cyclical fluctuation, but in the long run the country is having problems with economic development.

The Catholic Church controlled education in Brazil during the colonial period and for 150 years after independence, and supported curricula in law, philosophy, theology, and related areas. However, after the 1960s, it became necessary for the country to adopt curricula in business, management, and economics. The Church did not oppose this adaptation because it was necessary for the survival of the country; furthermore, the old curricula remained intact. Brazil has a relatively good educational system, but serious problems exist at the elementary and secondary levels. The nation's higher education system offers all types of curricula at the undergraduate, graduate, and doctoral levels. Business, economics, and management curricula are widely available.

The Catholic Church did not have an impact upon the social structure and social mobility of the country, which depended upon the economic conditions that prevailed in each period and was influenced by economic cyclical fluctuations. The social structure in early Brazil was vaguely defined and had more than one structure. In the 1940s, Brazilian society changed and started to become more flexible. The subsequent industrialization of the economy played an important role in creating a flexible and dynamic society that is yet still affected by race issues.

The economic development of the country provided substantial assistance to the creation, sustenance, and development of industrialization. However, the educational system and social structure did not offer significant support for industrialization until recently.

Modern Brazilian labor unions are strong and provide sufficient support for their members; however, they are also centers of political activity that frequently causes counterproductive results. While trade unions can work to improve local work conditions and pay rates, wage rates naturally gravitate toward the national minimum wage across the country.

Industrialization supported the creation and sustenance of corporations in the country, but the majority were owned and operated by the government. Therefore, private professional management in the corporate sector was absent. Recent presidents started privatizing corporations, but even today the government sector is substantially active in the corporate area.

The development of management in Brazil has been delayed by government ownership and control of the corporate form of business, the small size of most Brazilian business organizations, and the non-commensurate education of managers. However, the country continues to privatize corporations; it has instituted academic and professional curricula in business and management in many institutions of higher learning; and it is providing informal managerial training programs for owners and managers of small business organizations. Serious efforts should be made to merge small business organizations in order to create more and better economies of scale. Emphasis should also be placed on changing the static mentality of owners and managers of private organizations in order to promote dynamic management and development of their organizations from both a short- and long-term perspective.

RUSSIA

The Russian Orthodox Church, like its Greek Orthodox and Roman Catholic counterparts, did not favor economic development. However, the imperial government of Russia placed great emphasis upon development during the last two centuries of its regime, similar to what the Meiji oligarchy did in Japan. The Communist Revolution that followed had a doctrine that fervently precipitated economic development under a centralized and totalitarian basis. After the fall of the Soviet Union, Russia has made tremendous efforts to create economic development under capitalist terms. Much work remains to complete this change.

Under the Soviet Union, education in Russia was strongly influenced by the communist doctrine and served as an instrument of communism. The extent of education was satisfactory and available to all citizens up to the completion of secondary studies. Higher education was available only to a fraction of those who sought it. Party affiliation played an important role in being admitted to an institution of higher learning, and academic curricula emphasized political indoctrination and the physical sciences. Studies in economics and related areas were excessively limited or completely absent. After the fall of the Soviet Union, the Russian education system started to undergo drastic and rapid developments, but it was not yet ready to provide the necessary education for the new socioeconomic system that was gradually developing in the country.

Russian society has been influenced by the Orthodox Church since the time the Czars accepted the Christian faith from the Greeks in Constantinople. It was a rigid society ruled by a small number of people at the top, while the lower classes were oppressed and enslaved. The introduction of communism in the country created a society that was based on the tenets of communism, with communists at the top of the social hierarchy and less privileged layers below. The fall of the Communist regime in 1990 upset the social stratification and created great turmoil in the country. A Russian society with new social stratifications has not yet crystallized.

After the fall of the Soviet Union, industrialization did not sufficiently increase because it did not receive the necessary support from the economy, social structure, and education system, as these three elements had not reached a state of stability. All three factors had to change as the economy moved from being a state-controlled system to a democratic system. Labor unions in Russia under the Soviet Union were instruments of the Communist Party and included both managers and employees. The functions performed by labor unions in democratic countries, such as collective representations before management and total support for their members, were not present. After the fall of the Soviet Union, Russian law allowed its citizens to form and participate in labor unions. However, labor unions are unstable, and have been infiltrated with leaders who are looking out for their own benefit, not that of members.

Under the Soviet regime there were no private corporations in Russia. After the fall of communism, a strong privatization process of the government-controlled organization took place, but many characteristics of the Soviet system were present in the new private corporations. Furthermore, former Soviet officials took key management positions in the new corporations. For all practical purposes, the private corporate form of business has not stabilized and has existed in continuous turmoil. Briefly stated, the private corporate form of business has not impacted the development of management in private organizations in the country.

Management was dictated by the centrally controlled system that characterized the Soviet Union and reflected the totalitarian socioeconomic nature of the state. Neither labor unions nor corporations had any impact upon management, managers, and employees. Labor unions were instruments of the totalitarian system and corporations were totally nonexistent. Because of the impact of the cultural factors, management authority and employee control were autocratic, and management's view toward change and development did not exist.

After the fall of the Soviet Union management, managers, and employees in the newly established private organizations went through dramatic changes and adjustments, yet remain in a stage of turmoil which is gradually phasing out.

JAPAN

The negative impact of religion upon economic development in Japan was superseded by government and military desire to glorify both the Emperor and the country. The military, with the help of the Meiji oligarchy, placed themselves at the top of the social echelon and created economic development through a powerful industrial network under governmental control.

After the end of World War II, Japan started developing an excellent education system that served the needs of the citizens and provided the type of education needed for the high socioeconomic demands of the new century.

Initially, Japanese society and its social structure were influenced by the Buddhist and Confucian religions, which had created a rigid social network serving religious interests more than the people. Subsequently, new internal power players appeared who changed the social structure. The biggest change came with the American occupation of the country in 1945, which promulgated a Western-type society that was never fully created. Democratic changes took place in some areas, especially concerning social mobility, but traditional power centers, under different names, continue to control the society of the nation. Nonetheless, Japanese society became more democratic and has a higher social mobility rate than in the past.

The post-World War II industrialization received substantial support from the economy, the social stratification, and the education system of the country. Japan became one of the most industrialized nations in the world.

Labor unions formed that followed the philosophy of industrialization, which was deeply imbedded into the culture of the country and included a profound emphasis upon paternalism. Each organization formed its own labor union which included all the stakeholders in the enterprise; labor unions were a power center, much like the rest of the stakeholders—government, employer, and others. Confrontation between labor unions and management was excessively limited because the protection of the employees and their strength in the organization emanated from the stakeholders, not from the union itself.

After World War II, the well-balanced industrialization contributed to the creation of more private corporations and precipitated the separation of ownership from management, thus paving the way for management development under the distinct cultural auspices of the nation. Both labor unions and corporations in Japan influenced the development of management in a substantially different way than their counterparts in the West, and created a unique type of management development that faithfully reflects the cultural factors of the country.

GREECE

The impact of the Orthodox Church upon economic development in Greece was initially negative, but it started to change after World War II, as was the case with the Roman Catholic Church in Europe and Latin America. The country attained substantial economic development, but inherent weaknesses still exist in the labor market, product competitiveness, and organizational effectiveness and efficiency.

The Greek Orthodox Church favored classical education, such as religion, art, law, medicine, and music, but it changed its position in the 1960s and started to favor curricula in economics, business, technology, vocational education, and related areas that are commensurate to a modern socioeconomic system. The Greek education system was centralized and remained stagnant until the 1990s, when development took place, especially in higher education, which was strictly under the auspices of the government. Graduate studies, distance education, and lifelong education were introduced and functioned relatively well but were not sufficient to satisfy the demand for such services. Private higher education was planned but not implemented until recently.

Since Byzantine times, the Church had a profound impact upon the societies of all Greek states under the Empire as well as the modern Greek state. Modern Greek society was disrupted by wars, the Ionian and Pontian Greeks, Armenian refugees from Asia Minor, and the communist invasion. Despite the political turmoil, the Church maintained a rigid society; when the mentality of the Church changed in the 1960s, Greek society started to become flexible and allow social mobility. Greek society has recently attained flexibility and mobility, but it is currently confronting issues with immigrants, an aging population, insufficient employment for the youth, and a defective welfare system.

Industrialization came late in the 1960s and continued through the 1980s. During this dynamic and short-lived period of industrialization, labor unions found the opportunity to establish themselves as strong entities in the Greek socioeconomic infrastructure. They became power centers that imposed their will upon the management of private and governmental organizations. The subsequent deindustrialization that started in the 1990s created an uneven economy that militated against the well-balanced development of the country. This negative state of industrialization did not allow the formation of new corporations or the mergers of existing small business entities, a situation that deterred the development of management.

Due to the mentality of Greek business owners, who demanded full control of the ownership and management of their organizations, mergers of small enterprises have not taken place. Therefore, such organizations were unable to acquire more and better factors of production through the corporate form of business and the establishment of new corporations, even during the dynamic short-lived period of industrialization. The clear majority of Greek business organizations are small, preventing the formation of an infrastructure that would lead to the development of management through the effective and efficient use of all factors of production. This situation has been a characteristic of underdeveloped nations. Greece, which has sufficient wealth and adequate socioeconomic and political influence both in the European Union and around the world, needed the presence of a strong corporate form of business in the totality of its business organizations. The ever-increasing evidence of the country's failure to be competitive rested upon the weakness of microeconomic development that pivoted around the strength of the corporate form of business.

Since the completion of my first book on Greek management in 1971, insufficient development has taken place in the management of private Greek organizations due to the stubborn mentality of owners of small business enterprises, who could not see the benefits derived from mergers leading to larger size organizations and the corporate form of business. Furthermore, the owners of these medium- and large-size corporations appeared to be reluctant to invest in management development. Formal management education and management development programs are now in their embryonic stages. Briefly speaking, in order to develop management during this critical period of the economic and social development of the country, there is a strong need for mergers of small organizations, formal management education, formal and informal management and employee training, emphasis on commensurate organizational designs and structures, advanced organizational policies, good communication channels, and leadership development.

A striking difference between my research in 1971 and that of the present is that in the latter case there was a strong presence of qualified and well-educated university professors, writers, and consultants of management who had great concerns about the predicament of the management of private enterprises in Greece. Such persons are a powerful force that could create miracles in changing and developing Greek management. In 1971, only a handful of university professors and consultants were cognizant of the true meaning of management; the rest of them viewed management as accounting, finance, or banking.

ITALY

The Roman Catholic Church in Italy initially had negative views about economic development because the process emphasized mundane benefits at the expense of religious practices. After the end of World War II, the Church changed its position and started to support economic development. The basic objectives in Italy became economic development; the industrialization and modernization of the country; the industrial, commercial, economic, and social unification of the North and South; and allegiance to the European Union.

The Italian education system, under the strong influence of the Roman Catholic Church, favored classical curricula such as religion, art, law, medicine, and music. Due to the dramatic changes that took place in the country after World War II, this influence substantially diminished and the education system was modified to serve the needs of an industrialized socioeconomic infrastructure without neglecting the need for classical curricula.

The Italian social structure was under the influence of the Roman Catholic Church until the beginning of the 1900s, a period during which the industrialization of the country necessitated qualified persons to work in the new economic environment. The end of World War II substantially diminished the negative influence of the Church upon the country's social structure and gave impetus to the creation of a dynamic and flexible society with a high degree of social mobility. After World War II, the growing economy, the modern education system, and the flexible social structure provided the necessary support for the growth and development of industrialization. Labor unions were influenced by the development in industrialization, and after the end of World War II, they gained tremendous power and contributed to the well-being of both their members and the entire population.

The lack of sufficient industrialization in Italy until the middle of the twentieth century had a negative impact upon the development of corporations. However, after the country started its rapid acceleration of industrialization, more private and larger corporations appeared, precipitating the separation of ownership from management, resulting in the development of management.

Italian labor unions were relatively weak until the middle part of the twentieth century. Furthermore, the number of corporations, their power in the economy, and their impact upon the development of management were limited. However, at the end of the 1970s, labor unions became stronger and the corporate enterprises increased. These events had a positive impact that accelerated of the development of management in Italy.

FRANCE

Although the Roman Catholic Church opposed economic development in the past, its power and control in France were attacked and limited by both the government and the people. The French Revolution and the governments that followed supported the economic development of the nation. Subsequently, the impact of religion upon economic development was steadily altered and eventually became positive. The country became one of the most economically developed nations in the world. The French education system was strongly influenced by the Roman Catholic Church for centuries, which favored classical curricula such as religion, art, law, medicine, and music. Due to the dramatic changes brought about by the French Revolution and the Industrial Revolution, the influence of the Church substantially diminished. The country developed one of the finest education systems in the world, whose purpose was to serve the needs of an industrialized socioeconomic system without neglecting the need for classical curricula.

French society was under the influence of the Roman Catholic Church for centuries. The incoming industrialization era that started at the beginning of the twentieth century and the end of World War II substantially diminished the influence of the Church, and allowed the creation of a dynamic society characterized by social mobility. The post-World War II industrialization process received the necessary support from a relatively good economy, a flexible social structure, and a modern and continually developing education system.

Labor unions in France were relatively weak until the end of World War II. The rapid advancement of industrialization that followed created stronger labor unions with tremendous power and influence over the well being of their members and the entire population.

As the result of France's well-balanced industrialization process, it became necessary that enterprises follow the corporate form of business in order to create the necessary factors of production demanded by an industrialized socioeconomic system. Therefore, the impact of industrialization upon the corporate form of business was of paramount importance, precipitating the strengthening of labor unions and the rise of the corporate form of business. Both entities have contributed to the continuous development of management in the country.

GERMANY

The impact of religion upon economic development in Germany has been positive ever since the Protestant Reformation. Economic, industrial, and commercial prosperity were traditionally emphasized in the county, thus making it one of the most economically developed nations in the world.

The German education system was positively influenced by the Protestant Reformation and the Industrial Revolution imported from England, and started to serve the needs of the people in a highly industrialized socioeconomic environment. The educational system since World War II and the unification of the country in 1990 has been continuously developing in order to effectively and efficiently serve the needs of German citizens.

The Protestant Reformation had a positive impact upon the German social structure, but the German history was characterized by the turmoil of wars, military occupations, and the socioeconomic destruction and dislocation of its population. After final unification into one German state in 1990, the country created a new dynamic society with strong social mobility.

After World War II, Germany rapidly developed a good economy, formed a flexible social structure, and created a modern education system. These three elements provided the infrastructure for the beginning of a strong industrial complex. Labor unions in Germany developed under the powerful influence of early industrialization and, although they went through many painful experiences before the unification of the country, they became strong and provided sufficient support for their members. German labor unions were responsible for the well-being of their members and the entire population.

The early industrialization of Germany precipitated the creation of private corporations of all sizes, which were characterized by having all the factors of production required for an industrial socioeconomic system. The impact of industrialization upon the corporate form of business is of paramount importance for the development of the nation. Labor unions appeared early in Germany during the industrialization process. Both labor unions and corporations precipitated the development of management with several interruptions until the end of World War II. Since the unification of Germany, the development of management has continuously evolved with great success.

THE UNITED KINGDOM

The impact of religion on economic development had always been positive under the auspices of the work ethic of the Protestant Reformation. The education system of the United Kingdom was positively influenced by the Protestant Reformation and the Industrial Revolution. Curricula in classical studies, economics, and business have been present during the last two centuries, especially in higher education.

The social structure in the United Kingdom has gone through a long evolutionary process during the last three centuries. Although society remained traditional, it was dynamic and flexible, and favored developmental changes. The mentality of society was that of problem-solving, not problem-creating. Although it adheres to tradition, it allows social mobility and change through its customary evolutionary movement and development.

The United Kingdom had a strong economy, a relatively flexible social structure, a cosmopolitan society, and an advanced education system prior to the first phases of industrialization. These elements created a strong infrastructure on which the oncoming industrialization phases were built, making the country one of the most industrialized nations in the world.

Labor unions were influenced by early and continuous industrialization and have followed the same developmental path. They have always been strong and democratic, and have provided all the required support for the well-being of their members and for the entire population. Corporations appeared during the industrialization process, and gradually corporate ownership changed to professional investors. It was this transformation in ownership structure and power that greatly affected the governance of organizations and the way that managers behaved.

Labor unions and the corporate form of enterprise appeared early during the industrialization period of the country and thus precipitated the continuous and uninterrupted development of management.

THE UNITED STATES

The impact of religion upon economic development in the history of the United States has been very positive. This strong impact, accompanied by the entrepreneurial motive, resulted in a decentralized and independently owned and operated industrial complex, a democratic education system, and a flexible social structure.

The education system of the United States has developed under the positive influence of the Protestant Reformation. It is continually developing to serve the increasing needs of the American people in a complex post-industrial socioeconomic environment.

Social structure in the United States has been flexible since its formation and has allowed social mobility. American society went through a number of evolutionary stages that allowed the American people to enjoy the fruits of a dynamic and ever-changing society. Prior to the Second Industrial Revolution, the United States had a strong pre-industrial economy, a flexible and democratic social structure, and a good and liberal education system. These three elements served as a strong foundation on which the industrialization process was built.

American labor unions were influenced by the Second Industrial Revolution and the continuous industrialization of the country. They acquired power early and were able to support the well-being of their members and of the entire socioeconomic fabric of the nation.

As the result of the Second Industrial Revolution, the American corporation appeared early and grew quickly, playing an important role in the economic and social spectra of the country by providing the necessary factors of production in the nation's dynamic socioeconomic system. In turn, the American corporation became a powerful force that precipitated the development of management.

The early appearance of labor unions and corporations, their rapid growth, and their increasing importance contributed to the early and uninterrupted development of management in the United States.

Conclusions

The following conclusions have been drawn about the impact of cultural factors on the development of management in the countries studied in this work.

The impact of religion (or any other belief system that replaces religion, such as communism in Russia under the Soviet Union) was strong upon the economic development, the education system, and the social structure of a nation. India personified an impact which was negative. In the cases in which the impact of religion changed from negative to positive, as in Japan under the Meiji oligarchy, the positive impact reflected upon the economic development, the education system, and the social structure of the country. In Brazil, the impact of religion was initially neutral because the Catholic Church was only concerned with the Christianization and enculturation of the native population and African slaves; however, the impact of the religion on economic development became positive when the Church got involved in protecting and supporting economic interests during both the colonial and post-colonial periods.

The characteristics of economic development, the education system, and social structure either retarded or supported the development of the industrialization in a nation. From the beginning, industrialization in the United Kingdom and the United States received abundant support from a strong economy, a supportive education system, and a dynamic social structure. On the other hand, the industrialization process in Italy came later, when the economy, the education system, and society were able to support the process. Likewise, In Brazil, which came into the industrialization process much later than Italy, industrialization is growing due to better economic conditions, a developing educational system, and a more flexible society.

Industrialization required the development of labor unions to protect the rights of employees and to promote the creation and development of the corporate form of business, which in turn had all the necessary factors of production to sustain and develop industrialized nations. The early appearance and rapid growth of industrialization in the United Kingdom and the United States had a positive impact upon the development of labor unions and corporations. Corporations and labor unions did not become strong and important in France until the industrialization of the country, which came later than in the United States and the United Kingdom.

Finally, both labor unions and corporations had a tremendous impact upon the development of management in a country. The limited number of labor unions and corporations in India and Ecuador, and the late arrival of corporations and labor unions in Russia did not provide the necessary support for the development of management in those nations. The early appearance of labor unions and corporations in the United States and the United Kingdom precipitated the early and rapid development of management in those countries. The disrupted development of labor unions and corporations in Germany did not precipitate the development of management until the beleaguered nation allowed labor unions and corporations to be reorganized, stabilized, and developed.

A special phenomenon existed in the unevenly developed nation of Greece in reference to the limited number of private corporations. During the dynamic and short-lived industrialization process of the country, Greek owners and small enterprises failed to enter into mergers in order to create larger organizations in the corporate form of business. During the same period, there were an insufficient number of new corporations. Small proprietorships and partnerships dominated the Greek economy. Hence, the country had problems competing in the European Union and international markets because the central force of microeconomic development, the private corporation, was profoundly limited in the country.

In reference to Theory X and Theory Y, India, Ecuador, Brazil, Greece, and Russia, fall under Theory X, whereas the United Kingdom and the United States fall under Theory Y. Italy, France, and Germany have entered into the domain of Theory Y, but not to the extent of the United Kingdom and the United States. However, their management development is rapidly conquering more and more Theory Y territory. Japan is entering Theory Y, but the culture of the nation requires closer supervision and control of employees by their managers, a characteristic of Theory X, thus making Japanese management substantially different than its counterparts in the West. Finally, India, Ecuador, and Russia struggled within the lower three levels of Maslow's Hierarchy of Needs, Brazil has been slowly moving from the lower to the higher levels of the hierarchy, while the remaining nations were concerned with the upper two levels.

In summation, I have reaffirmed my thesis that the development of management of a nation was not an isolated entity but an extension of that nation's cultural history. The history of the nation shaped its management development.

One must also be aware that a nation's management development is a constantly developing process. Therefore, this study is not a fixed or final analysis of management development in the nations under examination, but rather an up-to-date presentation of the stages in the ever-developing continuum of change.

Recommendations

I strongly recommend similar studies of management in regions and nations that have not been sufficiently examined to date, such as Islamic nations, Latin American nations, Eastern European nations, and former Eastern Bloc members that joined the European Union. Such studies will add valuable data to the relatively abundant studies dedicated to the economic and social development of these countries and regions. Furthermore, I advise my Latin American colleagues in universities and management consulting firms not to focus on North American or Northern European development models, but to fully examine the precipitants that caused, delayed, or retarded the development of management in private enterprises in the Greco-Latin area of Southern Europe (Cyprus, Greece, Italy, Spain, and Portugal) due to the common culture and mentality shared by Southern Europe and Latin America. Latin America is rich in raw materials and most of the other factors of production, but it needs to be more realistic about the strategies leading to the development of management within private enterprises in the region as the result of the development of the cultural factors specified in this work.

About the Author

Dr. John Theodore holds a Ph.D. degree in Administration and Latin American Studies from the University of Kansas; a Ph.D. in Management from the Aristotelian University in Greece, European Union; and a D.B.A. in International Business from the University of South Africa. He also has a B.S. in Business Education from Vanderbilt University, a M.A. in Business Education from Western Kentucky University, and a Specialist degree in Management from the University of Central Missouri. He has been teaching in higher education for four decades and has held several administrative positions. His teaching experience is mainly in the United States but he has also taught in several countries in Latin America, Europe, and in Canada. Dr. Theodore is also a Certified Management Consultant (CMC) by the Institute of Management Consultants in Washington, D.C., and president of JDT Management Consultants, specializing in management, organization, strategy, human resources, international business, and higher education. In addition to English, he is proficient in French, Greek, Spanish, and Portuguese.

Dr. Theodore has published two previous books dedicated to comparative and international management in countries with capitalist, socialist, and communist economy systems. He has also published a large number of articles pivoting around education, management, organization, strategy, and international business. He has resided in Florida since 1965.

About Lyseis Public Policy Publishing

Lyseis (Greek for 'solutions') Public Policy Publishing is dedicated to producing new works of scholarship in the field of Public Policy. It takes advantage of the recent revolution in publishing technology and economics to rapidly bring forth works that help solve today's challenges. Now, we are growing the future together.

Colophon

This book is made of Times and Optima, using Adobe InDesign. The cover was designed and the body was set by Sam Webster.

Visit our website at
www.LyseisPublicPolicy.com

CPSIA information can be obtained at www.ICGtesting.com
Printed in the USA
LVOW07s1804150614

390067LV00001B/28/P